Clean Coaching

Most coaches today see their role as mainly non-directive, helping to uncover their coachee's own wisdom. However, coaches may unwittingly and unconsciously constrain what their coachees talk and think about, getting in the way of unique, self-generated solutions. Clean Coaching provides a different, simple yet highly effective approach to one-to-one facilitation. It is a style, strategy and set of techniques that helps coachees gain insight and make changes through discovering more about their own 'insider' perspective: of themselves and the world around them. Through the use of specifically-phrased, structured coaching questions, the coach's own biased perspectives are stripped from their language, ensuring the coachee's unique personal experience is honoured.

In *Clean Coaching*, Angela Dunbar explains how this approach works in practical terms, with descriptions of how to structure a Clean Coaching session and the steps to take within such a session. The book gives detailed descriptions of the kinds of questions to ask and provides a wealth of analogues, examples and case studies to bring the descriptions alive, offering a clear blueprint for action. In addition, the book explains where Clean Coaching has come from, describing the development of Clean Language and other 'Clean' approaches by the psychologist and psychotherapist David Grove. It also tracks how 'Clean' approaches have been adopted and adapted by other practitioners. Dunbar draws on current research in the fields of developmental, neurological, cognitive and social psychology to demonstrate why Clean Coaching works so successfully.

Exploring Clean Coaching in detail, and informed by both research and practice, this book is a valuable resource for coaches at all levels, including executive coaches and those in training, as well as managers and executives acting in a coaching capacity.

Angela Dunbar is a highly experienced coach and coach supervisor, accredited with and a former council member of the Association for Coaching. As Managing Director of her own training and development consultancy since 1994, Angela coaches people on their professional and personal lives, and her passion is using and teaching 'Clean' techniques through The Clean Coaching Centre, www.clean coaching.com. She is the author of *Essential Life Coaching Skills* (Routledge, 2009), and has twice been nominated for the Association for Coaching's Honorary Award for "Impacting the Coaching Profession".

'Whether you are new to Clean Coaching or already have some deep exposure, there is a wealth of information and guidance in this book – from the basics of just two questions you can use in a profound way to get started, through the full range of Clean questions and techniques, to the capacities and world views that will help you to use it successfully. Angela's writing, her examples and stories, spur you on to explore and use these powerful techniques.'

—Caroline Talbott, coach and author of
Essential Career Transition Coaching Skills

'I loved this book for its clarity and simplicity. It gives a thorough representation of the work that David, Angela and I did together during the years leading up to his death, as well as the way in which she has gone on to develop and progress our work. It provides a detailed description of what coaching is, what Clean coaching is, the differences between them, and how they complement each other, and will guide coaches towards a more neutral style of coaching. I regard it as essential reading for those studying or delivering Clean techniques, and a valuable resource for anyone studying and/or practicing coaching more generally too.'

—Carol Wilson FILM FAC FPSA, *www.coachingcultureatwork.com*

'A hugely valuable addition to the field of Clean Coaching, this book will surely become a seminal text. It contains a rich explanation of the benefits of a Clean approach to coaching plus practical know-how for coaches to apply to enhance their effectiveness through Clean strategies, mindsets and techniques. Angela shares her in-depth knowledge and understanding of Clean in relation to the art of coaching and the application of psychological and systemic models, all in a hugely warm and accessible style.'

—Lynne Cooper, Executive Coach, Coaching Supervisor, co-author of
The Five-Minute Coach and managing partner of Change Perspectives

'Angela's latest book is an excellent addition to the current literature on coaching and how Clean Coaching is distinguished from other approaches. In one volume, the reader can explore the theoretical underpinnings of coaching, our unconscious bias towards being directive and how Clean Coaching offers an alternative. Discover ways to build your Clean Coaching capabilities and strategies for structuring Clean sessions, peppered throughout with case studies, transcripts and insights drawn from Angela's rich experience in the field. An indispensible resource for both novice and experienced coaches alike.'

—Anne Munro-Kua Ph.D, CEO AMK Transformations,
Kuala Lumpur, Malaysia

'This book is a comprehensive overview of Clean coaching by someone who learnt from David Grove himself. Angela Dunbar puts Clean coaching into context by showing all coaches how we should "Clean up" our coaching approach, even if not using Clean methods primarily. She explains how and why Clean works, and provides "how to" sections for basic Clean questions and the more evolved Emergent Knowledge variations. Coaches will find this book useful and challenging, as well as informative.'

—Gill Smith, UK Chair, Association for Coaching,
Partner in The Brain@Work

Clean Coaching

The insider guide to making change happen

Angela Dunbar

Routledge
Taylor & Francis Group

LONDON AND NEW YORK

First published 2017
by Routledge
2 Park Square, Milton Park, Abingdon, Oxon OX14 4RN

and by Routledge
711 Third Avenue, New York, NY 10017

Routledge is an imprint of the Taylor & Francis Group, an informa business

© 2017 Angela Dunbar

The right of Angela Dunbar to be identified as author of this work has been asserted by her in accordance with sections 77 and 78 of the Copyright, Designs and Patents Act 1988.

British Library Cataloguing in Publication Data
A catalogue record for this book is available from the British Library

Library of Congress Cataloging-in-Publication Data
Names: Dunbar, Angela, 1964– author.
Title: Clean coaching : the insider guide to making change happen / Angela Dunbar.
Description: Abingdon, Oxon ; New York, NY : Routledge, 2017. | Includes bibliographical references and index.
Identifiers: LCCN 2016011365 | ISBN 9781138816367 (hardback) | ISBN 9781138816374 (pbk.)
Subjects: LCSH: Personal coaching. | Counseling.
Classification: LCC BF637.P36 D858 2017 | DDC 158.3—dc23
LC record available at https://lccn.loc.gov/2016011365

ISBN: 978-1-138-81636-7 (hbk)
ISBN: 978-1-138-81637-4 (pbk)
ISBN: 978-1-315-73866-6 (ebk)

Typeset in Times New Roman
by Apex CoVantage, LLC

Contents

Figures and table

Figures

Table

Foreword

A number of years ago, I recall a lively discussion on the Association for Coaching member's online forum, debating what does and does not make a 'Clean coach'.

From memory, the discussions went something like: as professional coaches, shouldn't we always ensure that we are 'clean', in that we don't contaminate our client's agenda?

Others argued that even the most highly trained coaches, who have honed their craft of not sitting in judgement of their clients, and asking open, inquisitive questions, will to some degree still be influencing – or worse interrupting – their client's agenda.

The above was making reference to the work pioneered by the late David Grove – which author Angela Dunbar beautifully articulates, and builds upon, in this gem of a book.

As someone who runs a Board and Executive coaching practice, and also Chairs the Association for Coaching (AC), I was eager to read this book, looking at this through the lens of a practitioner, as well as how it can contribute to the body of work within our profession.

I found myself reading, and rereading this book, due to the profound effect it had on me. Following a deep level of reflection, and a discussion with a fellow coach, I now realise why.

First, having known Angela for a number of years, I have the highest level of respect for her as a coaching professional. When she was in her role as Head of Professional Forums for the AC, she generously donated her time to bring together the highest level of learning events for members, including the popular Co-coaching forums still in existence today.

She is committed to the highest standards, a great role model for a coach approach, and someone who cares deeply for the value that coaching – and coaches – can bring to others.

So when I initially read through the pages of the book, I knew they would be written in a way that was well researched, authentic and a true testament to David Grove's work, whose legacy Angela (alongside other colleagues) is passionate about carrying forward.

Equally, I was struck by the clarity and 'cleanness' of Angela's writing, in such a natural and engaging style, in a way that truly reflects the nature and intention of the subject matter. There is so much to learn throughout, and I was soaking up all the content like a little girl sitting in the front of the classroom, asking all the annoying questions!

Mainly, though, what inspired me the most – considering all the other excellent coaching books stacked within my four bookshelves – is that this little book made me think *most* about my own practice. Without giving too much away, I'll let you draw your own pearls of wisdom for yourself.

However, for me it has helped to shine a light around what's most important:

- Coaching, in its purest form, is *helping others to do their best thinking*, in a way that encourages the appropriate actions needed for change.
- It's also about *creating the conditions for others to see their best selves*, so they realise greater levels of success, fulfilment and meaning within their personal and working lives.

The benefits of focusing on just these two facets of coaching alone can lead to better decision-making, engagement, and ultimately performance, within business today.

This is also fresh on my mind following a recent visit with Sir John Whitmore, and ordering a hard-to-find copy of Timothy Gallwey's *Inner Game at Work* book, for a client. These are two men who have undoubtedly left their mark on coaching globally by promoting these two principles.

Additionally, as the demand for coaching accelerates and continues to gain greater acceptance within the workplace as a highly effective leadership tool, one of the most frequent usages of coaching currently is in the areas of change management (Sherpa, 2016).

This is why *Clean Coaching: The Insider Guide to Making Change Happen* comes at a timely period for both coaches and leaders alike.

So enjoy this book, as I have. It certainly has been useful to remind me, beyond the very useful Clean Coaching models and methodologies skilfully presented in this book, of what coaching is all about.

Katherine Tulpa, CEO and Co-Founder,
Association for Coaching; Executive
Director, Wisdom 8.

Reference

Sherpa Coaching LLC. (2016) *Executive Coaching Survey, 11th Annual.* Available at: http://sherpacoaching.com/survey.html [Accessed 29/3/2016].

Acknowledgements

There are so many people I'd like to thank for this book, I don't really know where to begin nor where to end.

First I offer heartfelt thanks to members of the Clean community and our own Clean Coaching graduates who read parts of the book and offered their feedback.

In particular I would like to thank Jacqueline Suyin, whose journalist experience and editing expertise was of huge benefit. Also Andy King, whose grounded feedback helped me revise and condense much that I initially felt was essential to tell at length. Thanks also Gill Smith, Chair of Association for Coaching in the UK, who took considerable time to read and review the entire first section and offer her feedback and support. Special thanks also to Lynne Cooper, another former AC Council member, advocate for Clean and author: your words of encouragement and suggestions for improvement were greatly appreciated. And similarly, thanks to Gina Campbell, Clean facilitator, author and trainer based in the US, for your generous and thoughtful advice.

Others who offered feedback and to whom I am eternally grateful are Brian Cullen, Bernie Croft, Caroline Talbott, Sarah Fenwick, Lorraine Biggs, Adrian Goodall, James Cumming and Jo Tregear.

Stepping back a level, I'd like to thank those who helped me learn about Clean Coaching in the first place. To Carol Wilson, who had faith in me and invited me to become Course Director for the Clean Coaching training programmes. To David Grove for his willingness to have me on board and of course, for creating the concept of Clean in the first place. And to Penny Tompkins and James Lawley, who initially introduced me to Clean Language and set me off on my voyage of discovery.

I'd also like to thank all at Routledge, in particular Susannah Frearson, who is a pleasure to work with.

Finally, I'd like to thank my partner, Mark, for his unwavering support of me and my writing, even when it meant I was distracted and busy with writing for a very long time.

Angela Dunbar, December 2015

The foundations for Clean Coaching

Section 1

The foundations for
Clean Coaching

Chapter one

The art of asking 'stupid' questions

Asking stupid questions?

When I was in my early 20s, I earned myself a reputation for asking 'stupid' questions. I was working in my first proper corporate position, in an internal sales support role. I was part of a team and attended regular meetings. Sometimes the meetings were about planning ahead and making forecasts. Sometimes they were more creative, aimed at generating new ideas for solving existing problems. I was curious about and questioned *everything*. I wanted to check and double-check what people meant when they talked about things like 'raising the bar' or 'tightening our belts'. I wanted to be clear on jargon, vague terms or buzzwords like 'profitability' and 'customer-centric'. When meetings invariably overran and I was *still* raising my hand to query another point, my colleagues would groan.

People who didn't know me thought I was new or dumb. Those that did know me knew I was neither of those things, but still didn't understand why I was asking so many questions. They would tease that I was being attention-seeking or being manipulative by playing dumb. But the truth of the matter was that I was asking questions about stuff that everybody *said* they knew, but no-one ever actually discussed. These were the taken-for-granted rules of working: the situations that everybody knows full well; the assumptions we all thought matched everyone else's; the limitations we just have to put up with. I quickly learnt that once a question like this was raised, the 'truth' was up for debate! People saw these supposed universally agreed areas very differently once you scratched beneath the surface. I learnt that when I said, "This may be a stupid question, but . . ." what followed was a very necessary and important clarification. To do this I needed to be both brave and a little bit naive.

Over the years I've continued to ask so-called stupid questions and it's become the cornerstone of my career. Clean Coaching could be considered the art of asking stupid questions. By asking another person to clarify the meaning of his or her words, you raise questions about apparently obvious things that need no explanation or exploration. But the answers you get are far from obvious, as the assumptions we make about people's meanings are rarely correct. Clean questions hold a mirror up to the coachees, so they can see their own meanings reflected back at them. This allows them to explore and develop their own thoughts in sometimes astounding ways. So-called stupid questions can evoke especially clever answers.

Insider v outsider perspectives

This book's subtitle highlights it's an *insider* guide to making change happen. By this I mean it takes the view that the answers required to bring about self-directed change originate from within the person making the change, and not from anyone else.

This presents an interesting challenge for coaches, employed to help make change happen. My view is that any attempt to do this from an *outsider* perspective will only fail. We cannot see the world as our coachee does, even when we think we understand our view is distorted. Our perspective is inevitably coloured by our own 'map' of the world. All perspectives are biased as there can never be an impartial objective position through which to assess the coachee and his or her situation. What seems the obvious solution for our coachee from where we are looking may be completely inappropriate from that person's unique, first-person position.

Of course the coachee is also biased and blinkered by his or her own beliefs and experiences; however as coaches we must work with these biases as they are the only reality our coachee knows. When you start from the *insider* perspective, from where the coachee is *now*, part of the change experience includes shifts in perspective and ways of thinking about things. In fact many would argue that concrete changes in behaviour and action are often the result of an initial, more abstract change in thoughts and ideas.

The structure of this book

The book is segmented into four key sections. In this first section we cover the *foundations* of a Clean Coaching approach, addressing the reasons why it has value for both the coach and the coachee, in all kinds of situations. Chapter one serves as an introduction, setting the scene and explaining where 'Clean' came from. We continue by exploring definitions and descriptions of what coaching is about and the difference between directive and non-directive approaches. After reviewing the reasons why directive coaching is more commonplace than you might think, this section concludes with a chapter covering the basic principles of Clean Coaching to support a non-directive, client-led approach to coaching.

The second section focuses on the Clean Coach, and the typical *qualities* needed to be able to adopt this method successfully. It covers how your basic views about people and the world we live in will fundamentally shape how you coach. It looks more broadly at the capacities required for Clean Coaching, with a separate chapter highlighting a Clean approach to language and communication. The final chapter in this section covers one key quality – the ability to focus attention, highlighting a range of basic Clean questions that can be used to support that quality.

The third section covers Clean *strategies*. A chapter is devoted to metaphor exploration – a key aspect for many Clean Coaching approaches. A further chapter looks at modelling and systems thinking – two important frameworks through which to view your coachees and the work you do with them. The remaining two chapters cover the structure of a Clean Coaching session, addressing beginnings, middles and endings and presenting clear guidelines for identifying outcomes, exploring issues and agreeing on actions.

The final section of the book deals with *applications*. The first chapter offers a range of additional Clean questions and techniques to help your coachees expand their attention beyond what they already think and know in order to reach new insights and deeper understanding. The other chapters address typical issues and outcomes for coaching, offering many case studies, transcripts and step-by-step Clean processes to inspire you further.

This book alone will not teach you all you need to know about Clean Coaching. You need to practice the skills and gain feedback on how you are doing. I recommend that you also attend training as well as undertake some coaching for yourself, so you can directly experience a Clean approach as well as have a dedicated opportunity to build your competence and confidence in an appropriate setting.

Where did Clean Coaching come from?

'Clean' was created by David Grove, who originated from New Zealand and was part Maori. He lived an almost nomadic lifestyle, as he explored the world and the people in it to practise his craft and develop his innovative and unique approaches to people-change. He tragically passed away at just 57 years old, on 8 January 2008 in Kansas City, USA, after suffering a heart attack. He was an exceptional man who will be remembered for a life dedicated to his pioneering work in language, metaphor and spatial techniques in Clean Language, Clean Space and Emergent Knowledge.

Back in the late 1970s, Grove came across Neuro-Linguistic Programming (NLP), having originally studied business administration. This kick-started an interest in therapy, particularly phobias and trauma (Lawley and Tompkins, 1996). In the 1980s he began working with patients suffering from traumatic memories, travelling between mainly the UK and the US to practise his craft. During this time he pioneered the groundbreaking technique of Clean Language as he discovered that people used metaphors as well as memories to structure their experience.

Grove developed a unique way of communicating with another person that limited the typical two-way information flow of a conversation. Instead it enabled the client to pay much greater attention to his or her own experience, including his or her 'inner' mental world of thought and imagination. He discovered that patients would often speak in metaphor when describing their experience and that he got the best results when he honoured those metaphors by asking open questions which reflected back the patients' exact words.

The approach was coined 'Clean' as, like a surgeon who scrubs up before an operation, the questioner prevents any 'contamination' of bias by asking only questions that have been cleansed of any and all words that might lead or influence. The origin of the term 'Clean' has been explained through the extraordinary tale of Hungarian physician Ignaz Semmelweis (Grove and Panzer, 1989) who recognized that doctors were causing patient deaths by neglecting to wash their hands. This was in the 1840s and germs not yet discovered. So if your hands looked clean, then they must be so. The physicians considered themselves above and outside of the patient's problem and just couldn't conceive that this kind of detrimental influence was even possible.

During the 1980s, Grove identified 13 core questions for therapists that would least influence their patients in their metaphorical journey, and he gave this process the name 'Clean Language'. By the early 1990s, the technique was observed by neurolinguistic psychotherapists Penny Tompkins and James Lawley, who devoted several years to codifying and developing it into a methodology they called 'Symbolic Modelling' (Lawley and Tompkins, 2000).

Although Grove originally created Clean techniques for working therapeutically, Lawley and Tompkins helped spread the word of Clean beyond this into education, business and research. In particular, Clean has a wide application within other kinds of people development, especially coaching where it has grown in popularity within organisations as a tool for change. For example, the last decade saw a major UK institution, the British Broadcasting Corporation (BBC),[1] undertake a series of Clean Language training workshops for its internal coaches.

Grove was continually updating his ideas and improving his techniques. In later years he developed his linguistic work into spatial methods, known as Clean Space. This concept was germinated whilst he was voyaging on a container ship in 2001, to explore how this unusual setting affected his relationship with space – both of the physical and the perceptual kind (Lawley, 2009). Clean Space evolved into an entirely new 'suite' of ideas he called 'Emergent Knowledge', inspired by the notion of Emergence. Emergence is the science of how things are achieved through connections. It involves the theories of chaos and networking principles and explains how ant colonies are formed and search engines operate, through repeating, iterative cycles of connection rather than being controlled by any one leader. 'Emergent Knowledge' became Grove's overarching theory of how people change and how to facilitate that change. From the early 2000s, David Grove began working with Carol Wilson, an expert performance coach trainer and author, to adapt his Clean techniques into something appropriate for coaches. This came about because of the growing number of coaches drawn to Clean Language and attending Grove's workshops. The coaches were inevitably different from the more typical counsellors and therapists that learnt from Grove, especially in terms of their depth of psychological training. Grove and Wilson developed a six-day workshop aimed at offering a definitive guide to 'Clean' for coaches, named simply 'Clean Coaching'.[2] Over time this has grown into the Clean Coaching Centre,[3] which offers a series of modular courses and an accreditation process, recognised and endorsed by the Institute of Leadership and Management (ILM).

Carol Wilson has described Grove as a "man of contradictions" and being "many things to many people" (2016). He worked with different practitioners throughout his life and encouraged them to contribute to his work. He explained to Carol that this approach was like having a trunk with various branches, each branch being cultivated by his work with a different practitioner. He said he valued each branch equally and was emphatic that none of the branches constituted the trunk. Carol's branch was the application of Clean Language and Emergent Knowledge within the field of coaching.

My own affiliation is with the Clean Coaching Centre, after immersing myself in learning about Clean for many years. I started my learning with Penny Tompkins and James Lawley and attended many of their Clean training courses from around 2000. By 2004 I attended a Clean 'Personal Journey' workshop facilitated by David Grove. I attended the very first Clean Coaching training course in 2005, following an initial pilot course, co-facilitated by Carol and David. By this stage I was totally enthralled with Clean and keen to devote all my time to learning more, and so offered my services as an assistant/apprentice. I was able to fulfil this role when the course was repeated the following year, for the first time as a distance learning course supported by telephone-based classes with e-mail follow-up. Carol was able to transcribe exactly what happened during the calls so we had Clean handouts too. I was already a Clean enthusiast and my closer association with its originator was a privilege and a pure delight.

In time Carol passed over the reins of the Clean Coaching Centre to me, and for some time I worked in partnership with David Grove, on the design and delivery of the Clean Coaching courses. I never got to co-facilitate a course with David Grove as his fateful heart attack in 2008 happened before any took place.

David Grove's Clean techniques and the work of Penny Tompkins and James Lawley in Symbolic Modelling have created a growing number of Clean enthusiasts, all around the world. Some, like me, are hooked and there is a growing number of Clean training courses, and Clean specialists in coaching, coaching supervision, mediation, etc. The worldwide community of Clean practitioners, advocates, experts and trainers is still small enough to feel almost like a family where we all know or know of each other and many of us collaborate together. And it is growing fast. There is a central website, developed by Penny Tompkins and James Lawley, where you can find out more about the range of Clean training, facilitation and practice activities taking place around the world, as well as read many articles and papers about Clean techniques and related topics.[4] There is also a Clean Forum and since 2008 there has been a regular International Clean Conference (held in London most years).

Clean Coaching is accessible to all. Anyone can learn to coach cleanly by using the Clean principles and techniques covered in this book, and this would be best supplemented by attending a specialist training course on Clean Language and/ or Clean Coaching skills. What can you expect to learn? The 'language' of Clean is deceptively simple. Beneath the handful of carefully constructed questions is a vast body of knowledge and collection of skills, technique and step-by-step processes to support you in learning a radically different way to think as well as ask questions.

Notes

1 To read a full case study of how Clean Language training was implemented at the BBC, go to: www.cleancoaching.com/#/ourclientsbbc/4528643155
2 Not to be confused with The Clean Coaching Company Ltd founded by Ned Skelton in 2002: www.cleancoaching.co.uk. Grove sought agreement from Skelton to use the term for his developing work with Wilson.
3 You can learn more about this comprehensive distance learning training through the website originally created by David Grove and Carol Wilson in 2005: www.clean coaching.com.
4 www.cleanlanguage.co.uk

References

Grove, D. and Panzer, B. (1989) *Resolving Traumatic Memories: Metaphors and Symbols in Psychotherapy*. New York: Irvington.

Lawley, J. (2009) *The First Clean Space Process – Notes from a David Grove Training Workshop*, Auckland, February 2002. Available at: www.cleanlanguage.co.uk/articles/articles/254/1/Clean-Space-the-first-workshop-2002/Page1.html [Accessed 3/4/2015].

Lawley, J. and Tompkins, P. (1996) *And, What Kind of a Man Is David Grove? An Interview by Penny Tompkins and James Lawley*. First published in *Rapport*, the Journal of the Association of NLP (UK) Issue 33. August 1996. Available at: www.clean language.co.uk/articles/articles/37/1/And-what-kind-of-a-man-is-David-Grove/Page1.html [Accessed 3/8/2015].

Lawley, J. and Tompkins, P. (2000) *Metaphors in Mind*. London: The Developing Company Press.

Wilson, C. (2016) *The Work and Life of David Grove: Clean Language and Emergent Knowledge*. Leicester: Troubador Publishing.

Chapter two

The scope and spectrum of coaching

Coaching expectations, best practice and reality

When I first met my partner and told him I was a professional coach, I was initially impressed by his apparent understanding and enthusiasm. He earnestly told me: "You know, lots of people have suggested to me that *I* should be a coach . . ." Then he smiled and added: "Because I'm very good at telling people what they should do." We've been together for over five years now, and he has reluctantly begun to accept that this particular talent of his is not necessarily a true reflection of what good coaching is all about! Yet it continues to be an accurate impression of what many people expect from coaching. However, look in any good coaching book and the description of coaching is quite different. Coaching is focused on helping people to find their own answers, and *asking* them to explore their own thoughts rather than *telling* them whatever the coach happens to believe is the way forward.

This mismatch in coaching expectations is partly due to where coaching has come from, and how it has already evolved and diversified within its relatively short lifespan. This has created a dilemma between directive and non-directive approaches that many coaches struggle with. In this chapter, we'll look at the spectrum of coaching as a continuum along which the coach can freely move, choosing to be more or less directive, moment by moment. But are directive approaches appropriate for coaching at all, if the direction is not owned by the coachee? The alternative, non-directive approach can be highly purposeful and provides the essence of what differentiates coaching from other forms of people development.

The directive roots of coaching

The term 'coaching' has been used in different ways at different times, changing its meaning in more recent years. It came into common usage from the 1950s to describe an on-the-job instructional process. It was precisely about telling people what to do and the coach was directive in offering advice and imparting skills.

By the early 1990s coaching developed into a specialism, and non-directive approaches began to emerge as the gold standard. Influential books such as Tim

Gallwey's *The Inner Game* (1974/1997) and models such as GROW (Whitmore, 1992; Alexander, 2006) began to shape coach training courses and best practice. Even so, the modern perspective of coaching as being largely non-directive is a fairly recent development and it's hardly surprising that many clients still expect their coach to deliver answers. Coaches can find it difficult to avoid giving coachees what they want in this regard, despite what's considered best practice. Moreover, it's not easy to stop giving directions. It is a hard habit to break, as executive coach author Peter Bluckert points out. He highlights that even when the benefits are recognised, coaches "regularly fall back on the instructional, advice giving, expert mode" (2006:4). As habits are largely unconscious and automatic, coaches may end up inadvertently directing the coachee, even though they intended to be non-directive.

The upshot from these outdated expectations, habits and confused terminology has created a mismatch between what coaches think they are doing and what actually happens. Other influential voices from the coaching profession have come to similar conclusions, including Myles Downey (2010). Some even argue that non-directive coaching is a myth anyway and that coaches "inevitably steer the process towards achieving the desired results" (Blakey and Day, 2012:34). It seems that there is far less non-directive coaching going on in the profession than we might think!

The scope of coaching

The field of coaching has grown tremendously over the last decade or so, from humble beginnings to a multi-million-pound industry on the brink of becoming a fully fledged profession. It is supported by associations and institutes that have defined best practice and ethical standards, and introduced coaching accreditation schemes to differentiate and recognise experience and expertise. And even so, pinning down a definitive definition of what coaching actually entails, and how it's different from other forms of 'people helping' activities is more troublesome than you would think. There are abundant coaching providers coming from many different backgrounds. Inevitably a wide variety of coaching methods has emerged. A myriad of coaching suppliers offer their own special brand of coaching, with a unique blend of approaches, models, styles and emphasis. It's therefore no wonder that the market is confused as to what to expect.

Within the corporate world, the boundaries between the roles of a trainer, mentor and coach remain fuzzy. Many coaching providers add to the confusion by offering a flexible approach to coaching, suggesting that the activity label is not as important as the results. Bringing an eclectic mix of styles, approaches and models is seen as an advantage. And to a busy learning and development purchaser, an all-inclusive 'one stop shop' service is more appealing than a 'one trick pony'. Therefore, coaching is often seen as a pick-and-mix menu of approaches to choose from with many coaches also offering training and mentoring. The current consensus within the coaching community supports taking a mostly non-directive approach.

However, the extent to which imparting knowledge can be a useful aspect of good coaching practice remains an unresolved question (Hemphill, 2011).

In fact, many leading coach thinkers consider it impossible to be completely non-directive (Thompson, 2013). A 'dash' of directive is considered the accepted norm, with some writers positively supporting a more directive, challenging approach (e.g. Blakey and Day, 2012). Although a purely directive approach is generally seen as incompatible with coaching, these days it seems almost anything goes. Some have suggested we may even be witnessing a "partial return" (Ives, 2008:105) to the more instructional approach.

My concern is that this wide acceptance of such diversity means that coaching becomes ever more vague as a distinct activity and therefore increasingly difficult to assess good practice. If 'anything goes', then we could conclude *any and all* kinds of conversations about a person's development could be construed as coaching, which is clearly untrue. Something should and does separate coaching from other kinds of learning facilitation, and it is important to clarify and define what that is.

How do you know it's coaching?

Although the two activities are often confused, coaching is easily differentiated from teaching. Teaching, or training, is generally instructional, and involves imparting information, sharing models and showing people how to do things. Typically conducted in groups, teaching is a necessary activity to impart information and build knowledge and basic skills. But gaining the ability to interpret knowledge and develop skills in a creative way to solve real-life problems is more likely to happen when learners are encouraged to think for themselves. Indeed many teachers and trainers include facilitative exercises within their delivery. In contrast, coaching is mostly one-to-one, related to specific real-life situations requiring unique and meaningful solutions. A third kind of service falls somewhere between training and or coaching: mentoring. Mentoring is a one-to-one relationship, usually informal and longer-term than coaching, with mentors generally selected for their experience and expertise. Mentoring can include both training (instructional) and coaching (facilitative) approaches. But terminology describing coaching and mentoring is 'confused and confusing' (Brockbank and McGill, 2006) making it difficult to draw lines between them. Additionally, many believe the boundaries between people-development activities are even more blurred than is generally articulated and documented (Passmore, 2007).

If you are a coach, ask yourself this: when you are coaching, rather than practicing a different kind of people-helping approach, *how do you know it's coaching?* This is an important and useful question for all coaches and those involved in coaching to ask themselves. Although results clearly matter, clarity around your scope of coaching activity is also crucial, for many reasons. For instance, for establishing appropriate boundaries and managing client expectations, for providing clear guidelines and responsibilities as part of contracting, and to ensure the quality and relevance of coach training.

There are useful coaching definitions available to help establish the distinctions. For example, Whitmore (2002:8) clarified as: "Unlocking a person's potential to maximise their own performance. It is *helping them to learn* rather than teaching them." This simple and clear description separates coaching from more instructional activities, such as teaching. It is not about telling people what to do; the ownership for learning is with the coachee, not the coach.

The coaching spectrum from 'ask' to 'tell'

John Heron's (1990[1975]) six-category intervention framework allows for a 'spectrum' of different approaches ranging from extreme directiveness to complete non-directiveness. Developed for use by any kind of people helper, it has been adopted by the coaching community. It first defines two cores styles:

- The *authoritative:* This style is more directive, as the helper acts – and is seen – as an authority figure holding greater power than the person he or she is helping. The helper has 'gravitas', his or her advice carries a certain weight and the helper fulfils the role of an expert. It involves *telling* people what to do and how to do it.
- The *facilitative:* This style is more non-directive, as the helper sees his or her role as an enabler. Even when the helper has expert knowledge, he or she avoids giving answers. Instead, the helper uses his or her knowledge for *asking* well-crafted questions, so that the person forms his or her own solutions.

Within each broad style are three intervention patterns.

For the *authoritative* style, the interventions are:

- *Prescriptive*: The coach provides the answers. Like a doctor the coach diagnoses the coachee and tells the person what to do.
- *Informative:* The coach shares models, stories and examples. He or she guides the coachee towards the answer. The coach teaches or instructs how to do things, sharing his or her knowledge and expertise. The coach suggests possible solutions and leaves the coachee to accept or reject.
- *Confronting:* This is when the coach challenges the coachee's opinions, decisions, actions (or lack of actions) and/or beliefs. The coachee's usual way of thinking, perceiving and/or behaving is questioned and reframed.

For the *facilitative* approach, the three approaches are:

- *Cathartic*: The coach allows the coachee to express and/or feel certain emotional reactions that he or she may have been bottling up or avoiding. Once released, the coachee can let go of them and move on.

- *Catalytic*: The coach uses questions and listens carefully to the coachee so as to effectively track the coachee's own learning journey. The aim is to help the coachee discover his or her own wisdom.
- *Supportive*: Focusing on positive actions and qualities to build up the coachee's confidence and self-esteem. Believing in the coachee and acting with 100% certainty that he or she can succeed.

Heron does not stipulate any style as more appropriate than the other, but suggests the aim is to feel comfortable at both ends of the spectrum and all points in between. However, he also stresses that for those in more facilitative roles (i.e. coaching), the balance of time and emphasis should be weighted heavily to the three facilitative approaches. Carol Wilson, in her book *Performance Coaching* (2014), suggests no more than 10 per cent of your time should be in 'prescriptive', for instance. This is a good guide, however as explained in the next chapter, once drawn into an authoritative approach it's hard to get out of it.

But can complex human behaviours and intentions really be turned into this kind of linear scale? The 'spectrum' model polarises the directive style as being goal-focused and the non-directive style as people-focused. But are these two considerations mutually exclusive? It depends on whose goal it is.

Whose direction is it anyway?

Ownership of the outcome is always a tricky issue for corporate coaching, as the paying organisation may wish to outline what it expects the coachee to achieve from the coaching. If the coachee's personal outcomes seem out of line with the organisation's expectations, in which direction do you go to remain client-led? Your client is both the coachee and the organisation.

Jon Blakey and Ian Day (2012) are two voices within the coaching community who believe that non-directive coaching encourages a self-centred "me, me, me" attitude within the coachee, neglecting the wider organisation paying for the coaching service. They argue that coaches need to focus more on what's best for the organisation paying for the coaching, not the individual coachee. From this perspective, the direction of the coaching must lead towards organisational outcomes, and clear contracting is crucial to ensure such outcomes are clearly articulated to all involved. Leaders can be inspired through coaching, according to Blakey and Day, to pursue courageous goals, not in the service of individual egos but towards a broader, collective purpose.

But organisations already exert huge power over the individuals who work for them. The culture of an organisation represents the unspoken, taken-for-granted 'way we do things here' as well as the official mission and values, which push leaders to behave in certain ways, sometimes regardless of their own personal preferences. Giving priority to the individual's personal aims, and contracting with the organisation to that effect, helps re-balance the power. And people inevitably change for their own reasons, not because they are told to. We are all essentially goal-directed organisms and constantly juggle multiple goals, consciously and unconsciously, within a hierarchical arrangement of differing importance (Grant, 2012).

There are usually many people in a person's life who are 'expert' advisors, be it professional, family and/or job related. Most of us have an abundance of people prepared to tell us what we should do, and at times it can be crucial to get some good advice and clear instructions. However, it can also dis-empower people from facing up to their own decisions, as well as de-motivating to those who may never feel responsible for any actions agreed on. It can be hard to separate personal needs from others. People are intrinsically linked to others in their lives: at work, through family and other close personal and professional relationships. We carry within us the voices of those others, so much so that it may only be through quiet reflection with a coach that we learn to recognise our own voice and begin to develop some self-direction. As Grant (2012) highlights, "self-concordant" goals, determined by the individual and aligned to his or her values, are crucial to a person's motivation and likely success. Non-directive coaching allows the coachee to set deeply personal goals and these are what matter the most.

Is non-directive coaching pointless?

Coaching literature, professional bodies' descriptions of standards and coach training are all biased towards non-directive support, according to Blakey and Day (2012). From their perspective, providing feedback and challenge is not possible if a non-directive stance is taken. Their assumption is that non-directive coaching is not purposeful, nor does it challenge the client hard enough. But does the term 'non-directive' really mean 'directionless' as it may imply? It could be assumed that a directionless coach may simply focus on whatever the coachee says next in the conversation, following a possibly random and unstructured chain of thought, with no regard to heading towards any particular direction. The session would become a 'cosy chat', as Blakey and Day warn against, that ends up nowhere in particular. Non-directive could also be taken to mean being 'indirect', sounding like a rather vague, ineffectual approach where ideas and feedback are hinted at rather than overtly stated, and questions are hedged with uncertainty, such as "Don't you think it could maybe help if you were to try . . . possibly?"

Initially, the term 'non-directive' was coined to remind people of what to avoid, such as pushing their own direction, consciously or inadvertently. The best intentions of the coach for the coachee may not result in the most helpful question or intervention. But without the coach's direction, instead of an *absence* of direction the approach adopted could orient towards the coachee's solution. By continually checking the coachee's emerging understanding of where he or she is now against where he or she would like to be, the coach can help the coachee navigate the best route towards his or her stated and agreed outcomes. You can be purposeful without being directive. When purposeful you continually define and redefine what the coachee wants. Rather than 'non-directive', perhaps a more useful term to describe facilitative coaching would be 'multi-directional'. Rather than a lack of direction, the coach is constantly working with the coachee to negotiate the multiple outcomes and/destinations that the coachee could choose to focus on, moment by moment.

Non-directive coaching is not a soft option. It takes considerable skill to resist telling the coachee your opinions. Being non-directive is far from an easy option for the coachee either, who must step up to the challenge of taking responsibility for where to go. You must learn how to keep out of the coachee's way whilst keeping attention channelled towards coachee-defined, ever-evolving outcomes. This is where a Clean approach to coaching becomes very useful, as we will explore in later chapters.

In conclusion, the field of coaching has grown quickly and offers something distinct and different from other forms of people-development. Although many approaches to coaching are available, being facilitative, non-directive and client-focused offers maximum value. It is precisely because of what coaches *don't* say or do, that defines coaching as a unique and distinct activity, potentially worthy of becoming a profession in its own right. Non-directive coaching can still have purpose and focus, following the coachee's ever-evolving personal outcomes. But there are many pulls towards the more directive, authoritative coaching approach, including client expectations and habit. In the next chapter we will further explore the dangers of a directive approach, and how coaches may be unconsciously biased towards an authoritative style. It is not enough to *intend* to be non-directive, and this is where Clean Coaching comes in, as a discipline and practice to support a truly facilitative, non-directive approach.

References

Alexander, G. (2006) Behavioural coaching – The GROW model. In J. Passmore (ed.), *Excellence in Coaching: The Industry Guide*. London; Philadelphia: Kogan Page, 83–93.

Blakey, J. and Day, I. (2012) *Challenging Coaching: Going Beyond Traditional Coaching to Face the Facts*. London: Nicholas Brearley Publishing.

Bluckert, P. (2006) *Executive Dimensions of Executive Coaching*. Maidenhead: Open University Press.

Brockbank, A. and McGill, I. (2006) *Facilitating Reflective Learning Through Mentoring & Coaching*. London: Kogan Page.

Downey, M. (2010) Interview by D Hallett. In Four Quadrant coaching: A conversation with Myles Downey. *Integral Leadership Review*, Issue 3. June 2010. Available at: www.archive-ilr.com/archives-2010/2010–06/2010–06-interview-hallett.php [Accessed 5/7/2015].

Gallwey, T. (1974/1997) *The Inner Game of Tennis* (Revised ed.). New York: Random House.

Grant, A. M. (2012) An integrated model of goal-focused coaching. *International Coaching Psychology Review*, 7(2). September 2012. Available at: www.coachfederation.org/files/includes/docs/161-an-integrated-model-of-goal-focused-coaching.pdf [Accessed 2/7/2015].

Hemphill, P. (2011) *The History and Future of Coaching* [pdf]. The Association for Coaching, International Conference. Available at: https://app.box.com/s/e6d45f42419288d 5cf6e [Accessed 23/7/2015].

Heron, J. (1990 [1975]) *Helping the Client* (4th ed.). London: Sage Publications. (Original edition published in 1975.)

Ives, Y. (2008) What is 'coaching'? An exploration of conflicting paradigms. *International Journal of Evidence Based Coaching and Mentoring*, 6(2), 100–113.

Passmore, J. (2007) Coaching and mentoring – The role of experience and sector knowledge. *International Journal of Evidence Based Coaching and Mentoring Special Issue 1*, Summer 2007, 10.

Thompson, B. (2013) *Non-Directive Coaching: Attitudes, Approaches, Applications.* Cheshire: Critical Publishing.

Whitmore, J. (1992) *Coaching for Performance*. London: Nicholas Brealey.

Whitmore, J. (2002) *Coaching for Performance: GROWing People, Performance and Purpose.* (3rd ed.). London: Nicholas Brealey.

Wilson, C. (2014) *Performance Coaching: A Complete Guide to Best Practice Coaching and Training.* London: Kogan Page.

Chapter three

The directive bias

Getting drawn in

Directive coaching is magnetic. Coaches are drawn towards it without meaning to be, and it can be hard to pull away. This chapter highlights how unconscious, unintentional biases can bend us towards the authoritative position in coaching. We will also focus on the 'middle ground' between directive and non-directive extremes. The greatest risk is here, as there is maximum potential for confusion and misrepresentation. This is where coaches may believe they are being largely non-directive whereas in fact their approach, intention and language may be leading their coachee towards a pre-determined solution of their own.

The directive challenge

Blakey and Day (2012) have challenged the non-directive, client-led "sacred cow," suggesting it's a hangover from the field of counselling and therapy, irrelevant for coaching robust, healthy executives. They argue for coaching that goes beyond what they feel is the "traditional" client-led model, advocating the value of the coach's direct feedback, provocative challenge and the disclosure of personal experience. Coaches should speak their truth, and encourage the coachee to "face the facts," reconnecting senior leaders with reality through specific, direct and concrete interventions. Leaders thrive on challenge, and they need it because strong, confident leaders often end up surrounded by people who don't challenge them enough, if at all.

Perhaps you really do know better than the coachee and surely it would be irresponsible *not* to guide him or her towards a more viable option than his or her own suggestion? If you are certain of this, I recommend that you re-contract on that basis and name your intervention appropriately as a mentoring or training service. Being told solutions can be very useful for certain kinds of problems, but explicit instructions and clear advice do not necessarily result in the appropriate decision or action being taken. According to Bonaccio and Dalal's research (2006) most people take little notice of good advice because simply being told the solution does not enable people to actively construct new ways of thinking beyond their stuck-ness. It can even strengthen their resolve to take their own chosen path, reinforcing any potentially unfounded beliefs.

Apart from its potential ineffectiveness, directive coaching can be unhelpful for the following reasons:

- You may be an expert coach, but it's highly unlikely that you know more than the coachee about his or her own unique situation. Any advice – however well-intentioned – really could backfire and be wrong.
- Your position in the coaching relationship as a paid-for service carries invisible power. Your advice and/or judgement could be held in greater esteem than would be otherwise and may even exert undue influence.
- By presenting your own, or another's 'expert' opinion, you may deny your coachee the possibility of exploring and understanding his or her own path. Advice-giving undermines a person's sense of empowerment and encourages learned helplessness.
- When the coachee expects to be given answers it feels like an easy option, but avoids the depth of thinking actually required by the coachee to bring about sustainable change through reaching creative solutions and insightful decisions (Kline, 1999).
- Some coachees dislike being led and will resist, consciously or unconsciously, which obstructs effective coaching.
- Even in the best-case scenario, where your advice is sound and the coachee takes it and succeeds in his or her endeavours, the coachee is left believing that coaching is an instructional process and future expectations of coaching will be unrealistic.

The authoritative bias

With 21 years of being a coach/people-developer, I've been privileged to witness many coaches engaging in their craft. For instance, through my involvement with the Association for Coaching in setting up co-coaching forums throughout the UK, and running my own local group in Berkshire for five years. In addition, as Course Director for the Clean Coaching Centre, I receive recorded coaching sessions from students, which I listen to and provide feedback on. Finally, as a coaching supervisor, I have many coaches describe their actual coaching activity to me in great detail. In my experience, there is often a disconnection between what coaches *say* they do and what actually happens in practice. *Most coaches think they are more facilitative than they actually are.*

Myles Downey agrees that although coaches will say they are enabling the other person to think for himself or herself, in reality they are "leading the other person by the nose" (2010). I personally have found that very few stay firmly grounded at the non-directive end of the spectrum. Most, despite describing themselves as 'mainly facilitative', actually adopt a more consultative approach. Even though they try to avoid giving the coachee answers or suggesting solutions, many do just that, to meet client expectations and possibly their own comfort factor in the relationship. It can be very hard to withhold potentially valuable information from the coachee if you believe it could help the person.

There is a bias leaning towards the opposite direction to the profession's stated approach, i.e. away from facilitative and towards the authoritative. This bias is like a trap – once fallen into it is hard to get out of, for four key reasons:

1   Habit and relationship dynamics.
2   Making assumptions.
3   Putting words into people's minds.
4   Unconscious 'Rescuer' drives.

1. Habit and relationship dynamics

It's easy to fall into the trap of the authoritative. For example, let's say your coachee tells you that she is struggling to manage her time. You may initially respond in a facilitative style, and ask questions to clarify how the coachee currently manages time, what she wants instead and how would she know if she had achieved it. In answering your questions, your coachee might continue to look and act as if she is not in control of her time. For instance she appears harassed, struggling with conflicting priorities and desperately searching for a quick fix. That sense of urgency could easily rub off on you as the coach, as the hour's session is passing quickly and the client fails to produce answers or make any progress, as far as you can see.

Your desire to move things forward brings forth a tentative but definitely more directive question when you ask: "Do you think you might be avoiding responsibility here?" The client grabs this like a life line, because she wants badly to define the issue too. But you may both be colluding to follow a false path. Your client further fuels this direction by asking what tips you have for taking responsibility. You spend the next 20 minutes of the session explaining a model about taking responsibility. The session ends with both you and the coachee feeling good about the session. However, by providing answers, you may be fuelling the very problem the coachee came with by further stripping away her sense of responsibility.

Sadly, the above example is not unusual. People are creatures of habits that extend beyond their personal actions: we suck others into our patterns and relationship dynamics often reinforce an individual's expectations and any resultant behaviour. And, when a coach doesn't know what to say or where to go next, it can be reassuringly tangible to share models or 'how to' examples. Although we know models don't capture the complexity of real life, they provide neat packages that can be useful for simplification. For both the coach and the coachee, models can feel concrete and constructive. But models can also be constrictive. Knowing about a model is not the same as learning how to do something differently. What the coachee learns, perhaps unconsciously, is how to give the responsibility over to you.

Many directive interventions seem perfectly legitimate – assuming you are the expert and have appropriate authority. But once you have adopted an authoritative style within a coaching session, for instance prescribing a certain approach, it is difficult to step out of. You have already shaped the mould that may continue to influence the coachee's subsequent ideas. And with many issues and outcomes brought to coaching, matters are not straightforward. When a coachee wants help in 'time management' for instance, can you correctly interpret what that means for this particular coachee and provide a meaningful strategy? For example in the past I have used various time management models as a trainer, such as Stephen Covey's 'importance v urgency' matrix (Covey et al., 1994) to help people look at how they prioritise activities. For many people however, this model is so different to their current way of thinking about time that it's difficult to adopt the principles, despite sounding like a good idea.

2. Making assumptions

It is difficult to imagine a world, a relationship, a conversation, where nothing is taken for granted. Assumptions are the mental short cuts we use in order to have time to get on to the more important messages.

Our ability to infer more than we can see is part of our unique gift as human beings. For instance, an important idea in psychology is that most people are blessed with a mental mechanism known as the 'Theory of Mind' ('ToM'). This is the innate human ability to recognise that others have minds of their own, and although we cannot directly experience them we intuit they are different from our own. It's what enables us to put ourselves in another's shoes and imagine how we would respond if we were to see things from their perspective. Children learn this from about age three, before which time they find it hard to imagine that others do not know all they know and find it difficult to lie.

But, assumptions can be dangerous. For example, because of our ToM assumptions, we imagine what others are thinking, feeling, wanting and needing and then act as though that was known reality rather than guesswork. We do this so effectively we can forget we are not really mind-reading and the other person's viewpoint is concealed from us. When the coachee says he or she needs to work at being more confident, for instance, what you believe that might mean to the person is not the same as what it actually means. Words alone fail to convey the whole story and the other person means more than you can possibly hear or assume to know.

For example stop reading this for a moment and think of a tree. And then notice what kind of thought you had. For many people, in their mind's eye they will conjure up a mental image. Some may have pictured a real tree that exists somewhere, perhaps in their own garden. For some, it was purely an imagined representation of a typical tree. Each of us is likely to think of something slightly different and unique. But more than that, for some people that visual picture may be clear and distinct, for others it could have been a mere outline or silhouette. Some may have imagined a whole scene with the tree located somewhere with other flora and fauna around it. Some may not even see a picture at all, but a word. Some may have a different kind of sense of it, like the touch of bark, the sound of rustling leaves or the smell of a forest. All these sensory aspects have connections with other thoughts, memories and emotions, all totally unique to each individual, and to the particular moment. Moreover, repeat this exercise later and a very different set of images, feelings and memories may be evoked.

When you assume you know what the other person means, you deny the person the opportunity to explore the implicit meaning that person has uniquely assigned to that particular word or set of words. By asking questions to check your assumptions, your coachee can learn more about his or her own pre-existing but unexplored personal viewpoints, sometimes resulting in surprising discoveries that lead to a reframe in understanding.

Asking questions instead of giving information doesn't guarantee that you are being non-directive. Questions are easily framed so that they are biased towards the questioner's perspective, steering coachees towards what the coach already thought was true. The coachee's choice of response gets narrowed down to fit the coach's perspective. You may argue that you are following your intuition in exploring one particular aspect or theme rather than another. However those little 'inklings' could be red herrings, and reveal more about what's going on in your own mind rather than your coachee's.

The potential effect of these red herrings is highlighted by Robert Dilts and colleagues (1990) in the tongue-in-cheek story of the psychoanalyst who was under the impression that people who had serious problems would invariably dream about fish. Because of his preconceived model of the client, all of his questions were focused on dreams and in one way or another would be directly or indirectly searching for fish. If the patient said he or she was lying on a beach, the therapist would ask about the sea, and what was under the sea, for instance. Or, if the client dreamt of eating at a restaurant, the therapist would ask about the menu . . . was there fish on it? Regardless of whether the client thought there were any fish, the therapist was so sure of their presence that he would keep searching until inevitably, the possibility of fish would emerge. People tend to see what they expect to be there and already believe is true and as coaches we are not immune to this tendency. Your perception of the client, the outcome and what may be hindering him or her will inevitably affect what you notice and – unless you guard against it – which questions you choose to ask.

3. Putting words into people's minds

Suggestions are suggestive

In reviewing Heron's coaching spectrum, you may feel that the 'prescriptive' approach is just too far towards the extreme authoritative end of the spectrum to use regularly. But, the 'informative' option feels more comfortable for coaches, especially those who offer training and mentoring. This 'middle ground' coaching approach is common practice, I believe. Rather than 'show and tell', it's 'show and ask'. The coach makes suggestions tentatively, presenting a model or a story, and then invites the coachee to reflect further, potentially developing an alternative idea. This approach is appealing and one I have used myself at times. However, the impact can be easily underestimated.

Suggestions are, by their very nature, suggestive. People tend to be more easily influenced by subtle hints than overt orders, as Elizabeth Loftus and her colleagues discovered when researching the reliability of eye witness testimonies (Loftus and Palmer, 1974). Their experiment involved showing their research participants a film depicting a head-on crash between two cars. Different groups of participants were asked slightly different questions, varying from "How fast do you think the cars were travelling when they *bumped* into each other?" to "How fast do you think the cars were travelling when they *smashed* into each other?" The difference in responses from each group was measured, and those asked questions with more impactful descriptions thought the cars were travelling faster. By altering just one word in the question, participants appeared to have their perception of an event altered.

This may seem inconsequential; however even more striking was when a follow-up question was asked: "Did you see any broken glass?" The film did not show any such damage, however a high percentage of those asked did in fact agree that there was. The question contained an *embedded assumption* – a subtle but hugely influential factor that introduced the possibility of broken glass. For many people, this was enough to create an inaccurate memory and a totally false belief.

As an example of how easily this can impact on your coaching, I once innocently asked a coachee at the start of a session, "What would you like to pay attention to?" The word 'pay' metaphorically transformed my well-intended question into something that the coachee experienced as costly and difficult. Fortunately this coachee was able to notice and explain to me how my question conjured up images of being back at school with teachers forcing her to 'pay attention . . . or else!' Not a good start to a session!

Just consider how insidiously and unconsciously we choose our words when we ask questions, and how easily we may unintentionally alter our coachee's perception. Worse still, the effect seems to be enduring and possibly even permanent: you cannot take a suggestion back. Once a seed is planted it may take hold, as Loftus's (1975) further research demonstrated when a debrief was carried out to explain to participants how the phrasing of the research questions was designed to influence their beliefs. Although the participants were then given the opportunity to reconsider their previous answers, most still stuck to their guns and held on to their erroneous belief despite being told of the manipulation.

A wealth of evidence is available on the effect of biased questions and the power of suggestion, concluding that subtle language influencers can distort perception without conscious awareness. Because of this, biased questions are stringently controlled within some professions, for instance the police force, the legal profession and psychology research. However in other fields, without those controls our bias creeps in unguarded, whether we like it or not. This can trigger a number of biased responses, such as:

- The *observer expectancy effect* – where the coach unwittingly pushes the coachee towards the answer the coach expects.
- The *expectation bias* – the coachee gives the answer he or she thinks the coach wants to hear.
- The *confirmation bias* – the coachee searches only for information/ideas, etc. that match current preconceptions, both the coachee's own and those of the coach's.

It is not only leading or closed questions that influence, even the use of hypothetical questions (Moore et al., 2012) exerts unconscious bias.

Being truly impartial and non-directive as a coach means addressing your unspoken intentions as well as your verbalised questions. Even without words, we could unwittingly direct attention to the areas that we deem useful and important, with personal opinion leaking through our voice tone and body language. Coaches 'point' to where they think the coachee needs to go, with visual as well as verbal language, through hand gestures, eye movements and signposting with voice emphasis and tone.

A further example of the power of suggestion is so ubiquitous in scientific research that it's taken for granted and virtually ignored, and that is the power of *placebo*. Placebos highlight the potential benefit of positive suggestion for the coachee. The positive psychology movement and influences from solutions-focused counselling and therapy have found their way into coaching approaches, and there is considerable value in helping the coachee pay attention to the positive. Indeed, many people contaminate their thoughts with an overly negative commentary. Cognitive behavioural coaching approaches, which are highly directive, can be instrumental in counteracting that negativity and bringing the coachee into more balanced thinking.

Even so, prescribing positive thoughts, although in principle seems worthwhile, can backfire. Telling others what positive messages they should say to themselves is like dressing someone else in your clothes: they are not likely to fit or feel comfortable. However, steering the coachee towards his or her *own* positive and resourceful messages and away from any negative and/or problem-focused language can be very effective.

Paraphrasing

Paraphrasing is when you replay another's message with your own words. It is supposed to demonstrate that you have listened and understood them. However as soon as you introduce your own language and interpretation, you run the same risk of suggestion and bias. Whenever someone responds to me with "So what you're saying is . . ." I notice that his or her summary often contains a very different message from the one I had originally intended. Just one word can make a difference to the meaning. What I hear is my own message distorted through another person's viewpoint, influenced by that person's perceptions, beliefs and intentions.

I first learnt paraphrasing skills as a sales person, and some sales training courses capitalise on the persuasive effect of paraphrasing. When the prospect said "It's too expensive," I was taught to answer, "So what you are really saying is you can't yet see how valuable it would be for you?" This is a powerful persuasion technique that quite literally puts words into people's mouths that reflect what you think or want their message to mean, not what they actually intended. As well as putting words into their mouths you put words in their minds as well. This is another inadvertent way coaches may end up leading the coachee towards the prescriptive solution they would like to see happen.

A more effective and accurate way to show your attentiveness is to summarise using only the coachee's own words. This demonstrates that the coachee has been truly heard and his or her thoughts honoured and respected. If you have never tried this approach, give it a go. Most find it initially very difficult to remember and repeat back exactly the same words as the other person, mistakenly replacing the words with their own. It highlights the extent to which people hear what they want or expect to. We all quickly forget the other person's language in favour of our own interpretation. But this skill – a core part of Clean Coaching – can easily be improved with regular practice. This is a far more impactful way to show your understanding without risking any remoulding of the coachee's meaning.

4. Unconscious 'Rescuer' drives

Coaches are just as human as everyone else and sometimes driven by unconscious desires, fears and patterns of relating. Within the field of Transactional Analysis, people are thought to adopt certain 'life script' roles, and the subtle relationship dynamics between people can trigger habitual roles in unfavourable ways.

Stephen Karpman's "Drama Triangle" model (2007) highlights how unconscious dynamics between people, including coach and coachee can reflect, reinforce and fuel our unconscious drives. These drives are often formed in childhood and then reinforced through the roles we take up as adults. For instance, common roles include being the eternal 'Victim' who is always helpless, and never to blame, compelling others to step in and take charge. There is also the 'Persecutor' who is forced to defend victims and ends up challenging and attacking others. And then there is the 'Rescuer' who on the surface seems almost heroic, taking responsibility and making things happen for everyone's benefit. However it is often the Rescuer, not the Persecutor, who enables the 'Victim' to stay helpless.

All professional helpers would be wise to reflect on their deeper drives for pursuing their particular career path. The very motivation to become a coach and help others to improve could come from a deep-seated need to be needed. Excessive helping behaviour is a common problem within executive coaching, according to coaching psychologist Manfred Kets de Vries (2010). A pre-disposal to rescuing tendencies – referred to as 'rescuer syndrome' – is not an official disorder. But it becomes apparent when coaches feel compelled to actively help, rather than stay outside of the issue. There is a very fine line between enabling someone to succeed, and actually doing it for the person. Once you've played the Rescuer role, it is very difficult to stop.

Most people like to help, but Rescuers get a strong sense of urgency when their coachee presents a problem. There is an uncomfortable urge to resolve things quickly and offer solutions. They put high standards on their own performance and expect themselves to always know the right answer, feeling inadequate if they are not able to jump in with instant advice and concrete answers. In addition, they tend to feel guilty "for not accomplishing the unrealistic goals they set for others" (Kets de Vries, 2010:8).

Another tell-tale Rescuer sign is being unable to accept your own feelings or emotions, because you are 'over-attuned' to the feelings of others. This could eventually lead to burnout for the coach, who may find the boundary between his or her own desires and that of the coachees become increasingly entwined to the extent that the relationship becomes a mirror of other significant, troublesome ties. When this happens, typically the Rescuer finds himself or herself unappreciated and resentful and ends up becoming a Victim. Another possibility is the Rescuer switches to Persecutor role, and feels compelled to punish or expose the failing coachee who just wouldn't take the help he or she was offered. Rescuer patterns are best brought to the open through personal reflection and regular supervision. In this way they can be consciously explored and new ways of relating to people established. Often the very act of bringing it to conscious awareness decreases its hold on us.

How to become more coachee-led

No one is immune to directive bias, but it can be identified and addressed by having a high sense of self-awareness. This is the capability in the coaching moment to step outside of your personal viewpoint and ask yourself: "What is my intention here?" and "Where am I going with this?" Clean Coaching, as we will see from the next chapter onwards, provides a discipline and practice for continually checking your orientation and focus.

Let us return for a moment to Heron's 'spectrum' model. More than a 'pick and mix' approach to interventions, it is meant to encourage facilitators to think about their own *motivation* in taking a certain approach, and to consider their *intention* in asking a particular question. Intention, according to Heron, takes us to the heart of the matter and he suggests you consider what the point or purpose of your question is about (Heron, 1990). I would add, you might want to catch yourself just after you felt compelled to ask a certain question, and check:

- Who is this question for? and
- In whose best interests is this intervention?

An important (and also Clean) question to reflect on is "Where could that (question) have come from?" It isn't always easy to follow one's own chain of thought from listening to the coachee's words to choosing your next question. Usually there is some internal processing that includes remembering/imagining our own experience and in doing so, personal motives can be awakened. An even more fundamental question to ask yourself is: "Where do I expect the solution to come from?"

I encourage all coaches to be self-reflective and spend time after coaching sessions exploring the actual questions and interventions they took. If you are able to record and transcribe the occasional coaching session, it can be very illuminating to explore and examine your own coaching style and degree of directiveness. Even without a transcript, you can try taking notes during the session that record:

- Your actual questions.
- The coachee's actual answers (just key words).
- Your musings.

You can divide your note paper into three columns to record each of these different kinds of information for later review.

Increasing the amount of time spent reflecting increases your ability to be more self-reflective in the moment. Coaching supervision provides an essential facility to do just this in a professional, supportive environment. Clean Coaching, as we will continue to explore, is an approach to coaching that encompasses intention, behaviours, interventions and specific questions. It encourages coaches to be more self-aware and self-reflective, as the questions help draw clearer boundaries between the coach's perspective and that of the coachee.

Practical exercise

Take a recent coaching session that you have ideally recorded and transcribed, or if that's not possible use accurate notes you have taken during a coaching session, divided into the three columns mentioned above.

You can examine each of your actual questions after the session, asking yourself the following questions:

- What was the intention of this question?
- Where was I going with this?
- Who was this question for?
- Where could that question have come from?

When looking at your coachee's answers, spot any different layers or levels of direction the coachee may have alluded to. Is there anything else you notice about what the coachee said? In what ways might you have helped the coachee explore any stated or implied directions more explicitly?

When looking at any musings you noted, what do you know now, with the benefit of hindsight?

What would you do differently if you could?

The purpose of this exercise is not to beat yourself up or conclude you are brilliant, but to help sharpen your ability to notice directions at a deeper level of awareness. The more often you do this exercise and work with a supervisor, the more you will gradually increase your ability to notice more in the moment and during the session itself where you can catch potential intentions and inferences and go with the coachee's own path more deliberately.

Navigating a 'Clean' direction

In summary, there are many pulls on the coach to adopt an authoritative, directive approach even when it is not our intention. So how do we avoid the dangers of being directive? Clean Coaching is a form of non-directive coaching that provides suitable frameworks that help keep the coach's sense of responsibility within appropriate limits, avoiding any Rescuer tendencies. It also provides a structured but flexible process for orienting the coachee to discover outcomes and where the coachee currently is in relation to them. In Clean Coaching, the direction to go next is not chosen by the coach, but always established from the perspective of the coachee, mapped through his or her eyes, ears and worldview. By taking this 'insider' perspective, the coach accepts the coachee as the world's most renowned expert on the coachee. As Bluckert (2006:4) insists, this is the most profound notion, and the essence of coaching: "Learning through the coaching method is an *inside-out* process, not an *outside-in* one."

When we start from the coachee's perspective, directions can emerge and coaching rarely travels along a single line between current situation and desired outcome. Instead, as the coachee becomes clearer on his or her situation, the outcome(s) are clarified and sometimes change completely. In turn, as outcomes become clearer, the coachee's sense of where he or she is now in relation to those outcomes can shift and evolve.

The coach remains focused on the coachee's perceived destination, as it currently stands and allows that to determine the overall coaching direction. However within the session itself, the coach holds responsibility for keeping the coachee on the right track. For instance even non-directive advocate Bob Thompson (2013:4) says: "I aim to be non-directive about the content but I am often directive about the structure." And Tim Gallwey (2000) distinguishes between **two** levels of directiveness: directing the coachee's attention versus directing the coachee's actions. By directing attention, you can still be non-directive in the wider sense that the coachee owns the outcome and decides on strategies. Whereas directing actions is inevitably a prescriptive approach.

Directive coaching is like an arrow, with careful aim the process can reach its target very quickly and precisely. However, unlike a real journey, a coachee's metaphoric journey is rarely as straightforward as finding the shortest path between A and B. With coaching, the journey itself often changes the desired destination. If you have taken a directive path with your coachee, there is the danger that you'll reach a destination only to discover it's no longer the right place. As the destination belongs to the client, it is only the client who can really know whereabouts to head for, moment by moment, to get to where he or she wants to be. Non-directive coaching is sometimes described as unfocused and directionless, but I don't believe that needs to be true. Highly effective non-directive but focused coaching can concentrate on tracking where the coachee wants to get to, compared to where he or she is now, in order to continually re-navigate the path ahead. *Like a compass*, a non-directive coach can help orient the coachee towards the outcome, but only the coachee can decide which path to take.

References

Blakey, J. and Day, I. (2012) *Challenging Coaching: Going Beyond Traditional Coaching to Face the Facts*. London: Nicholas Brearley Publishing.

Bluckert, P. (2006) *Executive Dimensions of Executive Coaching*. Maidenhead: Open University Press.

Bonaccio, S. and Dalal, R. (2006) Advice taking and decision-making: An integrative literature review, and implications for the organizational sciences. *Organizational Behavior and Human Decision Processes*, 101, 127–151. Available at: https://faculty1.colorado-college.edu/~afenn/web/EC303_8_04/FALL07/READINGS/Bonaccio%20Dalal%20 Literature%20Review%20Advice%20taking.pdf [Accessed 3/8/2015].

Covey, S., Merrill, A. and Merrill, R. (1994) *First Things First: To Live, to Love, to Learn, to Leave a Legacy*. New York: Simon and Schuster.

Dilts, R., Hallborn, T. and Smith, S. (1990) *Beliefs: Pathways to Health and Well-Being* (2nd ed.). Carmarthen: Crown House.

Downey, M. (2010) Interview by D. Hallett. In Four Quadrant coaching: A conversation with Myles Downey. *Integral Leadership Review*, Issue 3. June 2010. Available at: www.archive-ilr.com/archives-2010/2010–06/2010–06-interview-hallett.php [Accessed 5/7/2015].

Gallwey, T. (2000) *The Inner Game of Work*. London: Orion.

Heron, J. (1990) *Helping the Client* (4th ed.). London: Sage Publications. (Original edition published in 1975.)

Karpman, S. B. (2007) *The New Drama Triangles* [pdf]. USATAA/ITAA Conference Lecture. 11 August 2007. Available at: www.karpmandramatriangle.com/pdf/thenewdrama triangles.pdf [Accessed 16/6/2015].

Kets de Vries, M. F. R. (2010) *Leadership Coaching and the Rescuer Syndrome: How to Manage Both Sides of the Couch* [pdf]. INSEAD Working Papers, 2010/104/EFE/IGLC. Available at: www.insead.edu/facultyresearch/research/doc.cfm?did=46469 [Accessed 27/1/2015].

Kline, N. (1999) *Time to Think: Listening to Ignite the Human Mind.* London: Cassell Illustrated.

Loftus, E. (1975) Leading questions and the eyewitness report. *Cognitive Psychology*, 7, 560–572.

Loftus, E. and Palmer, J. (1974) Reconstruction of auto-mobile destruction: An example of the interaction between language and memory. *Journal of Verbal Learning and Verbal Behavior*, 13, 585–589.

Moore, S., Neal, D., Fitzsimons, G. and Shiv, B. (2012) Wolves in sheep's clothing: How and when hypothetical questions influence behaviour. *Organisational Behaviour & Human Decision Processes*, 117(1), 168–178.

Thompson, B. (2013) *Non-Directive Coaching: Attitudes, Approaches, Applications.* Cheshire: Critical Publishing.

Chapter four

What kind of coaching is 'Clean' Coaching?

Introduction

Clean Coaching is a style, strategy and set of techniques for coaching that incorporates the 'Clean' approach to personal change created by the late, great David Grove. Grove was a counselling psychologist from New Zealand who pioneered this non-directive approach within psychotherapy and personal development which has subsequently cascaded into other areas of business, education and learning. Grove's ideas were shaped over many years and include three important developments: Clean Language, Clean Space and Emergent Knowledge. Each has the same core philosophy but distinctly different methods, together offering a highly flexible approach towards coaching.

Clean Coaching is a tool that enables self-exploration. It encourages coachees to reflect on their situation and available options, providing the conditions for insight to emerge. It rests on the premise that the real value of coaching comes from allowing coachees the time, space and stimulus to find their own solutions.

There are many reasons for using a Clean approach within a coaching session. Using Clean Language helps clients to think differently from their usual, habitual ways by exploring the metaphors they naturally and spontaneously use to describe their experience. And Clean Space often results in coachees being able to step outside their current perspective, and – literally and metaphorically – see their situation from new positions. To paraphrase Einstein, problems are unlikely to be solved at the same level of consciousness that created them. And so it seems likely that in order to help your coachee find fresh answers, a different kind of question may be required. An unusual kind of question, unlike anything the coachee may have heard before.

Clean Language, Clean Space and Emergent Knowledge each use a different route for exploring inner experience. Clean Language focuses on the coachee's language, in particular the inadvertent and automatic use of metaphors that describe what's going on for the person. These metaphors capture the essence of that person's experience and provide a window into deeper intentions and inner wisdom. Clean Space uses the physical space around the coachee as an external 'placeholder' for internal thoughts, getting inner experience out in the open where it can be examined from different directions and perspectives. The space becomes like a container within which patterns of thought can be represented as tangible locations, directions, objects and events. Emergent Knowledge uses the principles of networking and emergence, along with Clean Language and Clean Space, to structure a series of questions that encourage the coachee to reflect over and over again on what he or she knows. More than simple repetition, the questions are iterative, as each builds on the coachee's previous answer as the start point for the next question. This creates a kind of 'feedback loop', stimulating a chain reaction of growing understanding which leads to insight and change. All of these processes are covered in detail within this book.

Clean Coaching is the perfect antidote to any unconscious directive bias, as the word-specific phrasing and sequence of the questions prevents the facilitator hijacking the conversation by having complete free rein over what to ask next. However, some flexibility remains. Coaches can use different kinds of questions depending on the coachee. They may even give feedback and be challenging within the Clean Coaching frameworks, without steering away from the coachee's chosen course. Clean Coaching provides a strategy to help you to become more self-aware of your own perspective and intentions and be able to park them to one side.

Defining and describing the language of Clean Coaching

A key aspect of Clean Coaching is the use of very specific coaching questions. These questions are structured in a certain, exacting way and are unlike normal conversation. Clean Language is like a language all of its own and the following 'Clean' authors provide their descriptions of what those questions are and how they are used.

Penny Tompkins and James Lawley, in their book *Metaphors in Mind*, define Clean Language as "a way of asking questions of client's metaphors which neither contaminate nor distort them" (2000:xiii). They go on to highlight that for them, Clean Language has three functions (2000:52):

- To acknowledge clients' experience exactly as they describe it.
- To orient client's attention to an aspect of their perception.
- To send them on a quest for self-knowledge.

They say Clean Language is an extraordinary language because everything that the facilitator says and does is intimately related to what the client says and does (2000:52).

David Grove himself described Clean Language as questions that "do not impose upon the client any value, construct or presupposition about what he should answer." He goes on to say: "The questions are not asked to gather information or to understand the client's perspectives. We ask our questions so that the client can understand his perspective internally . . . in a way that he has not experienced before . . . the client is going to experience rather than describe what the experience is like" (Grove and Panzer, 1989:10).

Clean psychotherapist Philip Harland, who worked closely with Grove and wrote the Clean Language book *Trust Me, I'm the Patient*, explains what Clean Language is by describing what it isn't. For Harland (2012:16), it is:

> *Non-directive*: The facilitator issues no instructions at the level of content. Questions are directed instead at the level of process, which is concerned less with the meaning of what we say and more with its underlying construction: how we came to create our problems and how we may resolve them.
> *Non-suggestive*: In that the facilitator makes no recommendations and offers no advice.
> *Non-intrusive*: In that the facilitator does not dispute or challenge anything the other person may say.
> *Non-interpretive*: In that the facilitator offers no personal version of what the other might 'mean' by what they say.

Caitlin Walker (2014), a Clean proponent who works with groups and specialises in 'Systemic Modelling', suggests the core value of a Clean approach is that whatever you're doing with your clients, you're training them to do it for themselves. This requires you to engage in ego-less leadership, holding your clients to their own outcomes rather than to yours; trusting the wisdom in their system over your desire for them to change in specific ways.

Clean trainers Wendy Sullivan and Judy Rees (2008:1) suggest the basics are around fundamentally very simple behaviours:

- Keep your opinions and advice to yourself.
- Listen attentively.
- Ask Clean Language questions to explore a person's metaphors.
- Listen to the answers and then ask more Clean Language questions about what they've said.

Finally, my definition is this:

> To communicate without attempting to alter another's perception or understanding by adding yours. To ask questions that are not pre-loaded with your own assumptions and intentions. First and foremost it is a discipline that supports a way of being, that can be maintained and developed through practice.

This definition forms the basis of the body of work covered within this book. It is more than a description of what we need to be *doing*, e.g. the kind of questions we ask and what we don't say. It's as much about *being*: how we show up as a coach inevitably affects the process. It is a discipline similar to Peter Senge's description given in his seminal business book *The Fifth Discipline* (1990:12).

Rather than an enforcement or punishment, discipline is something which must be studied and mastered to be put into practice. And you remain in a state of practising as it is a developmental path which has no final arrival point. To practise a discipline is to be a lifelong learner. 'Clean' is not an expectation of pristine perfection, but a realistic intention that with practise and dedication can be continuously maintained and enhanced.

Assumptions v acceptance

The key principles and descriptions of Clean may make it sound extremely easy and similar to many other non-directive coaching approaches; however the 'cleanliness' goes deeper than your words. It goes beyond your conscious behaviours and question choice, to your actual intention for and opinion of your coachee. You need to keep out of your coachees' way and totally accept them as they are, with a right to remain the same as well as to make changes they feel appropriate. The golden rule for working cleanly is to *assume absolutely nothing*. Don't assume that the answer you are expecting and waiting to hear from your coachee is the only or indeed the best answer. By creating space inside your own head you can acquire a state of wise ignorance and be okay with not knowing what will happen next, completely trusting your coachee to answer in whatever way feels right for the person. This state of mind can be developed with practice and the right kind of attitude, which we'll cover more fully in the next few chapters.

It is not easy to be truly present with people, accepting them and their thinking just as they are, without any attempt to influence. It is human nature to tell people what we think: the evolution of language and consciousness has led us to share personal perspectives. However, the real skill in a coaching conversation is to resist the seductiveness of making suggestions, keeping our messages as free as possible of personal bias, hints, opinions and beliefs. If achieved, this can be incredibly powerful. Psychotherapist Carl Rogers (1961) expounded the value of giving people 'unconditional positive regard'. More recently, Nancy Kline (1999:37) highlighted the incredible power of listening without inputting, asserting that "giving good attention to people makes them more intelligent."

Assumptions are like the windows through which we see the world, and we can fail to notice any grime that builds over time to cloud our view. Clean Coaching provides a way to become more conscious of your assumptions and wipe them from your language. It provides both a mindset and a process that limits any biased directiveness creeping into your coaching conversation.

For example, in Chapter two I mentioned how easy it would be, with a coachee having time management difficulties, to share a well-known model to help her conceive of time as something concrete and pliable enough to be managed. Instead, I often use an approach which follows Clean Coaching principles, using the following question to start exploring: "Does your sense of time have a shape or a size?" This Clean Language question invites the coachee to think of a personal, symbolic representation of something abstract and conceptual. For example, one lady client initially drew a triangle, which after further exploration became a three-dimensional pyramid, with each of the four pyramid points representing the different 'pulls' on her time from different people/priorities in her life. She realised her free time was what was left in the middle, which, as highlighted by her own developing 'model', was currently virtually nothing at all! This led to a more effective realisation than anything revealed from exploring pre-existing models. These would have only forced my coachee to squeeze her version of the real world into something designed by someone else, most likely with a completely different understanding and experience from that of my coachee.

Using Clean Language: three different levels

Clean Language is a way of communicating that is very different from other forms of everyday conversation. And you can describe it in at least three different ways (see Figure 4.1):

Level one: a set of non-directive (multi-directional) questions

In the first instance, it can be described as a simple set of non-directive questions. The actual, exact wording of the question is important, as the language used is stripped of any assumptions embedded within our conversation without our awareness. Rather like a toolbox, a selection of Clean Language questions available at your mental 'fingertips' allows you to reduce the level of influence from any

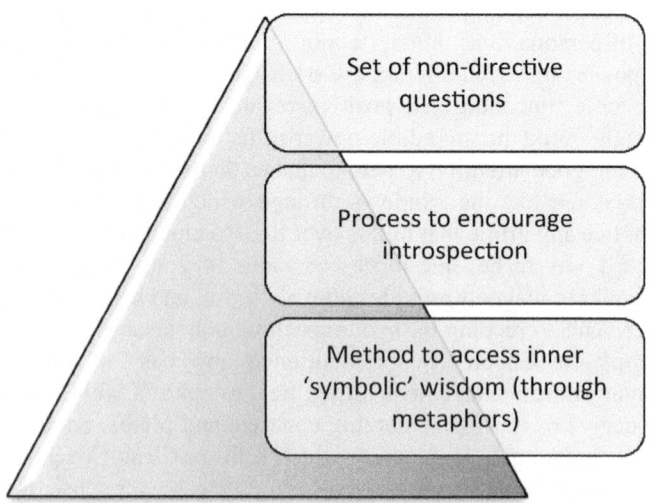

Figure 4.1 Applying Clean Language – three levels.

unconscious bias in your questioning. Any answer you get is more likely to reflect accurately what the other person really thinks and feels, unhindered by your own beliefs, opinions and desires. As a coach you might use Clean Language questions in a selective, occasional way, for instance choosing to use the questions right at the start of the relationship and/or today's session. In this way, it allows time and space for your understanding of the coachee and his or her situation to emerge.

Level two: a process to encourage introspection

The second application of Clean Language is more extensive. By sequencing a series of Clean questions together in a structured way, it becomes a process for encouraging introspection and mindfulness. When coachees continuously have their own thoughts reflected back at them along with Clean questions, they begin to pay less attention to the external world around them, including the coach's presence. Their attention becomes more introspective and focused on internal experiences and sensations as they answer a sequence of Clean questions. By focusing the coachees' attention on their own sensory experiences as they describe them, the questions help facilitate a meditative state of awareness. This awareness is focused on inner experience and deeper thought structures rather than the external world and surface-level reactions and responses.

Level three: a method to access inner 'symbolic' wisdom (through metaphors)

The third level is deepest of all. Clean Language questions are continually asked over a period of time, focusing attention on the coachees' metaphors that they use, naturally and unconsciously in response. Metaphors are more than just language embellishments. People use metaphors to describe experiences that would otherwise be hard to find words for. Metaphors occur frequently and spontaneously within everyday language and as David Grove discovered, people tend to use them more often when their attention is focused on inner experience.

This kind of introspection can gradually take the person into a state of altered consciousness, where the symbols and characters within their metaphors take on a tangible shape, form and location and 'come to life' within the person's imagination, almost as if they were dreaming. As the metaphoric 'story' evolves, its meaning may evolve, too. Changing awareness of the metaphor can translate back to the 'real' world situation, problem or outcome and surprising solutions to stuck patterns of thinking can emerge.

Using Clean Language as a coach

Clean Language questions are phrased in a specific and exact word sequence that remove any of the coach's own presumptions, judgements, ideas and opinion. It also strips the question of any subtle insidious metaphor of the coach's own formation that could creep into a more naturally spontaneous question form, distracting the coachee from his or her impressions. The question structure has a certain rhythm that also encourages the listener to reflect more deeply. The slightly hypnotic, repetitive syntax means the questions tend to 'land' deep and quickly generate an introspective state in the other person. This state is exactly the kind of quiet, reflective mental space that enables new kinds of thought to emerge.

Clean Language is a deceptively simple process. When facilitated by a person 'fluent' in Clean Language, the client often describes a complete freedom and total naturalness: it seems effortless. However, new learners of Clean Coaching sometimes experience the questions as 'clunky' and may doubt the client will find value from such simple questions. It can be almost painful for a coach to *not* say what he or she thinks is important, namely his or her own perspectives, opinions and judgements, and instead ask a Clean Language question, with the only additional content being the coachee's own words. Many Clean students are surprised by how difficult it is to communicate using nothing but a short list of simple questions, such is the force of our desire to influence and contribute.

Clean Language is a discipline, an aspiration and ongoing journey towards improvement. It is a practice and like mindfulness and meditation, on-going practice has a cumulative effect and a positive impact on the coach as well as the coachee. By learning to ask Clean Language questions, coaches can 'clean up' their act in general and become more aware of the subtle influence their own opinions, ideas and indeed metaphors have on their coaching interventions. Even when not choosing to coach 'squeaky clean', they are less likely to direct the coachee with their own thoughts, and more likely to predominantly use the coachee's own terminology and descriptions rather than replacing them with their own.

Clean Language is not a quick fix. It takes the willingness of the coach to devote time and effort to develop the skills. I believe this is best supported with dedicated Clean Language training and on-going commitment to practice. Clean Language is simple to pick up and try, and yet works on many levels so could take a lifetime to master.

Practical applications of Clean

These kinds of shifts in thinking can make very practical and real changes to how people behave. For example Carol Wilson delivered a coaching course within an NHS Trust, which included some training in Clean Language. One manager participant reported back that she successfully used the techniques to mediate during a breakdown in communication between hospital, patient and doctor. A discussion with the patient in metaphor enabled her to realise that some of her aggression towards the doctor was in fact arising from her own relationship with a relative, who was present at the time. Through Clean Language, the patient resolved not only the problem with the doctor, but the conflict with her relative as well.

Adrian Goodall, an experienced leadership and executive coach (PCC) working in the corporate sector,[1] completed the full distance learning programme on

Clean Coaching and went on to become an Accredited Clean Coach. Goodall works with leaders, their teams and rising talent who want better, different results. Typically, this involves the opportunities and challenges of leadership, promotion, confidence, teamwork, clarity of direction and communication skills.

He often uses a range of Clean techniques and believes these have helped him and his clients in a number of ways (Dunbar, 2010). He highlights the following core benefits:

- Establishing rapport (executives are surprised by accurate listening and reflection).
- Being efficient and direct with questions.
- Greater confidence in dealing with the client's organisational jargon.
- Additional confidence in handling unexpected emotional issues.
- Extra creativity.
- Greater systemic awareness.
- Dealing with blocks by helping people move away from stuck jargon/thinking.
- New perspectives which can be transformational and motivating.

He also says:

> I'm more able to be present with the client and their thinking because the Clean values help quieten my 'solutions' voice. Obviously there are times when clients want solutions and other 'content' more directly and we make a contract as to my role as coach and work together accordingly.
>
> I don't tell my clients when I'm using Clean Language so I don't have direct feedback on its impact. But my overall sense is that it builds a deeper confidence in coaching as something much more than just another conversation. Clients go away wanting to do things differently (rather than it being a duty). I'm often surprised at what makes a change land for the client, and I'm happy to go with that!
>
> (cited in Dunbar, 2010:3)

Common misconceptions about Clean Coaching

Most coaches these days seem aware of Clean Language, although David Grove's later developments with Clean Space and Emergent Knowledge are less widely familiar. Many coaching training programmes include some basic Clean elements within their standard curriculum. However, unless the learner has undertaken more in-depth training, limited understanding can lead to misconceptions and perpetuate a range of 'myths' about the pros and cons of Clean. When people tentatively attempt to be 'cleaner' with little or no experience of Clean in action, and without addressing their own underlying assumptions and intentions, those myths can become self-fulfilling. As with any technique or skill, the experienced can make it seem effortless. Although the basics can be picked up quickly, it takes a bit of time to get the approach right. Fundamentally, it is much more than a set of specialist questions, and this book intends to demonstrate this. Here are some of the myths I have heard, and in response, some more helpful ways of thinking about Clean Coaching.

It's more like therapy and not appropriate for executive coaching

Although it is true that Clean Coaching techniques tend to get to the heart of the matter – and therefore go deeper into the coachee's innermost thoughts, feelings, dreams and fears – getting personal is not the same as therapy. A psychotherapist works with people who have some kind of mental health issue that is usually serious enough to prevent them from normal day-to-day functioning in life. It is unlikely that your coachee is presenting with this level of difficulty and if so, it would be advisable to refer the person to a counsellor or psychotherapist, regardless to which kind of coaching you use.

An excellent resource for detangling any kind of coaching work from therapy is *A Guide to Coaching and Mental Health* (Buckley and Buckley, 2006). This book highlights how coaching and therapy can work side by side, as many mental health issues are surprisingly common and difficult to avoid in normal daily life.

It's too slow

The pace of the questions and the deliberate pausing to allow deep reflection can feel uncomfortable to those who are used to faster communication, including both coach and coachee. This slow pace is a key quality of the process, as it creates space for the coachee to become much more aware of what normally passes by unnoticed. But it is entirely appropriate to gradually slow things down during a session after starting at a more regular, conversational pace. And, just because the questions are delivered slowly, it does not mean that the coachee's progress is slow. Change can happen very quickly once a depth of understanding is reached.

It's too wishy-washy/vague

For the complete beginner, Clean questions can seem meandering and unfocused. However, the questions are highly precise and can get to the heart of the matter quickly. Clean Coaching provides a clear structure for identifying and exploring the coachees' desired outcome in relation to their perceived current reality. Practical action steps can be crystallised by using specific Clean questions designed for that purpose.

The coachee's metaphors are likely to have deep personal significance and a unique meaning that you may never be privy to. For some coaches, this lack of 'inclusion' into the coachee's experience can feel uncomfortable as they are curious about and motivated by the stories their coachees tell. Unfortunately, inclusion can feel like intrusion to the coachee, and coaches that feel compelled to know what's going on are possibly caught up in Karpman's Drama Triangle (2007) and trying to adopt their 'chosen' role. To be totally supportive and empathic even though you don't know exactly what the coachee is talking about – in any concrete tangible way – is an incredibly enriching experience for the coach and the coachee. It reminds me that in reality I never really know what the complete picture is for the coachee anyway.

It's only for creative people

Not true. Clean Coaching can be used with pretty much anyone, for many different purposes. Those who are visually creative may find it initially easier to engage with Clean Language and their metaphors. But more logical, conceptual people may find the process truly enlightening as it wakes them up to aspects of their thinking previously outside of their awareness. Even the barest glimpse of a deeper and different awareness can lead to insight and the inspiration to change.

It's not my style

This may be true, if you are a fast-paced, action-oriented person who is pragmatic and down to earth. I would describe myself as that kind of person. However, I recognised my approach often meant others would fail to keep up with my line of thinking and/or questions and I could easily 'steamroll' people along with my ideas. It also means I sometimes can't keep even up with my own train of thought. This can mean poor planning with lots of action but little progress! Learning Clean was the best thing to happen to me as it became a discipline to help me cultivate a gentler approach for teasing out answers from others. It's worth noting that I still retain the option to use my naturally quick, determined and single-minded style when needed, where it matters. For instance, having the determination and focus to write this book. Having greater choice over your coaching style is extremely useful, providing more flexibility, not less. Using Clean is always your choice, depending on the circumstance and context.

It's too restrictive/inflexible

Some Clean Coaching techniques follow a rigid structure. This can feel restrictive to the coach, but rarely the coachee, as the simple range of coaching questions frees up the coachee to answer in whatever way he or she likes. Questions are asked using specific, exact phrasing, the words themselves repetitive and predictable. This predictability is part of technique's effectiveness. The structure provides a sense of security for the coachee who doesn't have to wonder what the facilitator will ask next. For the coaches, it means they needn't devote their attention on deciding on their next question, so they can completely focus on the coachee. That depth of attention can be palpable to the coachee, sensing it as an extraordinary level of presence and complete acceptance.

Yet other Clean techniques are far more organic. Although the questions them-selves follow a repetitive rhythm, the flow of conversation within the session can diverge and the exploration go in different directions using different kinds of Clean questions and techniques. Both structured and organic Clean techniques may be applied in a single coaching session, giving the coach the flexibility to switch between approaches as appropriate.

It's an 'all or nothing' approach

Many trainers teach the discipline of an 'end-to-end' Clean process, as one direc-tive moment could greatly influence the coachee in an otherwise Clean session. However, you can operate at varying 'degrees' of Clean, from a generally con-versational 'Clean-ish' chat at the start to a more inward-focused, deeper Clean exploration in the middle; to a less formal 'Clean-ish' debrief at the end. Just because you have stopped being Clean in one part of a coaching session does not preclude you using Clean later on or in a subsequent session.

People are different. Some coachees will love Clean right from the start and some may take time to get used to this unusual way of communicating. For this reason, with new clients I often introduce Clean part-way through a session and return to a more typical conversational approach again before the end. In this way I can test the waters. It is not uncommon for the coachee to mention that the Clean part was a little strange and even to question its value. However, it often happens that within two or three sessions, once rapport has increased and a deeper level of trust established, this same client will request that we use Clean again to explore a deeper, personal area.

It's a bit odd

Yes! And hurrah for that. As I say to new clients:

> I am sure you already have people in your life that can listen to you and ask you the more usual kinds of useful question that you'd expect. What you get from me is something different: unusual questions that you may have never been asked before, which tend to lead to different, unusual kinds of answers, ones you have not thought of before.

It's also worth mentioning that when repeating back the client's exact words as the person stated them and with no grammatical alterations to the tense or the pronouns, the questions can sound weird to the coach. For example:

Coachee: "I want to decide on my next step."
Coach: "What kind of 'decide' is that?"
(Not 'decision')

However the coachees are unlikely to notice as their own words reflected back fall into the pool of their awareness without a splash, causing ripples that carry them along their own train of thought still further.

Coaches find it uncomfortable

For all the various misconceptions described in this section, if the coach is concerned about using this approach, no doubt he or she will feel out of his or her comfort zone. Due to its difference from normal conversation, initially it can feel alien not to put more of yourself in your speech. This further highlights the extent by which we are all normally seduced by our own self-perspective, including self-centredness and self-importance.

By practicing Clean techniques, first with willing experimenters happy to explore with you, holding no preconceptions or judgements, you can soon lose this sense of awkwardness and find yourself immersed in the slow rhythmic questions. By ridding yourself of more normal 'self' perspectives you can discover how to deeply connect with another person's experience, being truly present for the person in a totally authentic and unique way. Many coaches have described this level of connection with another as a privilege, a humbling experience that leaves them feeling both wiser and more compassionate afterwards.

Coachees find it uncomfortable

Inexperienced Clean practitioners who lack confidence and trust in the Clean process may introduce it with uncertainty. If the coach is feeling uncomfortable with the process, it's likely to rub off on the coachee – creating a vicious circle of discomfort. If the coach is feeling 'clunky' with these new-found skills and techniques the coach may inadvertently ignore more subtle signals from the coachee around acceptable pacing and patterns of speech.

If the coach is relaxed and takes time to 'ease into' a Clean approach, then far from being uncomfortable, many coachees find it an incredibly relaxing experience. For instance, one coachee described it to me as a "massage for my mind"!

It's not appropriate for my kind of coaching

Some coaches provide a very specific service for addressing a particular need or requirement such as getting a new job or learning new skills, the art of presentation or negotiation. If you coach on skills acquisition, you may need to impart knowledge and give specific feedback at times. However, even with this kind of coaching, sometimes Clean Coaching can be very useful, for instance to uncover and remove any confidence blocks; or to help inspire the coachee to practice; or to find ways for the coachee to develop a personal style of his or her own.

It's too difficult to learn

Many facets of Clean are simple to learn, and like many simple activities it can take a lifetime to reach mastery. Anyone can 'clean up their act' with a minimum of effort and some dedicated attention to their usual habits of conversation. Rather like learning another language, initially memorising questions 'parrot fashion' can take the pressure off recalling them. And using any mental aide memoire to help you select an appropriate Clean question in the moment will fast-forward your development and help build your confidence. After a while, the questions will begin to flow naturally. Many practicing Clean Coaches report that the right kind of question pops 'out of the blue' when they are completely immersed in the coachee's description of his or her experience.

Perhaps the difficulty is not so much in learning a new technique, but more around the challenge of letting go of old ways of doing things, and 'unlearning' the beliefs and thinking patterns that underline those behaviours. In the next chapter we will explore how your way of viewing the world and people in it inevitably influences the way you coach and how directive you are inclined to be.

Note

1 For more information about Adrian Goodall, visit www.adriangoodall.co.uk

References

Buckley, A. and Buckley, C. (2006) *A Guide to Coaching and Mental Health*. London: Routledge.

Dunbar, A. (2010) Speech therapy. *Coaching at Work*, 5(3), 42–45.

Grove, D. J. and Panzer, B. I. (1989) *Resolving Traumatic Memories: Metaphors and Symbols in Psychotherapy*. New York: Irvington.

Harland, P. (2012) *Trust Me I'm the Patient: Clean Language, Metaphor, and the New Psychology of Change*. London: Wayfinder Press.

Karpman, S. B. (2007) The New Drama Triangles USATAA/ITAA Conference Lecture. 11 August 2007. Handout. Available at: www.karpmandramatriangle.com/pdf/thenew dramatriangles.pdf [Accessed 16/6/2015].

Kline, N. (1999) *Time to Think: Listening to Ignite the Human Mind*. London: Cassell Illustrated.

Lawley, J. and Tompkins, P. (2000) *Metaphors in Mind*. London: The Developing Company Press.

Rogers, C. (1961) *On Becoming a Person: A Therapist's View of Psychotherapy*. London: Constable.

Senge, P. M. (1990) *The Fifth Discipline*. New York: Currency Doubleday.

Sullivan, W. and Rees, J. (2008) *Clean Language: Revealing Metaphors and Opening Minds*. Carmarthen: Crown House Publishing.

Walker, C. (2014) From Contempt to Curiosity: *Creating Conditions for Groups to Collaborate Using Clean Language and Systemic Modelling*. Fareham: Clean Publishing.

Qualities of a Clean Coach

Chapter five

What you see is how you coach

What kind of coach are you?

The Clean Coaching approach attracts different kinds of coaches for many different reasons. But some coaching styles seem more aligned with Clean Coaching than others. Some coaches discover a way of working that reflects and supports their underpinning values and beliefs. For these kinds of coaches, picking up Clean Coaching is surprisingly easy. One coach trainee I worked with once said on learning Clean that it felt like 'coming home'. For other coaches, the contrast between their usual way of operating and 'Clean' may seem like a wide chasm to cross. Still others find that what they can accept intellectually about the process does not easily translate across to their natural way of speaking and working. This chapter addresses how your basic way of seeing the world and the people in it fundamentally affects the way you coach. You can challenge your assumptions about the world and with perseverance, develop new ways of thinking that support the kind of coaching you want to do.

By looking more consciously at your current worldview, you can assess how compatible it is with the Clean Coaching approach and uncover potential learning snags. And by thinking more deeply about your current worldviews, you may develop a more open mind so you can ease your way more gently into Clean. Finally, most people rarely question their worldviews and the danger is that without conscious, mindful examination you may assume your personal view is the only view available. For any kind of coaching, this can conceal opportunities for more meaningful exploration, obscuring hidden agendas we don't even realise we bring to our coaching work. Having a closer match between your worldview and your coaching approach means you can be congruent and authentic: two qualities that will improve your coaching effectiveness.

Your coaching style

Your style of coaching is a reflection of who you are as a person as much as what particular coaching school, techniques or models you have been taught. It's like the 'flavour' that seeps through everything you do. It's so close to who you are that it's hard to pinpoint for yourself, though others may be able to sum it up. Your style is less of a personal choice, and more like the culmination of who you have become, given your personality, life experience and training. As Edna Murdoch (2010) wisely said: "Who you are is how you coach." Inevitably, your preferred choice of approaches is influenced by the kind of person you are and what you value most. Our beliefs are integral in shaping identity and values, especially our most fundamental beliefs about the world we live in. It's easy to confuse our personal worldview with the real thing, but they are not the same. We only ever get to see life through one set of eyes – our own.

The way the world appears to be for you *is* your worldview. It is your unique, personal philosophy about the world. It can be revised during our lives as we learn and experience new things. But we tend to arrive in the world pre-destined to see things a certain way. The time and the place we are born into will largely shape the possible viewpoints we are likely to take up. Rather than being a conscious choice, we soak up opinions from the vast cultural and social 'soup' within which we are always steeped. Our formal and informal education teaches us the way the world is as does our personal experience and the experience of significant others. Our beliefs are not solely our own as to some extent they are bestowed on us by others.

People's worldviews matter enormously, to the individuals who hold them and on a wider scale across various groups, organisations and society as a whole. Certain ideas spread and grow amongst people until they become the 'normal' way of seeing things, self-evident truths that may even end up forming part of future generation's formal education. Questionable opinions can become unquestionable truths, based on assumptions which are taken for granted. Over time, we have forgotten that they are not *really* real.

Coaching does not operate from a value-free and neutral position (Brockbank and McGill, 2006). Our personal philosophy or worldview affects our coaching style which makes sense to us precisely because of the cultural and social frameworks we live within. Our personal frameworks become the models we use to assume and predict other's beliefs, behaviours and motives. And it becomes a self-perpetuating cycle of feedback as our expectation of 'normal' behaviour from others becomes the reinforcement to our own ways of being. For the coach, this leads to expecting the coachee to see things as you do, having the same understandings and wanting the same kinds of solutions that you would. Our own perspective can mask what's really going on for the coachee, unless we can mentally step back and 'Cleanly' separate our personal view from that of the coachee.

So what kind of worldview do you have? How do you know what's real? Is it even possible to experience an objective truth about the world? How can people be understood? Can mental processes be independently measured? Is identity fixed or fluid? Is there such a thing as free will? You may seldom think about such deep philosophical questions, but your unexamined assumptions about their answers will affect your coaching style.

What matters gets measured?

We live in a world where if it can't be measured, it can't matter. Anything inexplicable is avoided, ignored and brushed under the carpet as it doesn't fit with what we consider is real and worthwhile of any attention. This is a legacy of the traditional, 'modernist' mainstream worldview. It is not a particularly modern view but as far as Western history is concerned, it evolved along with the birth of the modern, objective and scientific paradigm in the mid-nineteenth century and became known as *positivism*.

It's tempting and comforting to see the world as a positivist does: fixed and predictable. It's still the most popular perspective in the Western world, although it's not the way everyone sees things, nor has it always been the majority viewpoint. Positivism aims to classify, measure and predict natural phenomena in order to discover universal laws. When the field of psychology first became established, many abstract notions about people were given concrete status so that they could be studied in a similar way to that of physical objects. This led to the assumption that both the physical and the social world follow similar rules and could be measured in similar ways.

Positivists see the world as having an independent, knowable reality. They would say "I believe it if I see it" – indicating that their senses give a fairly accurate view of the real world, albeit some occasional filtering may occur. They believe it is possible to get a 'true' picture of reality by stepping outside of personal biases, to an impartial detached position free of any single individual's idiosyncratic and biased perspective. This is what scientists seek to do by setting up impartial laboratory conditions free of unwanted influence so they can isolate and accurately measure the things they want to research.

Some people see the world as having more shades of grey, and would rather say "If I believe it, I'll probably see it." This is more like the 'post-modernistic' or 'interpretivist' perspective, which believes our senses are not reliable photocopiers of reality, but part of a creative perceptual system that can never stand outside of itself. Each of us only gets to see the world from this limited, flawed and subjective perspective. We learn by playing detective and piecing together sometimes obscure clues to gain an impression (always distorted) of the world.

The 'map is not the territory'

This is the mantra of a typical interpretivist, such as Alfred Korzybski's (1933/1958) who first coined the phrase. As a pioneering scientist interested in what made humans *human*, this was a bold claim about the relationship between our perception of reality (called the 'map') with reality itself (the 'territory'). Rather than claiming reality does not exist at all, he meant that our interpretation of the world is an abstraction of it, rather than a complete fantasy or illusion. What we know of the 'real' world is limited by our perceptual capabilities and pre-formed conceptual frameworks. This statement (and underlying concept) has gathered momentum and become a core presupposition within the field of Neuro-Linguistic Programming (NLP).

For the interpretivist, we are always at least one step removed from the actual, original raw data of reality, relying on self-created mental maps to represent that. Our sensory channels provide only certain kinds of information which we have the capacity to know. From these 'shades of grey', we colour in our own picture of reality with guesswork and imagination. Most Clean advocates would support this view. For instance, Lawley and Tompkins (2000) argue that people build internal 'models' about how the world works from the day they are born. These models are based on our experience and interaction with the world, through our senses of seeing, hearing, physically sensing, smelling and tasting. We will cover more on models in Chapter ten.

The universe in our heads

Our models contain not just everything outside of ourselves, but also our image of self too. Some people from a *phenomenologist* leaning (one popular approach to interpretivism) would call this our 'lifeworld': we all have our own personal universe, with ourselves in the centre. Clean expert Philip Harland (2012:34) describes this as: "the world is a personal movie projected onto our private screens." Interpretivists would argue that maps are all we have as the 'real' territory always remains hidden from view. In which case, those maps *become* our reality as we construct frameworks for understanding the world, both individually through personal experience and socially by negotiating maps between us.

It is not surprising that most people end up believing similar things about the world and each other, especially considering how children learn within group classes. Our education system teaches fixed knowledge with right and wrong answers. But this may say more about our ability to influence each other than representing any overall impartial view of reality. This aspect of social influence on reality has been coined as *social constructivism*, which is another form of interpretivism – highlighting the co-creative way people build their versions of reality by sharing their views and telling/teaching others how it is.

Letting go of your reality

Our personal, idiosyncratic perceptions are: (1) very limited in capacity, (2) selective in terms of where attention is directed and (3) fallible in terms of distorting, deleting and generalising the picture of reality that we notice. If, as a coach, you accept that your perception is not reality, you are likely to interact with the world differently. First, you hold onto your version less tightly. Rather than blindly accept what your senses tell you, you question further and deeper, being curious about other ways of seeing this particular situation. If you ever find yourself completely *certain* of what your coachee should do, you would question yourself as thoroughly as you would your coachee.

It also means that you accept that your coachees' view of themselves, the situation and the wider world is unique and inevitably different from yours. Their map is also more comprehensive as they have been building it their whole lives. The expert on this coachee's reality and how it works is that coachee. In fact he or she is the only person in existence who knows what it's like to be him or her. Whether the person's version of reality or yours is 'truer' is actually a pointless question. There is no impartial, separate arbitrator that stands outside of any individual perspective and can determine degrees of accuracy. No one really knows. We assume that because people seem to agree on many aspects of reality, that the majority perspective has extra weight; however sometimes what 'everyone knows' is true is turned on its head when a 'truer' truth emerges.

You do not have to have an interpretivist perspective to use Clean Coaching although it helps. If the positivist expects there to be one real answer to the coachee's difficulty, and a single path towards a fixed desired outcome, the fluid nuances revealed through metaphor exploration may seem irrelevant and time wasting. Interestingly however, sometimes coaches discover a greater conviction for the interpretivist view once they begin to work more Cleanly. This is because it allows them to gain deep insight into another person's worldview, perhaps for the first time ever. In discovering its richness, they learn that it is no more or less valuable than their own.

What's there to know about?

Another kind of worldview is the way you think people can learn and gain knowledge about the world around them. *Objectivists* see the world as full of individual, independent objects that can be known about. This includes both physical things and non-physical ideas. An object has an essential, immutable core of properties that defines what it is, with a clear boundary or edge that separates it from everything else. Objectivists see people as being like any other physical 'object' in the natural world. This includes many abstract thinking processes like memory, learning and intelligence which are 'objectivised' into concrete, bounded 'somethings', lumping different aspects together into single broader concepts.

Subjectivists, on the other hand, see everything as being in flow, making it difficult to draw precise lines between things. Even within the physical sciences, the tide has been turning since Einstein upturned the idea of 'universal' laws by introducing the theory of relativity. The universe is not as clockwork as Newton imagined. The theory of relativity scientifically supports what many Eastern philosophers have long since believed, which is that reality depends on where you are looking at it from, if examined closely enough.

People are experiences

Although the objectivist position is still the majority viewpoint in the Western world today, it's under increasing challenge by more subjectivist thinkers

(Brockbank and McGill, 2006). Subjectivists view people and their experience as beyond objectivist understanding. They place greater importance on personal experience which is constantly changing, evolving and even contradicting itself, depending on many different uniquely personal factors.

How does this affect your coaching? The objectivist coach may be quick to draw boundaries around the coachee's stated outcome and consider it fixed and stable. However, the subjectivist coach would argue that goals are not single fixed objects. The coachee will have multiple goals that connect, cross over and even contradict. Goals are fluid and evolve and change during the coaching process. In other areas, the objectivist coach may view the coachee in a more mechanistic fashion, looking for linear relationships between thoughts and actions, beliefs and behaviours. Whereas the subjectivist will place greater importance on the coachee's current subjective experience and remain alert to changing perspectives and emerging understandings.

Brockbank and McGill (2006) suggest that a typical objectivist coach would emphasise rational elements of the coachee's situation and spend less time focusing on the coachee's personal and social world. These coaches would favour imposed objectives, and value tools for measuring inner experience such as profiling because they assume personality is a fixed component of the person. A subjectivist coach is more likely to place value on the coachee's subjective musings about his or her situation and outcomes. This coach listens for metaphors and imaginative descriptions as valid examples of what matters for the coachee. Additionally, he or she believes that time spent exploring subjective meaning can help the coachee find more helpful ways of experiencing the world.

Many everyday notions that 'everyone' knows about are likely to be cultural and far from universal. For instance, people in the Western world tend to see each person as a largely self-determined and autonomous entity. An *individualist* perspective is taken, which sees people as 'objectivised' into separate individual units. People are seen as being in control of and responsible for their own actions, and agents of their own lives. But other cultures, particularly Eastern outlooks, picture people as rather more joined up and connected. This is the *collectivist* perspective, which sees people as being more like leaves on a tree, or drops in an ocean. Individuals are seen less distinctly with more 'porous' boundaries between them. Surrounding social conditions are seen as largely determining an individual's beliefs, and shaping future possibilities. To a collectivist, trying to see a person as an autonomous unit is like looking at one fragment of a broken mirror. People only exist in relation to and because of other people. Collectivists are less concerned with individuals and more interested in the relationships between them, in line with 'systems thinking' and 'Gestalt' approaches to understanding people.

These different perspectives are important to coaching as they affect what kind of change you believe your coachee can make. In turn, this influences how personal change is handled within the coaching session.

How change happens

Change is a crucial factor within coaching, and can happen in different ways. Change can happen in an instant, or gradually over a period of time. Change may not be consistent, instead stopping and starting, with your coachee occasionally even taking a step backwards before moving forwards. The changes may be internal, such as changing beliefs and/or behaviours. And the changes may be external, such as changing the environment in some way. This could include major change such as changing a job or breaking up a relationship or minor things like changing the journey to work or meeting more regularly with a colleague. Sometimes change just happens to people, outside of their control completely, for instance through a chance accident or fortunate event. How much control an individual has over any kind of change is debatable, but change inevitably happens and often begins with an internal desire and decision to do something differently.

The more individualist perspective will see individuals as autonomous and self-directed. They believe that although people can be influenced by others, they remain capable of their own agency and control. Collectivist viewpoints of change look for patterns that repeat within individuals, societies, and natural and human-made phenomena. They wait for change to happen by attempting to create the right conditions for change to emerge.

Early psychologists such as Freud doubted that people were capable of controlling internal changes. He saw people as largely driven by unconscious parts of themselves that they may never be aware of, without the aid of an external expert who could analyse and interpret. Change happened by accident, or as a result of a slow, often painful journey. Carl Rogers had a more optimistic view of an individual's capacity for self-awareness and the ability to change. The humanistic movement saw change as coming from within the person, facilitated by another who gave that person unconditional positive regard. Rogers saw change stemming from identity and felt 'congruence' was key, being completely okay with who you are right now. He believed that most problems stem from individuals trying to be someone they are not. In reality, the paradox is that it is only through total acceptance of self that we are free to grow and make change.

The latest thinking in social psychology sees the image of an autonomous person in control of his or her own destiny as fundamentally flawed. Instead, like many other group structures within the natural world, each individual only comes into being due to the complex social network around them. From even before birth, we are already inextricably linked to other people and influenced in increasingly complex ways as we grow.

How individualist or collectivist you are will also influence your expectations of your coachee's ability to change and what needs to be in place to support any change. A more collectivist coach will pay greater attention to the surrounding context and social systems that may well hold the individual within certain patterns of behaviour and keep the person stuck. However, a certain level of belief in individualism is needed if the coachee is expected to take responsibility and make change happen.

Whatever you believe about people and their capacity for change, it is important to explore change with your coachees and find out what *they* believe about people and change. Your coachees' worldview about their autonomy levels is likely to be at least partially self-fulfilling. If they feel controlled by others, they most certainly will be.

A final consideration on worldviews is about the nature of 'self'. Most commonly, people are seen as having a single core, conscious identity that remains relatively fixed once we have reached adolescence. But more post-modernistic thinkers see each individual as a multiple of selves. The conscious identity we each assume to be the real 'self' is just one facet of who we are. Over the years many psychologists and psychotherapists have argued that there are a number of separate 'parts' contained within every whole person. People are a kaleidoscope of identities, competing moment by moment for conscious control or subconscious sabotage.

If you accept the possibility of multiple selves, you may find it easier to coach Cleanly at a different, deeper level, adapting more readily if your coachee thinks and acts in inconsistent ways. In Chapter fifteen we will further explore how the self can be understood as a collection of parts rather than a single entity. We will highlight some of David Grove's beliefs about working with people to address all the parts of themselves equally. Each of his core techniques – Clean Language, Clean Space and Emergent Knowledge – address the multiplistic nature of the person, seeking to uncover and explore hidden/lost parts of self and give them a voice.

Worldviews and coaching priorities

Now we have explored all these different ways of seeing the world and people within it, what do you think? Your opinions may closely match the examples above, or you may find your view is more selective, for instance seeing some kinds of things as more real than others. You may even hold conflicting worldviews at the same time, for instance what you see as true for yourself may be different to what seems true for everyone else. This exploration can help you think through your beliefs more consciously and even decide to change them. Or, you may become more interested in perspectives different from your own and decide to investigate further. But don't let all the 'isms' in this chapter bother you. Like all concepts, the subjectivist would argue they are just further examples of objectivist 'boxes' we try and squeeze our experiences into. I have used these terms so that if you would like to investigate philosophical perspectives in more depth you have some terms of reference to dig deeper into the core arguments beneath.

Your conscious awareness of your worldview and how it affects your coaching can help you become more congruent and authentic. If you have a strong objectivist perspective it may lead to confidence and certainty which in itself can produce positive results. But the more human-focused, subjective approach may make a more meaningful difference to the individual concerned, leading to deeper, more transformational change.

Table 5.1 Coaching values.

Positivist/Objectivist values	Interpretivist/Subjectivist values
• Actions • Results • Decisions • Moving forwards • Future oriented • Two-dimensional (thinking along straight lines) • Measures • Cause and effect	• Belief changes • Perspective changes • How the coachees do what they do • Staying still (and exploring more deeply) • Grounded in the current experience • Three- and four-dimensional (exploring across space and time) • Evidence criteria • Systemic

The coach's worldview will inevitably mean different things get prioritised within the coaching session/relationship. Table 5.1 highlights the main areas of emphasis and the extent to which the coach places value on them will shift the kind of coaching that takes place.

Clean Coaching lends itself nicely to the post-modernist perspective and the worldviews that tend to flow from that. From this perspective, working with the coachee's imaginary inner world makes as much sense as working with any so-called real world contexts, which will be seen as just a different level of subjective interpretation anyway. Those with strong black and white, objectivist views may struggle with understanding the value of Clean Language, unless they can relate it back to tangible actions and measureable improvement.

When worldviews collide

Few other writers have explicitly addressed the impact of worldview on coaching. The exception to this is the work by Ann Brockbank and Ian McGill (2006). They developed a matrix which explicitly addresses coaching orientation from different worldviews. They show the range of approaches open to coaches and/or mentors, dependent on current worldviews combined with expectations of change. The kind of change expected by all parties ranges from transformational (more radical and unpredictable change) to equilibrium (wanting to change the coachee to fit with the wider organisation).

An organisation's worldview is often imposed on all those connected with it. Does the organisation genuinely want this person to grow and develop? Or does it expect any individual learning or change to conform to the status quo of the organisation's current prevailing perspective? It is easy for this kind of view to be unspoken but condoned by all involved. Needless to say, this viewpoint will limit the effectiveness of coaching. It is vital this is discussed with the sponsor within the organisation as it will shape the level of non-directivenes that takes place during the coaching. The coaches themselves may see change differently to the sponsoring organisation and it's important to discuss this openly during the contracting stage.

Brockbank and McGill (2006) strongly advocate the merits of a subjectivist coach working within an organisation seeking transformational change. This leads to what they refer to as 'evolutionary coaching'. They suggest that coaching can be transformational providing the coach eschews advice, uses a non-directive process and the coachee has *ownership* of the purpose, a factor often unstated and assumed within organisational coaching. This could cover up hidden agendas where the coachee is coerced into saying he or she wants what the organisation expects of him or her.

In summary

Some coaches are more 'scientific' in their approach, relying on a static, real world where there is often one universal, knowable 'right' way to go. Some accept a more interpretivist, subjective perspective; choosing instead to have a looser hold on right and wrong ways. They rely on the coachee's perception of the truth that for the moment, matters more than any other.

There are no doubt effective and less effective coaches at either end of this spectrum just as there are many other factors that will determine success. However, Clean Coaching requires you to first clean up your own attitudes and beliefs about the world and people. You cannot *not* see through your own eyes, therefore your perspectives inevitably affect how you see the coachee and what you do with the person.

I recommend taking time to explore your personal perspectives and risk challenging yourself regarding those which you have previously accepted as unquestionable truths. Begin to question any taken-for-granted 'givens' that are handed to you, from the organisations within which you coach, from the institutions and associations within which you learn and affiliate with, and from your own assumptions. And of course, question your coachee's position too. You may never escape your personal perspective, but you can widen its boundaries to allow doubt and curiosity to have a stronger foothold.

References

Brockbank, A. and McGill, I. (2006) *Facilitating Reflective Learning Through Mentoring & Coaching*. London: Kogan Page.

Harland, P. (2012) *Trust Me I'm the Patient: Clean Language, Metaphor and the New Psychology of Change*. London: Wayfinder Press.

Korzybski, A. (1958) *Science and Sanity: A Non-Aristotelian System and Its Necessity for Rigour in Mathematics and Physics* (3rd ed.). Originally published by author, 1933.

Lawley, J. and Tompkins, P. (2000) *Metaphors in Mind*. London: The Developing Company Press.

Murdoch, E. (2010) *Who You Are Is How You Coach*. Available at: http://coachingsupervisionacademy.com/thought-leadership/who-you-are-is-how-you-coach/ (Originally published in Training Zone) [Accessed 5/9/2015].

Chapter six

Developing Clean Coaching capacities

Competencies or capabilities?

What are the core qualities you need to be a Clean Coach? One crucial factor has already been covered: how you see the world and the people you coach. Beyond your underlying beliefs, the areas of knowledge and skills needed complement those required by any good coach. Both the Association for Coaching and the International Coaching Federation (ICF) provide detailed lists of competencies for coaches seeking accreditation.

But can behavioural competencies really capture the essence of coaching excellence? Tatiana Bachkirova and Carmelina Lawton Smith (2015:128) argue that mastery "*transcends rules and modifies existing knowledge*" (emphasis in original) and cannot be translated into easily identifiable competencies. They point out that coaching cannot be separated into its component parts without losing an essential element that's woven into the complexity of the whole. Coaching is complex and unpredictable, and is not easily taught as a set of behavioural activities. They suggest focusing on internal *capabilities* rather than competencies alone. Capabilities emphasise the critical and reflective qualities that allow the coach to make choices in the moment of what to do next. They are harder to spot from the outside, but just because they cannot be observed and measured doesn't mean they don't exist. Capabilities reflect the freedom of the coach to opt for a certain action, given the moment by moment changing environment of a coaching session.

Many writers have supported the notion that effective coaching goes beyond a set of skills and techniques. For instance, Wang (as cited in Bachkirova and Lawton Smith, 2015) describes it as a state of being which stems from a profound coherence across how the coaches sees themselves and their role, with a consistency and congruence across:

1   Who they are.
2   What they believe in.
3   What they do.
4   What they say they do.

This authenticity influences the way they exercise their skills and techniques.

This chapter highlights some of the most important personal factors to cultivate in your Clean Coaching endeavours. The encouraging message here is that excellence is not an innate ability but something anyone can develop with deliberate, dedicated and sustained practice.

Being at your best

On our Clean Coaching training courses, one of the first exercises we invite participants to undertake is to consider the question: "When you are coaching at your best, that's like what?" This question encourages trainees to focus on their strengths and highlights the uniqueness of each and every one who coaches. The question has been adapted from an approach used by Clean Practitioner and trainer, Caitlin Walker (2014). There are two broad sections to the question: the first part referring to "at your best" has its roots in counselling and positive psychology. The rest of the question "that's like what?" is in the form of a very important Clean Language question, which will be covered further in Chapter eight. The question invites the recipient to think of a metaphor to describe his or her experience of excellence.

Later in the training we invite students to explore a slightly different question: "When you are Clean Coaching at your best, that's like what?" It's a really useful question to help people discover and explore the internal qualities and resources they need to be at their best for Clean Coaching. The exploration helps them to anchor their experience so they can access it more easily in the future.

Here is a small selection of the range and originality of metaphors that have cropped up when exploring Clean Coaching with those newly trained:

- Like a sunny day, when I'm completely relaxed.
- Like Tinkerbell, curious and playful.
- Like being supported in a pool of water.
- Like a tuning fork.
- Like pressing the pause button.
- Like a balloon, floating along.
- Like learning to walk in a new way.
- Like a tour guide – helping people find surprising places.
- Like a new jacket that's not broken in yet.

Having explored these kinds of subjective experiences with many learners over time, what follows is my list of the nine most important resource areas that people develop during Clean Coaching training.

Ten core capacities

Just as capabilities are more expansive than mere abilities, the term 'capacity' provides a deeper definition of the developmental qualities required, representing the potential for Clean Coaching. I believe everyone has these innate qualities, although to excel in them requires practice. Each capacity is like a link in a chain: developing one capacity supports further development in another, related capacity, creating a continuous cycle of growing improvement:

- Capacity for attention.
- Capacity for silence.
- Capacity for acceptance.
- Capacity for listening.
- Capacity to see the bigger picture.
- Capacity for reflection.
- Capacity to 'park' your own thoughts.
- Capacity to be genuine.
- Capacity for rapport, empathy and trust.
- Capacity to use one's voice.

Capacity for attention

Nancy Kline placed attention as her number one 'component' for creating a Thinking Environment: "Giving good attention to people makes them more intelligent" (1999:37).

Attention is like a spotlight that focuses our perception in one particular direction. We can adjust the beam and focus further in, concentrating on one narrow element, allowing for heightened sensitivity within a limited range. And we can also widen the scope and keep attention more broadly focused on our coachees and all that they say and do. To have the ability to both focus your attention and widen it at will is crucial for Clean Coaching, mirroring the same process we encourage coachees to experience during a session. The processes of focusing and expanding attention are covered in more depth in Chapters eight and twelve, highlighting specific Clean Coaching questions to support you.

'Evenly suspended attention'

A prerequisite to effective Clean Coaching involves emptying the mind of irrelevant thoughts, clearing the way for effective listening. This includes anything unrelated to the client and his or her circumstances. It sounds like a risky strategy, as an empty mind might not seem very useful. But you will be more effective if you can let your mind be like an open net, allowing thoughts to flow in and out as your coachee talks. You cannot *not* respond to what the coachee says. But you can develop the same non-reacting attitude to your own responses as you do for your coachees, separating yourself from your thoughts and just notice, with curiosity, where they come from and where they go to. Almost akin to a state of mindfulness, Epstein (1984) describes the state of 'evenly suspended attention': a core principle of Freud's approach which he deemed as fundamental to psychoanalysis. Freud described it as giving equal attention to all that the client says, withholding all conscious influences giving himself over completely to his unconscious mind. Likening the therapist to a telephone receiver, Freud (1923) believed that a state of 'attunement' can be reached, where the therapist can adjust his or her unconscious towards the client and catch his or her unconscious 'drift'.

Grove referred to a similar process of being an 'equal opportunity questioner' (Wilson and Dunbar, 2008) – which he described as treating all client information as equally important. This means not judging which takes priority but holding the possibility that everything the coachee says and does is of potentially equal importance.

Apparently, Freud did not take notes for this reason, preferring for all of his clients' words to wash over him without clutching onto any in particular to record with deliberate intent. He trusted in his unconscious mind, believing that it would retain and categorise whatever was important. "He should simply listen, and not bother about whether he is keeping anything in mind" (Freud, 1912:112). Grove also refrained from note taking. He was exceptionally good at retaining accurate information about his clients' metaphors, sometimes years after working with them. Being able to *retain* what you attend to is not an optional extra, and requires a good memory. But most of us need to support that memory with some kind of aide-memoire, in the form of notes taken so we can accurately reflect back the coachee's words. In Chapter ten we look at 'rich pictures' as a method of representing what we notice more helpfully than writing down words alone.

Focusing attention where it matters

Attention is the continuous, automatic process people use to select some kind of figure out of the ground. We pick up just a few salient details from the mass of data constantly bombarding our senses, spotting the melody from the background noise. We also have a wider capacity for awareness, working like a radar constantly scanning incoming signals from the world around us.

Grove (2003:6.1) stressed the importance of noticing the ground: the background symbols surrounding the main subject within a session. He said, "By treating the figure and the ground with equal importance you will not limit the resources available for healing, because the person in the trauma may be the least resourced part of the experience." He was referring to working therapeutically with trauma victims, but this seems appropriate for coaching as well. When attention is focused on the ground and questions asked of the surrounding contextual 'scenery', the coachees' viewpoint can widen and lead to a reframing of their perceived situation. They can gain a new perspective of what they thought they knew.

Be able to adjust between expanded attention and focused attention

Like a camera, the Clean Coach must be able to adjust his or her lens from a wide, evenly suspended view to narrowing in on specific aspects. Additionally, I have noticed that skilful Clean Coaches have a kind of stereo awareness, where they remain in touch with the wide view even whilst zooming into something specific. My own personal metaphor for coaching at my best is like being a lighthouse, and this reflects the dual aspect of attention. When I imagine this metaphor, simultaneously I feel as though I am like the lighthouse itself, but at the same time I can imagine myself within a darkened lighthouse, on the spiral steps with a torch in my hand. The lighthouse's beam represents to me a kind of continuous, steady scanning of the entire (coachee's) landscape all around: a 360-degree awareness. Superimposed within that is the sense of a smaller, faster 'me' on those spiral steps. I can shine my torch anywhere around me and see up close and personal what's happening on any particular step. I can also quickly step up or down two or three steps to move around within a particular focus.

Capacity for silence

Nancy Kline (1999:41) considers that in order to maintain attentiveness, one must break the habit of interrupting, something we seem 'unable to resist'. She points out that when you give people the space to finish off their sentence, it helps them understand and develop their own ideas. Moreover, when people learn that they definitely won't be interrupted by you, it is sheer bliss. They are free to really explore their thoughts in ways they simply do not even bother with, in the company of others. But the common tendency is to respond quickly once another person has finished speaking, to show we are 'keeping up' and being attentive. Whereas, the opposite response of pausing after the coachee stops speaking and before you respond is a much better demonstration of attentive listening. Pausing shows that you are taking the time to reflect on what the other person has said. You are also giving the coachee time to continue to speak, to further develop his or her thoughts or even change his or her mind. Grove referred to pauses as 'response inviting gaps' – see Chapter seven. The pause is an invitation to the coachee to say more if he or she wants, letting his or her current train of thought continue onwards, if the person wishes.

I have noticed that very often coachees *do* have more to say if you leave the silence to hang for just a few moments after they stop talking. Grove likened the pattern of his client's response to a 'bimodal distribution' (Wilson and Dunbar, 2008) which is a term used within statistics to describe a typical pattern of variable responses where there is a double peak with a dip in the middle. Many natural phenomena display this kind of pattern, and Grove noticed it was true of how clients reach insight. Once the client gets to a point of insight, often there is an initial 'wave' of information which he or she can express out loud, followed by a silent, thoughtful dip. If you remain silent for long enough, then this wave is typically followed by a second, even greater, wave of information.

Pausing also gives you the opportunity to reflect on what the coachee has said and give consideration to your response. It provides time to censor any automatic non-Clean reaction and instead mindfully consider where best to focus the coachee's attention next. You can use the 'three-part syntax' (covered in the next chapter) to enable you to gradually focus in on a specific aspect of the coachee's message and consciously and deliberately choose which question to ask next.

Kline described the silence that allows another to think as 'busy' quiet. It is like letting the other person go for a walk, knowing you will be waiting on the person's return. We should not confuse 'not talking' with 'not thinking', as people need silence in order to think at their deepest and most creative. She adds that "Listening to their quiet, you will not know *what* they are thinking. But you will know *that* they are thinking . . . ideas are forming, insights are melding, most of which you will never hear about" (Kline, 1999:51).

In cognitive psychology, the process of 'thinking aloud' is sometimes used as a research protocol to help capture subjective introspection. For instance, to analyse and understand moments of sudden, insight when solutions seem to appear 'out of the blue'. With 'thinking aloud' protocols, research participants are asked to literally speak about whatever thoughts appear, moment by moment, voicing their emerging trains of thought. What seems to be true, however, is that the very act of conscious concentration on turning thoughts into language might prevent insight from happening. Silence is indeed golden for allowing new ways of thinking to surface.

Yet many people, even coaches, are uncomfortable with silence, believing it is an awkward social gap to fill with activity. Some coaches feel anxious about 'empty space' within a coaching session, thinking it represents wasted time, lost opportunities and poor value for money. But silence doesn't mean nothing is happening. The silence is actually allowing something to happen. It is dedicated space in which you give your coachees permission to take the time they need to think. However much alone time they may have, it is not the same as having a witness. A person to wait at the end of the path, so when they return from their thinking 'walk' you are present to hear what they have to say.

Patience is a quality that helps strengthen our capacity for allowing silence. And patience is fostered by having a calm acceptance of how things are.

Capacity for acceptance

Acceptance involves respectfulness. It means letting go of the need to get everything right. It does not mean being sloppy or less committed. It is striving for continuous improvement without beating yourself up. It is also about tolerance for ambiguity and vagueness. Some coaches thrive on their coachees' ever growing 'to do' list of actions as an indication of a job well done. But Clean Coaching can result in significant internal change for the coachee, without instantly observable evidence.

Accepting yourself as 'good enough' means you have a solid ego and don't need to prove yourself in coaching sessions. You are emotionally stable and can be okay with being almost invisible in the session with strong, personal boundaries that keep you centred come what may. Acceptance of 'good enough' can lead to exceptional coaching as your coachee does not feel judged or pressurised into performing for you. You are also being a role model by demonstrating an accepting attitude, enabling your coachee to learn how to become more accepting too.

Acceptance like this prevents rigidity and stuckness. When we accept things don't always go as planned, we can be more flexible and creative during a coaching session, adapting to what's coming up and trying something different. When we are not wedded to things being a certain way, we can improvise and adjust our approach with a light touch. There is no single 'right' way to help your coachee. There are no right or wrong questions to ask.

Capacity for listening

Much has been written in other coaching books about the capacity for listening and its crucial importance to the coach. Nancy Kline (1999:37) said of people "we think we listen but we don't". Listening without pre-judgement or assumption is very difficult. We hold preconceived, tacit notions about the world around us that colour what we see and hear. This affects the relative importance we place on others' messages.

Laura Whitworth's co-active coaching model describes listening as functioning on different 'levels' (Whitworth et al., 2007). The metaphor highlights how active listening is different from passively hearing a message, with a scale along which listening can be enhanced still further. Bob Thompson (2013) suggests that the non-directive coach needs to listen not only with the head, but also the heart and guts. He describes listening levels as a ladder with five rungs:

1   *Not listening:* At the lowest rung of the ladder, we are present in body but mentally we are distracted by other matters. Some people at this level may appear to be listening and go through the motions of responding, nodding and making appropriate acknowledging noises. But internally they are doing something entirely different.

2   *Listening, waiting to speak:* This is a very common kind of listening in everyday conversation. At this level we assume that by not speaking and leaving a gap in the conversation for the other person to fill, we are listening. However, although our attention is engaged in the conversation, we focus on composing what we want to say next. People often indicate they are listening at this level when they jump in with their response instantly when they feel it's their turn again. This is as soon as the other person stops speaking, or even a fraction of a second before the person stops.

3   *Listening to disagree:* Many educated people are trained to listen like this, with a critical eye they focus on what's wrong with the other's message so they can attack it and argue for their own case.

4   *Listening to understand:* For many people this is the pinnacle of listening. It involves attempting to put yourself in the other's shoes and see things as he or she does. This kind of listening is more than a skill, it involves attitudinal qualities too, such as empathy.

5   *Listening to help the client understand:* At this level, your purpose in listening is to help you follow what's going on closely enough that you can select the most useful question to ask next. This helps the coachee stay with his or her own internal tracks of thinking and increases his or her own understanding. Although to some degree we listen to understand, when you accept that you can never understand completely, you can let go of that need, along with the fear and uncertainty that accompany it. Instead, this kind of listening is less pressured and more accepting. This is the level of listening required for Clean Coaching.

I would add that there is another, *sixth* level of listening, which is different from more usual coaching conversations. It is: *Listening to the structure of the message as well as the content.* The structure is more about how the coachees are choosing to express themselves and tell their story. The structure of their language represents their pattern of thought and the narrative of their story. It is often the glue that holds their logic and beliefs in place. Listening for the narrative gives clues as to where the story may have come from and where it may be going. Clean Coaches listen for patterns in how the coachees are organising their thoughts and behaviours. These structures are not random, and patterns of repeating thoughts are often revealed through the coachees' metaphors. Chapter ten on Modelling and Systems Thinking covers this idea in more depth.

Clean listening is like what?

Listening is an active, all-encompassing activity and is the initial and primary step towards working Cleanly as a coach. Before we do anything else, we must first take on the coachee's message without distorting or shaping it in any way. I have a metaphor for describing what Clean listening is like for me. It's like I have to put on my 'Clean Ears', which when I think more deeply about I can visualise as being rather like Spock's ears from the *Star Trek* movies. Like some kind of space-age hearing aid, the Clean Ears improve my listening by increasing the range and depth of information that I can hear. They also freeze my brain somewhat. They slow down my inferential thought tracks and help me to take on the message I hear completely at face-value, without attempting to make greater sense of it by seeking my own examples or experience. I imagine myself a little like an alien on a strange but wonderful world, and adopt a stance of 'wise ignorance'. If I think I understand, then I assume to myself that I am probably wrong and force myself to check and test any understandings over and over again. When I am Clean listening at my best it is like being completely in tune with another person without second guessing his or her meaning, simply being attentive to his or her own emerging messages and watching them with curiosity and awe. You can see from this description how skills merge with attitudes, demonstrating the difficulty in placing importance on competencies alone.

Capacity for self-reflection

As highlighted in Bachkirova and Lawton Smith's model (2015), this is considered a crucial capability for all coaches. For Clean Coaches I believe it's even more vital, as there is little opportunity for the coach to express his or her own thoughts and opinions during the coaching session itself.

A definition of self-reflection is "The purposeful contemplation of thoughts, feelings and happenings that pertain to recent experience" (Kennison and Misselwitz, 2002:239). Examining thoughts and feelings make it easier to look at them objectively. Supervision helps cultivate the ability to self-reflect, and the more practiced you become at doing this after and outside of the coaching session, the more skilful you be at keeping that objective distance from your thoughts during the session as well.

Capacity to 'park' your own thoughts

We are not robots. When you coach Cleanly, you cannot completely switch off your own thoughts and reactions to another, nor would it be desirable to do so. Being Clean doesn't mean that you have no opinion, nor that you can get beyond or outside of your own view of the world. This purist view of Clean is unrealistic. We are never completely Clean in our thoughts and it is more honest to own up to the fact that you can be influenced and biased. Being 'Clean enough' means noticing your own thoughts when they come up, acknowledging them but not acting on them (except in rare cases). 'Epoche' was an expression used in ancient Greece meaning 'Suspended', and was popularised by phenomenologist philosopher Edmund Husserl, describing it as the process of 'bracketing' your own thoughts for a while, putting them to the side and not letting them decide where you go next. If you can observe your own thoughts in this way, they can be helpful as indicators of your own emerging biases, showing you where you need to gain more clarity about the coachee's own perspective.

For instance, your coachee tells you a story about how his boss was unfair. You notice that your own response is that the boss did the best he could, maybe your coachee was not appreciating the pressure the boss may be under. As you notice that thought, you recognise it is no more true than the coachee's perspective, in fact probably further removed from reality as you have no direct experience. But even so, the fact that this is your reaction may be useful. What is it that makes you interpret this as unfair? Could it be your personal history is somehow reflected in the coachee's story? Have you been in a similar position to that of the boss and are you adopting that perspective? If you see your own previous experience could be biasing your perspective, then it would be best to park the thought completely. On the other hand, taking a more collectivist view, what is it about the way the coachee told the story that has enticed this kind of reaction out of you? If you can find the 'hook' that drew you in, then you can ask more questions about that to see whether your perspective changes. If not, what's actually happening between you and the coachee? These difficult, potentially conflicting moments within coaching provide a great opportunity for massive growth, if you can unhook yourself and speak from an impartial perspective and describe, for instance what you are noticing about what's going on. You can also invite the coachee to reflect at a relational level by asking "And what's happening right now, in this session, between you and me?"

Nancy Kline (1999) points out that people seem to assume that the place to look for the answer to a problem is somewhere other than the mind that formulated and expressed the problem. When you genuinely accept that the answer will come from the coachee, it means that you look for it there. Your questions will point to the coachee's own developing line of enquiry, not towards your own.

Capacity to be genuine

Carl Rogers (1951) described this as authenticity: simply to be yourself with self-awareness. This may seem contradictory to Clean; however, it is not. Being present and true to yourself is not the same as burdening your clients with self-disclosures or monopolising the conversation with your own stories and perspectives. But you do not have to deny them to yourself or disown those feelings or responses, or hide behind a 'mask of professionalism' (Rogers, 1951). Coaches can become acquainted with the constantly shifting flow of experiencing within themselves.

Authenticity has two facets: an inner and an outer side (Rogers, 1951). The inner side is our congruence – how closely we can be aware of what's happening within us. Rogers felt therapists cannot remain totally distanced and impartial; they have to be personally involved as congruence can be sensed by our clients and it's what leads to their sense of trust about us. In this way, the coachee knows that, in essence, we are who we appear to be. Congruence means being honest when you don't understand something or you make a mistake. It's the willingness to be less than perfect. This inner authenticity is what makes up our personal presence. As coaches we hold up a mirror to our clients with purpose. But that mirror also reflects back to the coach. We sometimes recognise ourselves in our coachees, seeing reflections of our own lives, fears and desires through our clients. This parallel process is inevitable and can be very useful if we can openly accept and admit to ourselves when it happens. We need genuineness to be responsive and adaptive when such processes occur, and non-judgementally explore where they may come from.

The outer layer of genuineness and authenticity is transparency, which is the explicit expression of the coach's inner thoughts and feelings. Client-centred therapy evolved from 'non-directive' to 'experiential', which allowed the therapist to bring in something from his or her own frame of reference, as long as the client's experiential track is regularly returned to (Gendlin, 1970). For Clean Coaching, explicit expressions are not generally part of the process. But, very occasionally it may be very appropriate and useful to say exactly what's on your mind. As a Clean Supervisor, I am more open to the learning potential this can bring and will allow it to happen more frequently. In this way I am a role model for honesty and openness. Sometimes my self-disclosure gives the coachees permission to be more honest themselves and share something they may not have otherwise said. If you have a strong urge to say something and it can't be contained, it could fester and skew the rest of the session. For this reason it may be best to voice it and let it go. But it may be better to voice it somewhere outside of the session. For instance at supervision, or written and reflected upon in a coaching journal.

If there is an occasion to voice your thoughts or feelings, you can keep it 'Cleanish' by:

1   Directly owning the thought/feeling and expressing in its natural form, not masquerading as a suggestion or question.
2   Making it clear this is a personal and possibly temporary perspective: "This is what I think/feel just now."
3   Allow the coachee/supervisee to reflect on your thoughts: "What does this mean to you?"

Gendlin (1968) points out that if a person is troubled, the person can't fail to rouse difficulties in others that he or she relates to. This refers to the psychodynamic concept of 'transference', where people-helpers may find themselves so embroiled within the coachee's story that they begin to experience it directly, through feelings, ideas and reactions that seem to belong with them, not the coachee. For this reason, when you notice you have a strong emotional response to something your coachee has said or done, proceed with some caution. Ask yourself: "What does this feeling/reaction have to do with me?" If this is clearly your own stuff, for instance a memory from your past has been triggered, then your self-disclosure would serve no purpose for your coachee. But if something less attributable keeps cropping up, then the 'transfer' may have come from the coachee and into you. Describing what's going on for you could help the coachee face his or her own thoughts and feelings. Another question to self-reflect on before divulging would be: "Will my self-revelation serve the coachee's growth process?"

If and when you do voice your own thoughts and feelings, do so in a simple, brief fashion where you *name* it and *claim* it as your own. Then move the conversation back to the coachee:

1   "What's happening now for me is . . ." (describe what you notice in an impartial way).
2   "What's happening for you?" (check if there is any relationship between your reactions and the coachee).

Capacity for rapport, empathy and trust

Rapport is like a bridge between people, along which all communication flows more easily, maintaining a trusting relationship. Rapport is often born out of similarities: people like and feel comfortable with people like themselves. But your desire to build rapport can make you eager to voice your similar thoughts and experiences, with a 'me too' message. In normal social contexts this kind of echoing works well, but as it means the focus of attention is switched to the coach, it is not appropriate for Clean Coaching. Instead, we want the coachee to be focused on his or her inner thoughts and experience, not externally, centred on you.

We want to establish rapport with the coachees' internal 'landscape' of thoughts, and we do this by attempting to see through their eyes as though we were accompanying them on their inner journey of exploration. One way to do this is to follow the coachees' gaze when they look off, up or down into the space around them. David Grove was drawn to find out, when people look away into the distance, where are they going? Look where they look, point to where they point. There is an NLP process called 'Mirroring' used to build rapport, where all the movements and gestures the coachee makes are reflected back like a mirror image. This technique can be effective in everyday conversation; however for coaching, we are not looking to create such a strong rapport that the coachees identify with us. We want to blend into their background as subtly as possible, exploring their terrain without leaving our footsteps. You can do this by picking up on gestures and body language and instead of mirroring, try honouring their space by keeping things where the coachees put them. For instance, if they put their hand on their heart you can reflect that movement by making a similar gesture but pointing to *their* heart, not your own.

Having a sense of curiosity about other people helps with rapport building, and balanced with a sense of detachment, provides solid boundaries to keep yourself out of your coachee's way, avoiding any entanglements with his or her situation.

You can encourage the coachee to trust in you and the process, by first trusting it for yourself: having self-trust and then trusting the coachee to know what to do. Trust tends to happen between people, rather than originating from just one person. Your trust is likely to grow as you experience more and more successful Clean Coaching sessions. Initially however, you may need to take a leap of faith: to have the courage to try something different from your usual coaching approach.

Capacity to use one's voice

This is one of the more tangible skills for Clean Coaching, and something which distinguishes it from other forms of coaching. Vocal pace, pitch, resonance and timbre all help to convey many of the qualities covered above. The right kind of tone supports the curious, open, non-judgemental qualities we want to display. Keeping the pitch down at the end of your questions, and delivering them with a slow, steady pace helps carry confidence, trust and patience.

Grove was interested in what he referred to as the 'shape' of a question. By that he meant how it sounds when spoken out loud, from the experience of the listeners as they hear the question. Grove, being from Maori descent, seemed to pay greater attention to non-Western notions of communication, such as rhythm and beat: saying for instance: "The acoustical parameters in Clean Language, the rhythm and tonality, are such that a person can reject the question very easily without much ego affect. I want the client to chuck out any question that doesn't feel right" (Lawley and Tompkins, 1994).

In the next chapter we will look more closely at how a Clean Coach can use his or her voice as an instrument to aid communication.

Developing good habits

With Clean Coaching, no amount of reading about it, or even listening/observing others in action, will, in itself, develop your expertise. It takes the actual experience of being coached and coaching others to get it 'into the muscle' – a term I learnt from James Lawley and Penny Tompkins, although they tell me it they heard it first from Judith deLozier. Further research reveals that it originates from the Azaro tribe of Indonesia and Papua New Guinea who say, "Knowledge is only a rumour until it lives in the muscle" (Brown, 2015:7).

Acquiring excellence requires you to move from a position of incompetence to one of competence, and along that journey, your confidence levels are likely to first dip before gradually rising. This is because as you initially practice and experience Clean Coaching, you may become more consciously aware of your incompetence in the process. The following diagram (Figure 6.1) shows how, when learning something new, confidence shrinks when consciousness increases.

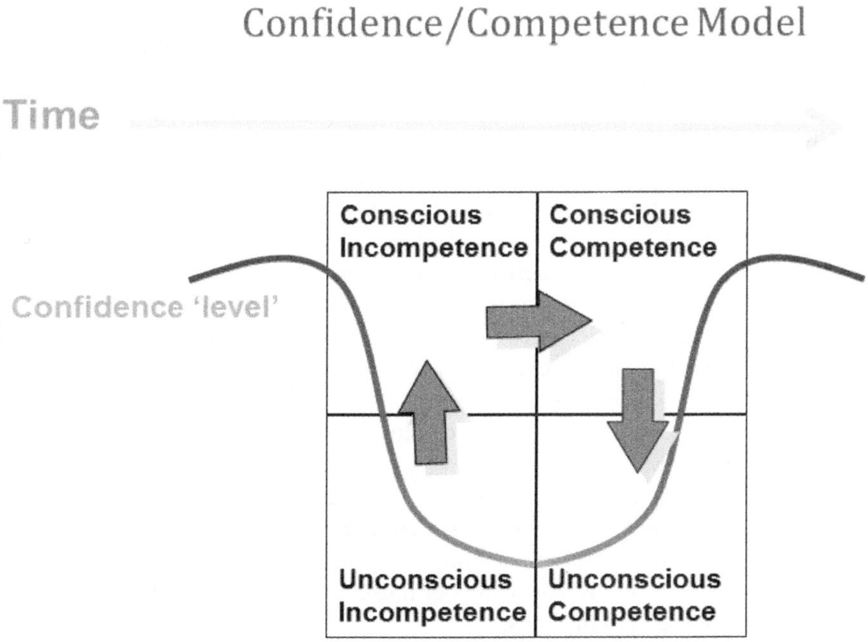

Figure 6.1 Learning – from unconscious incompetence.

Whatever they are learning, most people find they feel self-conscious and clunky in the early stages. For instance, when remembering learning to drive, most people can conjure up some pretty uncomfortable feelings from their first lesson. But it is reassuring to know that perseverance pays off. Continued practice, learning from experience and trial/error eventually leads to competence.

As competence is slowly mastered, confidence gradually grows. At the conscious competence stage of learning we may excel, but need concentration and effort. However, that is not the final stage of learning as we eventually progress towards unconscious competence. With any practice/skill-set that we continually use, eventually our conscious mind stops paying it so much attention, to free up headspace for something new. At the level of unconscious competence we can be masterful. However, because we are no longer consciously aware of our behaviours, if we are not careful we may over time slip back to incompetence as we fail to update our knowledge and become sloppy. The danger comes from being overconfident and believing we know all there is and can do all that's required. A healthy dose of humility is, I would say, the final quality or capacity that keeps Clean Coaches grounded and on a path of continuous development.

Practical exercise

It takes about 10 years to become an expert at anything (Ericsson et al., 1993) but you can learn the basics quickly and build from there. To become masterful in a given discipline, you can focus your attention on one piece at a time. With conscious and deliberate effortful practice, in just 21 days you can turn a new behaviour into a habit.

For example with Clean Language, you could take one question at a time and give it your total attention, commitment and concentration for a fixed period, say one week or even a single day.

Make that question your best friend. Keep it close by you and get to know it. Write it down, make an acronym of it, draw a picture that represents the question to you. Examine each word and become so familiar with it that it takes on a solid presence, even when you don't remember to look at it or think of it.

Ask the question as often as you can to people around you within everyday conversation.

Ask the question of yourself too as often as possible.

Notice what kinds of answers it generates and reflect on when this kind of question is most useful in coaching.

Once your question is firmly in your muscle, then select a different question for the same kind of focus.

References

Bachkirova, T. and Lawton Smith, C. (2015) From competencies to capabilities in the assessment and accreditation of coaches. *International Journal of Evidence Based Coaching and Mentoring*, 13(2) August 2015, 128. Available at: http://ijebcm.brookes. ac.uk/ [Accessed 7/8/2015].

Brown, B. (2015) *Rising Strong*. London: Penguin Random House.

Epstein, M. B. (1984) On the neglect of evenly suspended attention. *The Journal of Transpersonal Psychology*, 16(2), 193–205.

Ericsson, K., Krampe, R. and Tesch-Romer, C. (1993) The role of deliberate practice in the acquisition of expert performance. *Psychological Review*, 100, 363–406.

Freud, S. (1912) *Recommendations to Physicians Practicing Psychoanalysis* (Std. ed.). Republished: London: Hogarth Press, 1955, 12, 109–120.

Freud, S. (1923) The ego and the Id. The standard edition of the complete psychological works of Sigmund Freud (1923–1925). *The Ego and the Id and Other Works*, XIX, 1–66.

Gendlin, B. T. (1970) A short summary and some long predictions. In J. T. Hart and T. M. Tomlinson (eds.), *New Directions in Client-Centered Therapy*. Boston: Houghton Mifflin, 544–562.

Gendlin, E. T. (1968) The experiential response. In E. F. Hammer (ed.), *Use of Interpretation in Therapy: Technique and Art*. New York: Grune and Stratton, 208–227.

Grove, D. (2003) *Summary of David Grove's Ideas – as of 2003*. (Reorganised in March 2004 then published on the Clean Language website in 2010). Available at: www.cleanlanguage.co.uk/articles/articles/278/1/David-Grove-summary-of-ideas-as-of-2003/Page1.html [Accessed 15/7/2015].

Hill, P. (2004) *Concepts of Coaching: A Guide for Managers*. London: Institute of Leadership and Management.

Kennison, M. and Misselwitz, S. (2002) Evaluating reflective writing for appropriateness, fairness and consistency. *Nursing Education Perspectives*, 23(5), 238–242.

Kline, N. (1999) *Time to Think: Listening to Ignite the Human Mind*. London: Cassell Illustrated.

Lawley, J. and Tompkins, P. (1994) *And What Kind of Man Is David Grove?: An Interview by Penny Tompkins and James Lawley*. Available at: www.cleanlanguage.co.uk/ articles/articles/37/1/And-what-kind-of-a-man-is-David-Grove/Page1.html [Accessed 28/6/2015].

Rogers, C. (1951) *Client-Centered Therapy: Its Current Practice, Implications and Theory*. London: Constable.

Thompson, B. (2013) *Non-Directive Coaching: Attitudes, Approaches, Applications*. Cheshire: Critical Publishing.

Walker, C. (2014) *From Contempt to Curiosity: Creating Conditions for Groups to Collaborate Using Clean Language and Systemic Modelling*. Fareham: Clean Publishing.

Wang, Q. (2013) Structure and characteristics of effective coaching practice. *The Coaching Psychologist*, 9(1), 7–17 as cited in Bachkirova, T. and Lawton Smith, C. (2015) From competencies to capabilities in the assessment and accreditation of coaches. *International Journal of Evidence Based Coaching and Mentoring*, 13(2), August 2015, 124. Available at: http://ijebcm.brookes.ac.uk/ [Accessed 7/8/2015].

Whitworth, L., Kimsey-House, H. and Sandahl, P. (2007) *Co-Active Coaching: New Skills for Coaching People Toward Success in Work and Life*. Mountain View, CA: Davis Black Publishing.

Wilson, C. and Dunbar, A. (2008) *Clean Coaching with EK* (training course manual).

Chapter seven

The language of Clean Coaching

What is communication?

Communication is a big topic, covering many different concepts all in one. It's often explained by using the metaphor of a conduit, with two people passing along a message like some kind of 'package' between them. This helps highlight some of the key ingredients for communication, first that it requires two roles: that of the message sender and message receiver.

Like a two-way street, people take turns in being sender or receiver and in this way, conversations take place. Despite this common view of the duality of communication, it is not limited to two people and depending on the type of message, there may be multiple receivers. Generally however, we usually think of the message as being owned – and sent – by a single person. But is that really the case? All our messages must have come from somewhere and more likely as not, someone else. Rather like an eternal game of 'pass the parcel' we continually pass messages along from person to person, although instead of unwrapping the layers when it stops in our hands, more layers are added. In this way, we all learn meanings and carry important messages that have previously been received from others. What this means is that any and all communication is likely, at least in part, to contain a myriad of voices from other times and places.

Communication is complex. My own personal metaphor for communication is that it is like trying to share the picture from a 10,000 piece-jigsaw puzzle with someone else. The message sender sees the completed picture, but can only send information about it piece by piece. With limited time and patience to wait for the complete picture to unfold, the receiver begins to fill in the gaps and imagines the whole picture, when only a few pieces are in place. The person then assumes he or she has seen the real thing, rather than the version the person mostly created himself or herself. In this way, people infer meaning based on limited data all the time. Real communication is even more complicated than this, more like having dozens of puzzles being shared in many directions. No wonder we get our wires crossed and misunderstandings between people are so commonplace. Most communication is a messy melee of two-way messages flying back and forth, with outputs and inputs happening almost simultaneously between people. Like a kind of feedback loop each received message prompts a new response from each person, creating a fresh input into the 'system' that then generates the next output message. You cannot *not* communicate when with other people. Even silence communicates a message.

How then can any kind of communication ever be considered 'Clean'? This chapter explores the purpose of communication and how meaning is formed. We explain how Clean Coaching is different from regular conversations. We look at how people influence one another, how authority manifests in coaching and why Clean is so important. We examine words, voice and language as the components of communication and how to use each channel for Clean Coaching.

What do we mean by meaning?

The common purpose given to any and all communication is that we do it to convey meaning. The conduit metaphor implies that meaning is something that originates from the message sender. The message sender must then take this meaning already formed in his or her mind, and package it up neatly (usually referred to as 'encoding') into a clear message to transfer to another with minimal distortion. In an ideal world, effective communication is represented by two people at each end of the conduit sharing exactly the same thought, the meaning 'package' arrives with the receiver in one piece to be unwrapped (decoded) and understood completely. But this model of shared meaning doesn't seem to happen often.

Meaning can be elusive and people don't always say what they mean. Meaning can become confused between people. We sometimes imply what we mean rather than say it directly, and others have to infer it, reading 'between the lines' of our stated words. People sometimes don't even know exactly *what* they mean. When we speak, our meaning and intention is at best only 'half baked'. Ideas are born not as richly formed statements, but more like wisps of mental images coupled with a word or two, and a more ethereal 'sense' of something. Meaning is like a spark that needs to be fanned, before it can catch fire.

Traditional cognitive psychologists liked to think of the meaning of a message as something fixed and definitive, attached to language like a code to be cracked. The everyday concepts used to describe the non-tangible 'things' we know about in the world were thought to correspond exactly to inner mental categories (Lakoff, 1990). This objectivist viewpoint means that as long as you choose the right words that the receiver can understand, you can convey meaning. But current thinkers are challenging this 'message in a bottle' understanding of communication and meaning. Categories, according to George Lakoff (1990), are not formed according to some kind of universal translation codebook, but individually created by each person's actual bodily experience in the world. We literally make sense *through* our senses, and form internal mental images and sensations that represent our understandings of the world we live in.

Some social psychologists suggest that meaning doesn't even exist within the message sender at all. It is only once another had caught our drift that any kind of meaning becomes fully formed and in any sense 'real'. Clean Psychotherapist Philip Harland describes meaning as a subjective experience: not conveyed by the speaker but evoked in the mind of the listener (2012:33). It is constructed between people rather than owned by an originator. Meaning, therefore, is never fixed, as the communication exchange will shape it. Within the field of NLP, one core presupposition that practitioners abide by is that "the meaning of the message is the response it elicits" (Alder, 2002).

Influencing is at the heart of communication, and rather than a neat package passing between people, meaning is more like a breeze that circulates around them, never fully owned by anyone but contributed to by everyone. From this view, meaning is something fluid and constantly changing. Rather than belonging within some individual's mind, the social constructionist view is that meaning is co-constructed between people, rather like building sandcastles on a beach. We use the 'sand' we find all around, consisting of everyday 'discourse': that is, the common definitions and expressions used within the social environment around us.

But what would happen if the message receiver did not add and shape the meaning, but instead passed it back to the message sender untouched by his or her assumptions? What if a person was allowed to unwrap his or her own message parcel, and discover, layer by layer, what he or she really thinks? Clean Coaching provides a framework to help people unwrap their own message parcels to discover their unique and personal meaning, often containing insights and understanding they never realised were there.

Carl Rogers (1967) believed that we can encourage others to understand themselves better by making our own best attempt at understanding them completely. He suggested that even a minimal, 'bumbling and faulty' attempt can be very helpful as people rarely permit themselves to understand precisely what another person means. It can feel risky to lose yourself in another's thoughts. People fear that if they let themselves really understand another, they themselves may be changed by the experience.

Coaching conversations

Coaching is all about a certain form of communication – having a conversation. Conversations are a kind of social interaction, tending to be spoken, spontaneous, and involving two or more people. Conversations also follow certain etiquette – which help create and reinforce normal, acceptable forms of social behaviour. Conversations tend to be balanced with a 'to and fro' pattern of turn-taking, each turn is like a building block, becoming the base for the next person's contribution. This creates a chain reaction or feedback loop of dialogue and if people don't follow this expected pattern, conversation does not flow.

Grove (2003) referred to the 'seductiveness' of language, which draws both the coachee and the coach into a complicated and compelling story. Question after question that collects information around the problem can make it harder to get outside of it. Grove called this the 'tyranny of the narrative' as the coach ends up entangled within the story and becomes personally involved with it. This is quite normal but actually unhelpful for the coachee. Grove explained that Clean questions help the coachee enter into a dialogue with himself or herself rather than an interaction with another. Psychologists refer to this as an 'intrapersonal conversation' with our dialogical self. People often have multiple 'self positions' and this enables an internal exchange between the different representations of who they think they are. Most of us are aware of having conversations – or even arguments – with ourselves and it's a key aspect to how we make sense of things and make decisions. See Chapter fifteen for more on multiple selves.

It's not easy for people – even coaches – to keep our attention purely on the other person because, according to Derber (2000), we all suffer from conversational narcissism. Within the 'to and fro' pattern lies a subtle, unconscious competition for attention. Derber suggests that most conversational responses are *shift-responses*, which take the focus of attention away from the last speaker and refocuses on the new speaker. The famous line spoken by Bette Midler in the film *Beeches* highlights how people can become preoccupied with being the centre of attention: "But enough about me. Let's talk about you. What do *you* think of me?" In contrast, a *support-response* keeps attention with the previous speaker, an example of which would be a simple Clean Language response of "And is there anything else about that?"

Clean Coaching is different

Clean Coaching is unlike normal conversation, as priority is given to the coachee's meaning rather than any interpretation of the coach's. Rather than following the unspoken etiquette of sharing airtime, Clean Coaching is different in the following ways.

Not adding your own input

The conversation responses are supportive not 'shifty': focus remains with the coachee's train of thought. Even by mentioning yourself in your question you are subtly shifting attention away from your coachee and towards yourself. For example: "So . . . *I'm* wondering about the skills you mentioned earlier. Can you explain to *me* what you meant by that?" These kinds of references to self are to be avoided with Clean Coaching, as are expressions of empathy like "I've had that too" or "I know exactly what you mean" plus sharing your personal anecdotes or stories: "I had that happen too and this is what I did about it . . ."

Repeating back: mirroring

Rather than paraphrasing the client's meaning in your own words, the coachee's message is reflected back exactly as delivered, if necessary summarised using his or her actual words, not your own interpretation.

Pacing

Questions are delivered with a slow and steady pace, with pauses between each word to encourage the coachee to reflect further and deeper before deciding how to respond next.

Listening for patterns and metaphors, not the content

Clean Coaches pay attention to and listen out for the patterns, metaphors and implicit meanings within the client's message, not just the content of any story being told.

Linking with 'and'

Questions often start with 'and', creating a smooth continuation from the coachee's message and the coach's next question, instead of the pendulum 'to and fro' swing between competing message senders.

Sequence of questions

Clean questions can create an iterative and generative flow of information, as each question builds from the coachee's previous answers.

Structure of each question

The questions have a certain repetitive form and syntax, often repeating back the coachee's same words multiple times, even within one question. With only certain words being permissible, coaches could feel restricted because they cannot use normal conversational spontaneity. The upside is they allow the coachee greater freedom in response and for exploration. Although the raw ingredients of the questions are limited, there are as many variations as there are possible coachee responses as Clean questions are moulded from the coachee's own words.

Communication and influence

Social psychologists argue that the true objective of communication is to make something happen. Austin (1962) described language as a speech 'act': language serves a purpose as does any other kind of action.

Most people underestimate the extent to which we are all subtly persuaded and controlled by other people's expectations and desires for us. No wonder communication is complex: every single utterance could have a myriad of meanings, intentional and unintentional, full of echoes from the wider social world around us. Common refrains get repeated and reiterated like waves on the sea, washing ashore common cultural expectations, beliefs and values. Within typical groups of people, including organisations, normal practices and customary routines are rarely consciously created by a leader, but by a kind of group osmosis. We soak up what's 'right and proper behaviour' from what we see and hear around us, generally without much awareness or examination. This is particularly apparent within large, long-established institutions, such as private organisations or government departments where large-scale 'groupthink' creates clone-like opinions and decisions. People can become lazy about thinking for themselves, and instead recycle sayings and phrases heard so often they assume they must be true. Arguing against cultural norms is like swimming up-stream. It can happen, but not without hard work, conscious, sustained effort and the desire to change the status quo.

The field of NLP has capitalised on the impact of language for influencing, developing key interventions and processes to encourage people to change. For instance, 'reframing' techniques draw attention to different ways of perceiving the same thing. 'Future pacing' has a person rehearse what needs to happen so he or she can practice new ways of thinking and responding. And 'sleight of mouth' is an NLP conversational change technique based on the work by eminent psychotherapist, Milton Erickson. He found that he could help people make dramatic changes in their thinking and behaviour through making indirect, hypnotic suggestions within ordinary conversation (Erickson and Rosen, 1982). He felt that people were always in one kind of trance or another, with the unconscious mind always alert and ready to take on 'artfully vague' permissions to change. Politicians, sales people and writers regularly use these techniques, intentionally and unintentionally. It is quite commonplace and acceptable to persuade others: to believe in something; to buy a certain product; have sympathy for a certain character and to think or act in a certain way. To conclude, it is virtually impossible not to influence, and be influenced by others.

As a coach, you may find yourself intentionally persuading your coachees in positive ways. To believe in themselves, for instance. Or to take the actions they have said they need to in order to reach their outcomes. But, as covered in Chapter two, the power of suggestion is subtle and happens accidently. Clean Coaching heightens awareness of your own language and that of your coachee. By taking the time to repeat back exactly your coachee's own words, you hold the coachee in his or her own experience rather than 'flipping' the coachee over to your way of seeing things. As you choose and construct the next Clean question, you also have time to carefully select which part of the coachee's previous message to focus on.

New learners are often surprised how difficult it can be to ask such simple questions, giving the reason that their own intruding thoughts are 'begging' to be spoken. The urge to let go of the reins and run down your own trains of thought is very compelling. If experienced, it can be an alarming realisation of just how much you normally lead conversations unintentionally.

Influence is different from being influential. The whole point of coaching is to bring about a change in behaviour and thought. To some degree, all coaches will have a broad intention for the coachee to make some kind of positive change, but must resist pre-determining what kind of change that may turn out to be. But, something *is* supposed to happen as a result of the coaching experience and so questions need to be influential. Clean questions are often very influential in the sense that they have a significant positive effect on those being asked them. The questions help facilitate the coachee to make self-directed changes that tend to emerge naturally when people attend deeply to their experience.

The impact of authority on self-determination

Another aspect of influence within communication comes not from our message but from who we are and what we represent. To paraphrase Ralph Waldo Emerson (1875): "I cannot hear what you are saying, who you are speaks too loudly . . ." People already believe something about your communication before you even know what it is that you will say. Their beliefs about you will colour how they hear your message, which is imbued with the power of your authority.

How much authority do you have in any particular coaching session? The coachees' perception of that authority is what matters, which is mostly outside our control. Wider influences affect the coachees' perception, such as what they already know about you and expect from coaching. Even for senior leaders used to being in control, they are likely to regard their coach as an expert in their field and place trust in them. As coaches are generally paid for their time, what they do is seen to have value. The more expensive you are, the more authority you may appear to hold, all other things being equal. Authority causes other people to comply with their perception of your wishes. Compliance robs people of any empowerment, preventing them from thinking for themselves and becoming agents of their own change.

Stanley Milgram's (1963) obedience study is one of the most influential, controversial and widely known studies within social psychology. Milgram sought to find out the extent to which people will comply with perceived authority and follow orders even if against their own better judgement. Participants were told to administer seemingly increasingly severe (but fake) electric shocks to a stooge in response to incorrect answers given in a so-called learning exercise. A very high percentage of people went along with the experimenter's requests acquiescing to figures of authority despite clearly being uncomfortable doing so. The experiment demonstrated how *authority can be illusionary*, created by no more than a fancy-looking laboratory and a white coat.

Milgram's study was groundbreaking as it broke from the typical 'positivist' view of an impartial scientist using a pristine lab free of outside influence. Instead, the scientist and the lab *became* the influencers in the experiment. This highlighted how all scientific experiments involving people carry invisible authority which potentially bias results, as participants seek to comply with the researcher's wishes.

Like it or not, you probably already carry authority imbued in you by the coachees and they will place greater importance on your advice than on other people they consider on their 'level'. They may misinterpret your thoughts and read them as commands. I remember early in my coaching career a client saying "I took your advice and went for that promotion." I was absolutely certain I had given no such advice, but the client's expectation had coloured his memory of events.

Clean Coaching limits our use of words to just a handful of simple, clear terms, wrapped amongst the coachee's own expressions. This helps ensure that the coachee reflects on his or her own language and its deeper meaning to him or her, rather than focus on illusionary authoritative interpretations or advice.

Difference between communication and language

For the conduit metaphor of communication to work, as well as two communicators at either end, we need a channel along which to send messages. For humans, we use language for this. When face to face, people have three key language channels: words, voice and body language. A well-known and well-worn 'fact' states that different percentages of meaning are gleaned from each channel. Seven per cent of any message is carried through words. Voice accounts for 38 per cent of the message (known as 'paralanguage', including all our subtle voice nuances, tone, pace, pitch, emphasis, etc.). That leaves over half of our message – 55 per cent – coming from body language.

This misinterpreted fact is in itself a good example of how messages and meaning 'grow' from circulation. The original research by Mehrabian and Wiener (1967) was specifically conducted in relation to communication of *personal meaning*, particularly of attitudes and feelings. Albert Mehrabian (1981) subsequently explained that the low percentage of meaning placed on words is most relevant when there are incongruences within the message, as people will believe the voice and body language messages more. Above all, the research emphasises how we may communicate more meaning than intended. Meaning can be inferred whether we like it or not, pulled out from the sender, not just pushed towards the receiver.

As a Clean Coach, words, voice and body language are all important to help us understand our coachee and reflect back the coachee's experience.

Words

Every word we know has a distinctly different meaning to each of us, based on our personal history with that word. Despite differing levels of ability in conveying messages, our chosen words matter to us. Some people try to use too many words in one go and their meaning becomes lost within the complexity. Some people are mean with words and answer in short, sharp sentences. Freud said, "Words were originally magic and to this day words have retained much of their ancient magical power" (Freud et al, 1963). We *entrance* others with our words, but no words are more captivating than those we choose for ourselves to express our ideas and inner experience.

Clean Coaches repeat back the exact words used by the coachee. With Clean Language, before asking a question the coach would demonstrate he or she has listened and understood by reflecting back some of the coachee's dialogue. Instead of paraphrasing, the Clean Coach reflects back the coachee's language exactly as spoken without changing the words or switching to the coach's own understanding. In this way, it honours the coachee's message and helps highlight what's most important.

Reflecting back accurately requires a few highly attuned qualities and capacities as covered in Chapter six. Although your choice of response is limited to those words actually used by the coachee, you can still be direct and challenging. For instance, I once asked a coachee: "What the bloody hell *is* going on?" and it was completely, 100 per cent clean. How so? He had just said those same words to me, in a more rhetorical fashion: "What the bloody hell is going on?" By reflecting back his rhetorical question exactly as said, like a boomerang it came back to him, creating a kind of feedback loop, the coachee's output became my next input, asked as a question it became a Clean kind of challenge.

Grove (1998) described the repetition within Clean Language as being recursive. The process is like a spiral rather than circular, as each reflection does not return the coachee to the start of his or her thinking but helps him or her progress. It has a forward momentum. He pointed out that repetition creates a protective space, from which something new can be born. In part, it moves time forward and helps 'give birth' to creative thinking and new information which emerges from the client's attention on sometimes seemingly irrelevant and off-the-cuff remarks and comments that the client hears as if for the first time as you reflect them back. Your repetition of the coachee's words could be just a word or two or a more complete summary, depending on the pace of the session. In its complete form, there are three distinct parts to a Clean Language question, which together are known as the 'three-part syntax'.

The 'three-part syntax'

Part one is pure reflection of the coachee's message. *Part two* selectively orients towards the part of the coachee's message that your question is aimed at. *Part three* is the question itself, which will often have the coachee's words wrapped into its structure.

For example if the coachee said:

> "I feel like I'm drifting a bit. I kind of know roughly where I need to get to, but I'm not really pushing myself at the moment. I wish I was a bit more focused on a more ambitious career goal, something that would really fire me up."

> For Part one reflection, rather than repeat the whole narrative, you might just reflect back some of the key parts that summarise the whole piece, using *'and'* to help keep the pieces joined together. "And . . . drifting, not really pushing. And you wish . . . a bit more focused . . . and more ambitious career goal . . . really fire you up."

Or at times you may choose to reflect back simply the last few words the coachee said: "And . . . a more ambitious career goal that would really fire you up."

Once you have reflected back, the next part of the question orients towards the focus of the question. This part of the question starts with *'and when'*. So building on from the previous, the first *two parts* of your question might be:

"And . . . drifting, not really pushing. And you wish . . . a bit more focused . . . and more ambitious career goal . . . really fire you up. (Pause). And *when* you're a bit more focused . . ."

This middle part of the question provides you with extra time to think through exactly what question to ask, and allows the coachee further thinking time to focus his or her attention on a specific part of the prior message, in this case, being a bit more focused.

The third part of the three-part syntax is the question itself, so for example, a very simple and remarkably useful Clean Language question is: "What kind of (coachee's words) is that (coachee's words)?"

All three parts of the question would therefore include the following:

Part one: "And . . . drifting, not really pushing. And you wish . . . a bit more focused . . . and more ambitious career goal . . . really fire you up." (Pause).
Part two: "And *when* you're a bit more focused . . ."
Part three: "What kind of focused is that focused?"

Wherever possible, even if it doesn't sound grammatically correct, reflect back the coachee's words exactly as said, in the same tense, without changing anything. So, for instance if the coachee says: "I need to be more confident." You would be repeating back: "And when 'more confident' . . ." Rather than subtly changing to a more conversational response of: "And when you *are* more confident . . ."

Or as an another example, if the coachee says: "It's about not losing my way anymore." You would repeat: "And when 'not losing your way anymore' . . ." Rather than changing the tense to: "And when you've not lost your way . . ."

Sometimes the littlest words can make a big difference and it's important to reflect the coachee's language exactly as it has been delivered.

What not to say

You may notice from reading out loud the above Clean Coaching example that the sentence sounds a little incomplete and disjointed. But we are not having a normal two-way conversation, so any superfluous, additional conversational words are excluded which could detract from the coachee's own words and therefore his or her own experience. You would also resist referring to the person by *name* which could switch attention from his or her internal experience to responding in a social conversational context.

So for instance you wouldn't say, "So Jane, what you're saying is . . ." "If I heard you correctly, you said . . ."

As the coachee engages further into his or her own experience during a Clean Coaching session, it is best to avoid even changing the reference to himself or herself from 'I' to 'you' as that can jolt the coachee away from internal mind wandering and back to conversational dialogue with you.

So, for instance when the coachee says: "I feel warm." You repeat: "And I feel warm."

If you mirror the person's self-reference early on in the session it can be confusing as the expectation will be for you to refer to him or her as 'you'.

I often compromise with this dilemma by reflecting back: "And . . . you say 'I feel warm.'" Although not strictly Clean, in this way I pave the way for later on dropping the 'you say' part once the coachee is in the flow of self-exploration.[1]

Finally, with word reflection, remember *less is more*. If in doubt, it is best to repeat fewer words accurately than more with slight inaccuracies. Some Clean Coaching techniques (see Chapter ten) don't require much repetition of the coachee's words as the space and other 'props' around the coachee become containers for the coachee's words and can help echo back his or her meaning as the session continues.

What words to repeat back

By choosing which word(s) to repeat back and focus your next question on, you are influencing the direction taken. As the coach you are directing the flow of conversation even though you are not directing towards a certain strategy or outcome. It is important to choose that focus wisely, if in doubt ask the coachee what he or she would like to have happen next.

Here are some suggestions on which words to repeat back:

- Words that get repeated by the coachee – indicating these words matter to him or her.
- Words that have multiple meanings – Grove was drawn to ambiguity and any double-edged meanings that can help coachees reframe their understanding.
- Metaphors – this is where the juice for Clean Coaching is found.
- Verbs – are often latent metaphors – active words that involve doing something help signal change.
- Words that describe a sense – seeing, hearing, feeling, touching, tasting, smelling. These words signal a raw experience and the closer we get to that, the more likely the coachee will discover deeper, personal meanings.

- Unusual words, 'red herrings', 'asides', spoonerisms – Grove (1998) suggested the 'accidental asides' that the coachee introduces are often the key to underpinning assumptions that hold thoughts in place. Although it can feel like going 'off track' in the coaching session, sometimes we need to get 'lost' before we can find a new path.

In Chapter eight we will further explore how to focus attention.

Voice

Our voices are the melody to our language, conveying mood, authenticity and intention, amongst other things. We add harmony and resonance to our message with voice pitch, speed, emphasis and tone.

Pacing and pausing

For Clean Coaching, generally a slow, steady pace is used, with a distinct pause between the words within your question, as though separated with full stops:

"And what. Would you like. To have. Happen?"

Grove called the exaggerated pauses in Clean questions *'response-inviting gaps'*, as they invite a continually deepening state of reflection. He compared the importance of this pause with a certain style of drumming that emphasised the 'off' beat, where the space between the sounds is more important than the sound itself in creating the melody. I've since researched off-beats and discovered that in musical terms, this is called 'syncopation', occurring when a regular rhythm is deliberately skipped and the weaker accent stressed instead. Missed beat syncopation is known to cause a physical effect in the body of the listener as his or her body moves to supply the missing beat. And recent research has highlighted an impact on brain activity waves as the mind tries to synchronise with the expected rhythm. This, according to Annette Schirmer, leads to boosted cognitive performance and accelerated decision making (Escoffier et al., 2015).

Within the field of cognitive psychology, neurological measurement devices have shown that for the listener, their brain begins processing verbal messages before completion. The brain takes a 'best guess' approach to the actual meaning and starts formulating all possible answers. Research into 'garden path sentences' has shown how the meaning of a statement (or a question) often evolves as each new word is expressed, and psychologists have shown that people tend to hold open *any and all* possible meanings of the words used until the speaker stops talking. At that point we narrow down options. Some Clean questions have questions embedded within them and with each pause, multiple meanings are created, opening up a huge variety of possibilities. This encourages deeper stimulation of the brain and additional mental networks of ideas, concepts and memories are brought into service.

Reflecting back word emphasis

When emphasis is given to a certain word within a sentence, not only does it underline that word as being particularly important, it can in fact change the meaning of the sentence. For instance:

> I didn't really *want* the promotion, it just *fell* into my lap.
> I didn't really want the *promotion*, it just fell into *my* lap.
> For Clean Coaching, keep the intonation as the coachee has chosen and use the emphasis to select which words to pay further attention to.

Body language

We can learn a lot about the coachees from their body language, movements and mannerisms. As people explore their inner experience, they may begin to notice that the feelings and images they are imagining have a location. Although this location is within their imaginary 'mind's eye' space, that space is usually superimposed all around and inside a person. People literally paint pictures with their hands and show you what they are thinking about. For instance, a coachee I worked with once told me that she did not know what was stopping her from moving forward, and as she spoke, her hands seemed to be running along a verti- cal 'wall' immediately in front of her, and they even made a fist and thumped it. It was not until I drew her attention to that wall with my own body language, eye gaze and gestures that it came into her conscious awareness. She was then able to 'see' it for herself, in the space in front of her.

Lawley (2013) describes a crucial aspect of Clean communication is like reciprocal 'pointing'. Coachees continually point to aspects of their inner world through their gestures and the metaphors they use. Coaches are the recipients of these signals even though they can never actually see what is being pointed to, they can pay attention to what is going on. Referred to by Grove as the cli- ent's 'choreography', the clients' bodily movements show where their imaginary mental spaces and symbols are located, and the form they take. Lawley says, "Although I may not be able to see the symbols in a client's private world, with careful modelling I can know where they are from the client's perspective and attend to something like what they are attending to." You will learn more about modelling in Chapter ten.

What Lawley is suggesting is that you can use your gestures to reflect back what's happening for the coachee, being careful to honour the spaces the coachee selects, rather than reflect a completely symmetrical mirror image. So, for instance if your coachee talks about courage and gently touches the centre of his chest, rather than touch the centre of your *own* chest to mimic his movement, you would gently indicate towards *his* chest, reflecting his location. It is *his* courage and belongs with *him*, not inside you.

The role of the Clean Coach

Clean Coaching favours the coachee's meaning, not the coach's. In successful coaching sessions, the coachee does most of the talking. That's not to say that the coach is passive or has less to do. The Clean Coach's role is to help the coachee discover his or her own emerging meanings and make sense of them.

From this perspective, the coach is not communicating to impart his or her meaning, nor even to understand the coachee's meaning (although it usually helps). It is to help the coachee understand his or her own meaning, or put in another way, facilitating others to communicate with themselves. Philip Harland points out that Clean Language facilitates first-person reporting of internal truth uncontaminated by the fanciful assumptions, presumptions and suggestions of others. It is a 'model' of questioning that "effectively neutralises the unconscious beliefs and intentions of the questioner and sidesteps the distortions and re-interpretations we habitually place in the way of our communications" (2012:24).

Lawley and Tompkins (2000:27) argue that

> Your purpose is not to analyse or interpret the client's experience. It is not even to understand it. Rather, it is to offer them the opportunity to become aware of their (symbolic) perceptions with minimal 'contamination' by you (your metaphors).

Does Clean completely avoid any bias or direction?

Being 'Clean' as a coach limits the amount of your content you bring into the session and helps you avoid offering suggestions, solutions or prescriptions. However, as Steve Andreas (2006) points out, there will always be some room left for biased beliefs and orientation to influence the client. For instance, the choice of which of the client's words to repeat back to the person from a single word, phrase or everything that has just been said "depending where you want to direct their attention" (Andreas, 2006:134). He points out that different approaches may focus on the problem, or the solution, for instance. He suggests a second source of potential bias is in the choice of which questions to ask, for example whether the question points towards the coachee's past memory, current experience or imagined future, for instance.

Andreas questions the value of Clean Language, suggesting the 'protection' from content may be a double-edged sword as the coachee may be unable to think in any new way beyond his or her stuckness. "When you are inside a box, it's hard to think outside the box" (Andreas, 2006:133). This seems most likely and psychologists call this tendency towards stuck thinking 'functional fixity' which has been extensively studied in ingenious ways. For instance see Duncker's (1945) creativity experiments where participants were given a candle and a box full of tacks and told to find a way to fix the candle to the wall. Most people failed to do so, unable to see the box containing the tacks as being part of the available resources they could use. But encouraging uncommon thinking is just what Clean Coaching does, by helping the coachees stretch beyond their usual thinking patterns precisely because they build from their current frame of reference.

On the question of bias, James Lawley and Penny Tompkins (2000:52) set the record straight:

> Of course Clean Language influences and directs attention – all language does that. Clean Language does it cleanly because it is sourced in the client's vocabulary, it is consistent with the logic of their metaphors and only introduces the universal metaphors of time, space and form.

Note

1 Although there is a potential disadvantage in this approach as it introduces the coach's words 'you' and 'say' and could even be interpreted as a challenge. I justify my use of this phrasing as Grove himself used it as a question structure within his 'Clean Pronouns' process, developed to explore personal pronouns. See Chapter sixteen.

References

Alder, H. (2002) *The Handbook of NLP: A Manual for Professional Communicators.* Aldershot: Gower Publishing Ltd.

Andreas, S. (2006) *Six Blind Elephants: Understanding Ourselves and Each Other – Volume One Fundamental Principles of Scope and Category.* Moab: Real People Press.

Austin, J. (1962) *How to Do Things with Words.* London: Oxford University Press.

Derber, C. (2000) *The Pursuit of Attention: Power and Ego in Everyday Life* (2nd ed.). London: Oxford University Press.

Duncker, K. (1945) On Problem Solving. *Psychological Monographs*, 58, 1–113. Whole No. 270.

Emerson, R. (1875) *Letters and Social Aims.* Boston: James R. Osgood and Company.

Erickson, M. and Rosen, S. (1982) *My Voice Will Go with You – The Teaching Tales of Milton H. Erickson.* New York: W.W. Norton & Company.

Escoffier, N., Herrmann, C. S. and Schirmer, A. (2015) Auditory rhythms entrain visual processes in the human brain: Evidence from evoked oscillations and event-related potentials. *Neuroimage, 111*, 267–276.

Freud, S., Strachey, J., Freud, A., and Rothgeb, C. L. (1963). *The Standard Edition of the Complete Psychological Works of Sigmund Freud: Introductory lectures on psychoanalysis. pt. III* (Vol. 16). London: Hogarth Press and the Institute of psycho-analysis. (Original work 1917).

Grove, D. (1998) *Philosophy and Principles of Clean Language.* Available at: www.clean language.co.uk/articles/articles/38/1/Philosophy-and-Principles-of-Clean-Language/ Page1.html [Accessed 24/6/2015].

Grove, D. (2003) *Summary of David Grove's Ideas – As of 2003*. Available at: www.clean language.co.uk/articles/articles/278/1/David-Grove-summary-of-ideas-as-of-2003/ Page1.html [Accessed 25/6/2015].

Harland, P. (2012) *Trust Me I'm the Patient: Clean Language, Metaphor, and the New Psychology of Change*. London: Wayfinder Press.

Lakoff, G. (1990) *Women, Fire and Dangerous Things*. London: The University of Chicago Press.

Lawley, J. (2013) Pointing to a new modelling perspective. *Acuity*, 4, October 2013. Available at: www.cleanlanguage.co.uk/articles/articles/326/1/Pointing-to-a-New-Modelling-Perspective/Page1.html [Accessed 8/8/2015].

Lawley, J. and Tompkins, P. (2000) *Metaphors in Mind*. London: The Developing Company Press.

Mehrabian, A. (1981) *Silent Messages: Implicit Communication of Emotions and Attitudes*. Belmont: Wadsworth.

Mehrabian, A. and Wiener, M. (1967) Decoding of inconsistent communications. *Journal of Personality and Social Psychology*, 6(1), 109–114. doi 10.1037/h0024532.

Milgram, S. (1963) Behavioral study of obedience. *The Journal of Abnormal and Social Psychology*, 67(4), 371.

Rogers, C. (1967) *On Becoming a Person – A Psychotherapist's View of Psychotherapy*. London: Constable.

Chapter eight

Clean questions to focus attention

The art of questioning

People ask questions for many reasons. We may seek factual *information* – such as directions to the new cinema; or *opinion* – such as whether it's worth visiting. Sometimes we ask questions to confirm what we think we already know, or clarify further when we have only some of the story. In all these cases, information is sought for the questioner's benefit, to enrich his or her understanding.

But in coaching, questions are asked mainly for the benefit of the answerers, to improve *their* understanding, not the questioners. However, some exceptions apply. Occasionally we ask questions to get specific information about the coachee, their organisation and/or their circumstances. For instance, when:

- Gaining clarity on the coachee's expectations of coaching and how the person expects change to happen, so we can track progress against those expectations.
- Contracting – using questions such as:
  - How would you like us to communicate between coaching sessions?
  - Which is the best email address to use for you?
  - Are you happy for me to send a summary of our session and any follow-up notes to this email address?

Mostly however, coaches ask questions for other reasons. For example:

- To show we have listened.
- To communicate empathy and understanding.
- To help the coachee further explore and develop his or her own thoughts and ideas.

Within a coaching session, different kinds of questions tend to be useful at different times and under different circumstances. And Clean questions can be used for multiple purposes, sequenced in many different ways to bring about change.

Using Clean questions for different purposes

To check understanding/challenge assumptions

As well as using Clean questions for coaching, they can be used in any conversation to improve levels of understanding between people. For instance, if
your partner says he or she would like you to 'be more adventurous', rather than
guess what that means you could use Clean questions to find out more about the
kind of 'adventurous' he or she means. When you first learn Clean questions, it's
a good idea to look for any and all opportunities to practice them in everyday
conversations.

For self-improvement/self-discovery

You can ask questions of yourself, encouraging greater examination and deeper
understanding. For instance, as I write this book, I frequently wonder how best
to explain a certain idea or topic. I ask myself Clean questions to help clarify
how best I can explain things to others. Sometimes I might also ask myself Clean
questions when I am not sure what to do or how I feel about something; it helps
me sort out my opinion. But, I do prefer it if someone else asks me the questions.
Many find it helpful to write down both the questions and answers, and ponder
on them for a while. For others, introducing an element of surprise over what the
question will be makes it a more thought-provoking experience. You might do
that by picking a Clean question at random, written on cards for instance. And you
could randomly select where to focus attention by rolling dice and counting to that
number of words within your sentence as the target of the next question.

To avoid bias

As covered in Chapter three, at their most basic usage level, Clean Language
questions can be used like a set of tools within your coaching toolbox. You can
pick up a single question and use as required whenever you need to be more non-
directive to prevent any unconscious bias. In this way, you may simply select an
appropriate Clean question that fits the bill, without planning to use in any sequential way. For instance, when the coachee introduces an issue that has significant,
personal resonance for the coach. In such a scenario, it is all too easy for the coach
to jump in and explain his or her story or solution whereas the coachee's own version of events and potential solutions may be very different. The coach may even
find that the coachee's situation triggers unwanted or unpleasant feelings, with
knowledge/memories of his or her personal experience getting in the way of the
coachee's exploration.

   As covered in Chapter two, echoes of one's own past may trigger Drama Triangle 'roles' and along with it the urge to Rescue, or to become a Persecutor, or
even a Victim. If the desire is acted upon, even subtly, it could spark an equally

unhelpful transactional role within the coachee. There are many useful strategies that the coach can employ in this situation, first and most important noticing his or her own internal sensations, emotions and mental dialogue and recognising when personal 'unfinished business' may have been triggered. In itself, that may release the hold these experiences have and enable the coach to continue the session with more conscious control and freedom. Then, a careful selection of Clean questions can ensure that at 'critical moments' within the session, the coach's own understanding and beliefs don't overly influence the subsequent direction of the coaching conversation. Fortunately, the simplest Clean questions, like those given below, are most effective in these kind of situations.

Any action taken by the coach 'in the moment' should be supported after the session with further reflection, potentially by taking the issue to coaching supervision. Over time and with regular support, coaches can improve their ability to reflect on the deeper dynamics triggered through coaching. With a greater capacity for self-reflection and improved self-awareness, coaches can become better at recognising and dealing with personal triggers live in the coaching session.

To encourage reflection

When you sequence a series of Clean questions together in a structured way, it becomes a process for encouraging introspection and mindfulness. The coachee's attention is continually focused on his or her actual inner experience in the here and now. Each of the coachee's answers becomes the input stimulus for the next investigative thought forming an iterative effect: the answers build on and reinforce each other. You can use this process to enhance conversations, allowing the other person to reflect on any and all aspects of his or her words and experience, to discover deeper meanings.

To gain deeper understanding of a felt sense

You can also encourage deeper reflection by noticing and questioning further any sensory experiences the coachee becomes aware of. As you continually use more Clean questions, the coachees' internal mind wandering generally leads to a greater awareness of 'raw' impressions of their inner experience, often conveyed through sensory terms. For example, what they can see in their mind's eye; what they can feel: as an emotion but also as a physical sensation somewhere in or around their body; what they can hear in their own heads: their own inner dialogue or some other sound; and sometimes even tastes and/or smells. People make sense of the world through their sensory channels and descriptions of this kind are closer to real experience than our usual thinking processes involving 'rational' but abstract concepts.

Focusing on embodied experience or 'felt' senses is a well-known tactic in the counselling arena. Eugene Gendlin developed a process known as 'focusing' to bring about such an awareness. He described it as a way of accessing intuitive understanding contained within us but on the edge of our consciousness. Coming from a phenomenological perspective, Gendlin (1968) asserts that the body is highly influential in how people create meaning out of experience. All our lives, moment by moment we are in our bodies and live through our bodies, it is a consistent source of implicit, intricate knowing that we may find hard to put our finger on, but nevertheless can be substantial and detailed.

Our bodies affect how we think. And how we think can also affect our bodies. There is a wealth of neuroscientific evidence demonstrating that we have various 'blueprints' of our body literally mapped across our brains (Blakeslee and Blakeslee, 2008). Body maps of the somasensory system include the complex subset of touch senses: temperature, pain, balance, proprioception (awareness of the position of our body and its parts in space, and how they are moving) and finally interoception, which is our visceral awareness of what's happening within our bodies, internal tissues and organs. The body map for our interoceptive sense is held within the right frontal insula in the brain, which is also responsible for detecting our emotional state of mind. Brain scanning confirms that we really do experience emotions as coming from specific places within our bodies, with both physical pain and emotional pain lighting up the same brain circuitry within those regions.

In everyday language we often refer to this almost sixth sense as our 'gut feel'. Often we have a visceral sense of 'it' without having words to describe it or a form to define it. Gendlin's focusing process starts by simply relaxing and turning your attention inwards. People are used to attending to and engaging with the external world around them, but less so with their own internal body reactions and sensations, including images and sounds in their mind's eye and mind's ear. Gradually, attention is focused towards what the body senses (e.g. feels, sees, smells, tastes and hears). Gendlin's core idea is that by noticing and placing attention on any felt sense, it will reveal its wisdom. People can make explicit the often vague sensory inklings they have by finding words, images and pictures to describe them. When we find the right kind of symbols to represent our felt sense, often we reach a shift in our understanding, things fall into place and we take a step towards resolution of problems or issues.

'Focusing' questions are not the same as 'Clean' questions. However Clean questions can be used in a similar way, to help coachees focus on their internal, embodied experience. By asking Clean questions about any kind of bodily sense the coachee mentions, his or her attention can become more finely attuned. Asking a series of Clean questions about a felt sense helps the coachee become more aware of its qualities and characteristics, and gradually it may take on a clearer symbolic representation, with a location and form. The added value with Clean questions is they follow the coachee's own evolving thought process rather than a pre-established list. In addition, the added dimension of inviting metaphors helps the right kind of symbol emerge.

To aid creative original thinking through exploration of metaphor

Let's say your coachee describes her working life at the moment as being like a rollercoaster. You know she doesn't mean it literally, but the metaphor helps convey something about the essence of her experience that is quickly understood. However, if you follow up with "How could you find a less stressful way to work?" you will not be honouring her metaphor. For most coaches, this would be considered a non-leading, open question, but it is *not* Clean and definitely contains the coach's map of the world.

The word 'stressful' may be how you think of rollercoasters, but doesn't reflect your coachee's impression. To her it might be *exciting*, or *playful*, or *dangerous*, or *mechanical*, or *predictable*, or *fast* or some other experience. So, with a Clean approach, *you only use the actual words that the coachees have used themselves*, along with a scattering of totally neutral words to create very basic questions. This allows the coachee to reflect on his or her own metaphors and discover their personal meaning, often leading to creative solutions to stuck situations. This will be covered in more detail in the next chapter.

To help the coachee reveal personal deep emotions safely and confidentially

The coachee answers questions about the metaphors, which means the disclosures can remain one step away from actual experience or memory. The coachee can share facets about the metaphor which relates to the coachee in a deeply personal way, without the coach needing to understand that connection, therefore the coachee feels less exposed.

How many Clean questions are there?

Clean questions are limited and specific. Some people say there are only a handful of truly Clean questions. But, as Clean questions are usually asked in response to another's unique message, the actual form and wording of every Clean question is also unique. Therefore there is an infinite number of Clean questions, just as there is an infinite number of things that your coachee could choose to say next.

Clean questions follow certain rules in their structure, content and delivery. There is a core group of basic Clean questions that are easy to use in many different contexts and these are the ones to get started with. As you become more fluent in the language of Clean, you can expand your repertoire to include the advanced questions covered in Chapters twelve onwards, and also begin to devise your own questions that follow the principles of Clean.

The rest of this chapter highlights the basic Clean Language questions to get you started. Each will be explained in some detail, and a number of uses for them described.

Six basic Clean Language questions

- *To clarify:*

  - What kind of (coachee's words) is that (coachee's words)?
  - And is there anything else about that (coachee's words)?

- *To invite a metaphor:*

  - And that's (client's words) like what?

- *To locate and give form:*

  - Whereabouts is (coachee's words)?
  - Where is (coachee's words)?
  - Does that (coachee's word) have a shape or a size?

Questions to clarify

The two most useful and frequently used questions for Clean Coaching are:

"What kind of (coachee's words) is that (coachee's words)?"
"And is there anything else about that (coachee's words)?"

These two questions are useful in almost any situation. You need no special training or practice. You can ask them of any aspect of what the coachee says. You can use them in any kind of everyday conversation too. Although they are incredibly simple, they can also be used in more challenging and complex coaching situations. David Grove himself was said to use these two, most basic of all Clean question 60 to 80 per cent of the time in all client sessions. This means, you could stop reading this book right now and just concentrate on delivering these two questions, and you'll be well on your way to Clean Coaching, especially if you develop the underlying capacities and worldviews covered earlier in this book.

The 'what kind of' question helps narrow down the detail about the particular aspect of the coachee's thought in question. It causes the coachee to consider what category this particular aspect belongs to, and encourages the person to explore this aspect in more than one way. For instance, if the coachee says:

"I'm worried about redundancies. It happened last year and the rumour is there will be more again this year. I wish I had more security about my future."

As a coach, your initial reaction might be to try a strategy you know of to help your coachee with this concern. A Clean response would mean putting any judgements or solution thoughts on hold and instead, really explore and clarify what the coachee has actually said. In doing so, this helps the coachee explore the meaning for himself or herself. For example:

> "And when you wish you had more security, *what kind of* security is *that* security?"

Or:

> "And when you wish you had more security about your future, *what kind of* future is *that* future?"

The emphasis on 'that' stresses this is not a general question about the meaning of the word 'future', but a specific enquiry into the particular future that the coachee has mentioned just now, the one the coachee wishes he or she had more security about. Another example of a useful 'what kind of' question could be:

> "When you wish you had more security, *what kind of* wish is *that* wish?"

Almost any word the coachee uses could be followed up with a "What kind of" question. As soon as you get a new answer, you have a new set of words to ask further "What kind of" questions about. Although the question contains the same few words at the start, they are *not* repetitive; each question is always unique as it's directed towards the coachee's evolving thoughts.

So, let's say the coachee answers about the future:

> "It's a future I often worry about these days. I cannot see my future career path clearly anymore. It's cloudy and indistinct. Whereas a few years ago, I had a very bright sense of where my future was leading."

There could be many different aspects of this statement to focus further attention on. You could ask more about the future. Now there are two versions of the future being imagined, the one the person often worries about, and the one the person previously had a bright sense of.

You could ask the same "What kind of" question to explore either 'future':

> "And when there's a bright sense of the future, *what kind of* future is *that* future?"

There are always more "What kind of" questions that you can ask, each time it uncovers another layer of information, deepening the coachee's understanding of his or her own meaning.

Adding 'and' to the start of your Clean question effectively provides a link between what the coachee has just finished saying and your question. It helps the question blend into the coachee's own thought processes, showing that your question has been borne out of the previous answer. 'And' helps form a pattern between the coachee's answers and your questions which is similar to a feedback loop within a system. Each influences each other in equal measure. But rather than simply repeating the same question and answer over and over again, the process is iterative, each round of question builds on the previous. Rather than looping back to the same place, the coachee's evolving understanding forms like a spiral rather than a circle (Grove, 1998).

The "Is there anything else?" question is really useful and can be used in almost any situation. For instance, to invite the coachee to expand on what he or she has said. Interestingly, this question is phrased as a *closed question*, and many would think it an ineffective way to encourage a coachee to open up. However, it is less assumptive than asking "*What* else is there about that future?" where you presume there is more to say! Phrased in the 'Clean' way, it is more respectful to the coachee, leaving the person to decide whether there is anything and what that might be. Seldom will people say 'no', and if they do, that's fine too.

This question allows the coachee freedom to respond in whatever way he or she likes, and in whatever direction he or she chooses. The answer could bring in a totally different facet of meaning not yet explored. So, for instance, given the above statement, you may have chosen to ask:

> "And is there anything else about a future that's cloudy and indistinct that you often worry about?"

Note that the question is made up almost entirely of actual words the coachee has used, in the same form and tense. This question invites the coachee to answer in multiple ways. If the coachee is no longer interested in exploring this particular topic, he or she could just say, "No, that's all there is." It seldom happens, but occasionally avenues of thinking lead to a dead end, in which case you can simply back-track to an earlier point in the conversation and focus on another train of thought.

Or the coachee may say: "Yes, it seems I have no control any more about that future. In the past when it was brighter, I could see that my day-by-day actions were helping me on my journey."

This answer opens up further opportunities to explore more aspects. There are 'control' and 'day-by-day' and 'journey' and 'actions' as possible contenders for further exploration.

Or, the coachee may even use the question as a springboard to take the conversation in a very different direction by answering:

> "Yes. I think it's all due to the way my boss is treating me."

This answer reveals another aspect of the coachee's emerging thoughts, and a new path of questioning opens up to explore, this 'boss' and the kind of treatment he or she is giving.

With just two-question frameworks, you have an unlimited supply of non-directive, Clean ways to help your coachee further explore his or her thoughts.

You can move along the scale and be more directive, by focusing attention on particular kinds of words or phrases. Or you can become even more non-directive by asking about larger chunks of language. The most non-directive of all being ambiguously phrased, "Is there anything else about *that*?"

Questions to clarify the metaphors

In the above example, we didn't specifically focus on the metaphors, so as to demonstrate that Clean questions can be useful and revealing when asked of any aspect of the coachee's experience. However, focusing on and clarifying the coachee's metaphors to express his or her thoughts and feelings can be especially useful. For example, in the above statement, 'journey' may have been an interesting choice as it represents a metaphor, as did the 'path' mentioned earlier. When you ask questions directed at the metaphors people use naturally and unintentionally, it often leads them to realise the deeper significance and connection between their chosen metaphor and the 'real' thing they are exploring. For instance if you ask: "What kind of journey is that journey?" the answer may be:

> "Well, it felt like I was moving before, travelling fast towards a destination. Now I just feel stuck."

Further exploration might develop the 'my career progress is like a journey' metaphor in useful ways that could lead to some realisations about what can be done now to address that stuckness.

When you choose to ask a few Clean questions of any metaphors you notice your coachee using, it often brings about a new way of seeing things.

To continue with the example given earlier, if your coachee described her current working life as a rollercoaster, you might follow up with:

> "And, your working life is like a rollercoaster. And when it's like a rollercoaster, what kind of rollercoaster is that rollercoaster?"

That question may seem strange to read, however a coachee will hear her own words played back and feel listened to and honoured.

Or, you may ask: "Is there anything else about that rollercoaster?"

These two questions alone will help you to enter the world of metaphor and have your coachees learn more about themselves. By repeating back the metaphoric content of the clients' language, it helps draw them into their metaphoric experience, so they begin to imagine how that rollercoaster is the same or different to their working life, often discovering something useful about the real world from contemplating its symbolic substitute. The next chapter explains more about metaphors and how they mould our thoughts.

Inviting a metaphor

You can further encourage your coachees to express themselves in metaphor by using a certain Clean Language question specifically designed to invite a metaphoric description which is:

"And that's (coachee's words) like what?"

Like all Clean Language questions, it needs to be wrapped carefully into the coachee's own words to create a uniquely personal enquiry. For example, if the coachee described his current situation as 'calm and uneventful', you could invite him to translate that description into a metaphor by asking "And that's 'calm and uneventful' like what?" The question is asking for a *comparison:* a description of something else which is similar in some way to the expression already given, which may be too abstract or general to capture any meaningful understanding at a personal level. Metaphors provide a kind of translation of a person's real-life intangible experience into a more tangible, imaginative expression, revealing something essential about it.

Grove said, if you ask "And that's like what?" it's 'Clean' language as it directly addresses the client's experience and it goes straight to the metaphor. Whereas, if you ask "What's that like to you?" the client immediately goes to his or her cognitive processing, losing the direct relationship with the particular metaphor (Lawley and Tompkins, 1994). Asking "What's that like?" instead of "That's like what?" is a common error for those learning Clean questions. But I've witnessed many learners focus too much attention on avoiding the mistake, and in doing so, end up saying it even more! Although it is not as effective, I believe "What's that like?" is still Clean, as it is enforcing no assumptions or bias onto the coachee. The question's re-phrasing makes it an enquiry about detail, rather than asking for a comparison. So relax if you mis-phrase this question, you'll just get a different kind of answer, probably more conceptual than metaphoric. Ask "That's like what?" next time.

When you ask "That's like what?" you invite a metaphoric response, but it doesn't guarantee one. Some people find it easier to talk in metaphor than others. But in my experience, everyone uses metaphors and is capable of connecting with them in a more sensory way. For some people they may need some time to focus their attention inwards with Clean Language questions before anything metaphoric emerges. If this is the case, be patient and trust that this will be valuable time spent and useful for the coachee even when the person is not exploring metaphors.

For some people, the "That's like what?" question is less effective than gradually focusing their attention on their internal embodied experience and physical sensations. For them the 'route' to metaphor and symbol exploration comes from noticing felt senses and being given the time for them to gradually solidify into a clear shape. If you keep to the basic "What kind of" and "Is there anything else" questions, the coachee will eventually turn attention inwards and you can then focus on any sensory descriptions used. We explain that process in more detail further on in this chapter.

If the "That's like what" question generates a metaphor, your coachee discovers something different. For instance, following from the earlier example, when you ask the coachee "That calm and uneventful is like what?" he may reply:

"It's like a frozen lake in the middle of a winter's night."

The images, physical sensations and emotions that arise in response to that metaphor deepen the person's personal understanding of what 'calm and uneventful' means in ways the person may not have been previously aware of. And often when that metaphor is explored further, particularly images and sensations within it, a wider, wiser understanding begins to emerge. This gradually takes the person into a state of altered consciousness, where – almost in a dream-like state – the symbols and characters within the metaphors take on a tangible shape, form and location and 'come to life' within the person's imagination. For instance the person may imagine skating on the lake, or walking around it, or breathing in the cool air, or noticing a young fallow deer in the woods around the lake – that tentatively steps out into the open.

As the metaphoric 'story' evolves, the meaning of the metaphor may also evolve too. Changing awareness of the metaphor can translate back to the real-world situation, problem or outcome and surprising solutions to stuck patterns of thinking can emerge. The 'calm and uneventful' is no longer seen as boring and passive, but a space from which new adventures can take place for instance. The meaning will always be owned by the coachee and unique to that person.

Coachees may hint at metaphors in a less obvious way, for example:

"My life seems to be whizzing by so quickly, I can't keep up with it."

The implied metaphor is that life is like some kind of moving object, racing ahead. But it's not yet been stated so the same question can still help clarify:

"And when your life seems to be whizzing by so quickly, you can't keep up with it . . . *that's like what?*"

Reflecting back the metaphoric elements allows them to become clearer. The coachee may answer:

"It's like I've got this eager puppy on a lead that's always pulling ahead."

The metaphor has been clarified; life is like an eager puppy! But that's not the end of the exploration. In fact it's just the beginning. Now you can return to your two basic clarifying questions to find out more:

"And what kind of puppy is that puppy?"
"And is there anything else about that puppy, when it's always pulling ahead?"

"What kind of pulling?"
"What kind of lead?"
"What kind of eager?"

Our aim is to help this metaphoric image become clearer, until it's a 'rich picture' in both the coachee's mind and our own. Focus particular attention on the symbols within the metaphor. The symbols are the more tangible bits that could have a clear form and location. For instance, so far in this emerging metaphoric landscape, there are two stated symbols:

• The puppy

And

• The lead

There is a third symbol implied within this picture, presumably there is someone holding the lead, for the puppy to be able to pull ahead from. It will probably be a symbol of the coachee. But it's still part of the metaphor if the coachee describes himself or herself in the picture: "I'm trying to hang on tight but she's pulling away . . ." Although the coachee is obviously a real person, this is an imaginary version of the real person; it's not a real puppy and the person is not really hanging on. It is all still a metaphor.

Another common beginner's error is to ask "That's like what?" when the coachee has already given you a perfectly good metaphor to explore further. So for instance, if your coachee has just explained that her life is like a puppy on a lead that's always pulling ahead, it's not the time to invite a metaphor. If you say "That's a puppy like what?" the coachee will probably try and find something else to compare the eager puppy with. An excited rabbit perhaps, or an energetic kitten. But neither of these secondary descriptions is likely to fit the bill as well as the original version of the eager puppy. When the coachee shares a metaphor with you, don't ask for another, focus attention on the one the coachee has given you with plenty of clarifying questions. Once a metaphor is revealed, you can help the coachee explore it with plenty of "What kind of" and "Is there anything else" questions.

Other metaphors may come up too, even if you don't ask for them. If they are metaphors relating to different aspects of the coachee's experience, you may also want to explore these. Be careful not to flit from one metaphor to another however, as it can be distracting for the coachee. Instead, make a note of any new metaphors and you can return to them in a few questions time, when you have adequately explored the metaphor in hand. How do you know if a metaphor has been adequately explored? It's when all the symbols within that metaphor have a clear form and location. In the above example, that includes the eager puppy, the lead and the lead 'holder' (described in whatever way the coachee chooses, let's say the person calls it the 'owner'). For each of these three symbols, we can ask

"What kind of" and "Is there anything else" and any answers they generate will lead to further "What kind of" and "Is there anything else" questions.

To locate sensations and symbols

As coachees becomes more engaged with their metaphoric landscape, they relax into themselves, their speech starts to slow down and may begin to gaze into empty space. At this point you can ask two further questions to bring the metaphoric picture into life:

> "And *whereabouts* is that eager puppy as it's pulling ahead?"
> "When that puppy is always pulling ahead, *whereabouts* is the 'owner'?"
> "*Whereabouts* is ahead?"

As James Lawley (2006) said: "Whether I have the world on my shoulders or at my feet makes all the difference." Locations and spatial relationships are the most common kind of metaphor used in all languages, and when you help your coachees discover those locations and relationships, it opens their awareness to anything else happening in their experience.

After "What kind of" and "Is there anything else" questions, asking "Whereabouts" is worthy of being the next most frequent and useful question to ask. For any of the "Whereabouts" examples, you could replace with "*Where* is" instead.

Many beginner Clean Coaches struggle with the whereabouts question because if it's not asked at the right time and in the right way, it can be confusing for the coachee who won't know how to answer it. For instance, let's say the evolving metaphoric landscape continues when the coachee says:

> "This eager puppy always wants to get to the next place. It's never happy to sit still."

Practicing coaches often turn to the whereabouts question when they feel they have asked more than enough "What kind of" or "Is there anything else" questions. But then they ask the whereabouts question of something new that's just cropped up, or something that doesn't logically have a place, even in one's mind's eye. For instance, "Whereabouts is eager?" or "Whereabouts is never?" just doesn't make sense. Concepts have no location, but sensations do. Watch out for sensory words such as "I feel happy" or "I see that eager puppy." If there's a sensation, there will be a location. It's worth repeating back the sensory word too as it helps the coachee notice the 'whereness' of something:

> "And when you feel happy, whereabouts do you feel happy?"
> "And when you see that eager puppy, whereabouts is that eager puppy?"

With no sensory clues, you can still move on to whereabouts questions. But when you do, ask it of the symbols you have already explored and clarified in some detail. These are the ones that the coachee will most likely have a sense of place for. So, ask whereabouts is the puppy, the lead or the owner, for instance. Often people imply locations and directions in their language. In the example above, "next place" has an implied location, as does "sit still." You could ask "whereabouts" questions of both these aspects.

You might also focus specifically and intentionally on the sensory language, especially when there are few metaphors and the coachee doesn't appear to be engaging with them. Some people are more visual and can easily see and describe mental images that represent the symbols within their metaphoric landscape. For others, the visual view is less clear and they have more of an inkling or 'felt sense' of a metaphoric experience. You can still help the coachees explore and understand these more obscure aspects, taking a different route to their symbolic wisdom, through awareness of their embodied experience.

Clarifying and exploring a 'felt sense'

This is a strategy for exploration which follows all of the questions above, but narrows in on the emerging feelings and bodily sensations that the coachee describes. It's particularly useful for people who do not easily come up with vivid metaphors and even when they do, they cannot get a clear mental image of any symbols contained within those metaphors. As with many Clean strategies, rather than the coach deciding to take this approach, it's more about noticing when the coachee is naturally flowing along this path, and then to go along with the person in this way.

When coachees refers to any positive feelings they have or resourceful mental states that they wish to have more of, notice when they use any physical sensations to describe that feeling or state. For instance, if the coachee says:

"I need to develop my confidence to handle those unexpected situations."

Confidence sounds both resourceful and positive, so you may question further:

"What kind of confidence is that confidence?"

The coachee may give examples or describe more about it:

"Well, it's a natural, open confidence. I'm not scared. I just get on with it. It feels like a kind of energy."

Now you could focus further attention on the physical sensation:

"And when confidence is natural and open and it feels like a kind of energy, *is there anything else about that energy?*"
"*What kind of energy is that*, when it feels like a kind of energy?"
"When it feels like a kind of energy, *what kind of . . .* feels . . . is that?"

As your questions continue to draw attention to feelings and bodily sensations, the coachees' attention should gradually turn inwards, until they become more aware of their bodily experiences. When you notice they have become still and less engaged with the external world, you could try asking a whereabouts question:

> "And when energy is like (their words) and you feel (their words), *where-abouts* can you feel it?"

Your body language can help this question land well, as you ask your question look around the coachee's body as though you are looking for the feeling yourself. People then generally 'get' that feelings have a physical location as well as an emotional content. Typically, people will locate a feeling or state in a part of their body and say something like "It's in my heart" or "I feel it right at my core." It can be very helpful and clarifying to ask a further follow-up whereabouts question immediately after they have initially located the feeling:

> "And when that energy you feel is in your heart, *whereabouts* in your heart is that?"

The second whereabouts question gets a more specific location and can also help the coachee begin to associate into the feeling, here and now in your session.

Once the feeling has been located twice, you can help it to develop a shape and/ or form by asking:

> "And when that energy you feel is right in the centre of your heart, does that energy *have a shape or a size?*"

Often at this stage, many people will spontaneously use a metaphor, describing a particular symbol to represent their felt sense:

> "It's like a miniature sun that radiates heat and light from within me."

Once you have a metaphor like this you can explore further by returning to the basic clarifying questions.

If the coachee just gives a shape and size, you can question further using the "That's like what" question. Notice in the example below, how the question is asked very slowly and carefully, building in all the descriptive elements that the coachee has been using along the way to gradually build up his or her own awareness and understanding:

> "It's small, and round, and very hot."
> "And that energy you feel right in the centre of your heart is small and round and very hot. . . . And when it's small, round and hot, in the centre of your heart. . . . . that's small, round and hot. . . *like . . . what?*"

This gradual and careful process often leads to a meaningful metaphor that has a lasting effect on the coachee. The metaphor is linked to a powerful embodied experience and a felt sense. It also often develops a visual element too, and potentially involves other sensations too. This multi-sensory metaphor can be a very useful resource in future. When the coachee remembers the metaphor, he or she also generates the positive and resourceful feeling and/or state that's represented by that metaphor.

Within the field of NLP, the process of helping someone create a powerful visual and physical reminder that they associate with a particular positive state is known as 'anchoring', and involves asking coachees to remember a time when they had such a positive feeling, and then have them build up a representation of all the senses that were involved. These Clean Language questions enable a similar result without needing to access a past memory, which some people may find difficult. Those trained in NLP might consider combining the NLP anchoring approach with the questions above to help coaches get a deeper felt sense of any positive feeling or resourceful state.

How to get started with Clean questions

The simple answer to this question is just start asking Clean questions. As with all the examples given above, ask simple questions when an opportunity presents itself and continue for as long as it feels comfortable to do so. There is no need to stop and explain to the coachee what you are doing. Some beginners with Clean find it difficult to take the 'plunge' into Clean, fearing they may get it wrong or the coachee may not understand them or find the questions strange. But it doesn't have to be a 'plunge' at all, you can just dip your toe in and see how it goes. You can start with the two most basic questions to clarify, in a natural, conversational way and see where it leads you. Similarly, if you notice your coachee spontaneously use a metaphor to describe an experience, take that as an opportunity to learn something new about this coachee, through exploring that metaphor for five minutes or so. Chapter eleven covers more formal ways to begin a Clean Coaching session, but meanwhile getting used to asking Clean Language questions is an excellent first step.

When to stop asking Clean questions

Even with just a handful of Clean questions to use, I hope you can see that there is potentially no end to pathways of thought and metaphoric explorations you can take. However, conversations need to end in a timely fashion and I suggest the following pointers for bringing things to an appropriate pause:

• If you have moved naturally and conversationally into using a few Clean questions, you can move out in a similar, gentle fashion and just go back to asking your usual kinds of questions.

- If the coachee seems very engaged in the process, you can keep going for 20 minutes or more. Rather than wait for a total resolution or a complete understanding, notice when the coachee discovers a new insight or commits to taking a certain action. At that point, you can bring things to a close.
- If the coachee appears to have a 'light bulb' moment, stay with that light bulb for a few questions longer to help 'anchor' the insight.
- You can invite the coachee to take a short break and write down or draw anything that the person would like to remember or share with you. When you start again, ask whether he or she would like to share anything with you, then move back to your normal coaching approach.
- Two good questions to wrap up are: "Would this be a good time to pause?" (after a short exploration) or "And is there anything else you'd like to say or do before we bring this to a close?" Use this after a longer exploration and the end of the coaching session.
- Once you have taken a pause, begin again on a different note, with your usual coaching approach.
- If the coachee is looking at you quizzically and clearly not understanding your questions, just start asking different kinds of questions and stop using Clean. If this happens, it does not necessarily mean that Clean questions won't ever 'work' with this person, it just might be the wrong time today.
- However well things appear to be going, always bring to a close at least 10 minutes before the end of your coaching session, this allows time for the coachee to share any thoughts and most important come back to the 'real' world. Clean questions can be very hypnotic and you want to ensure the coachee is wide awake when they leaves, particularly if he or she is going to immediately drive a car, for instance.
- After your Clean questions, just move on, do not overly dwell on the experience nor ask the coachee to give a concrete explanation of what the metaphors 'meant'. You would dirty up the Clean in that way!
- You might ask more general, open non-directive questions to gauge reaction such as:

  - "How did you find that exploration?"
  - "What did you notice?"
  - "What did you learn?"
  - "Will you do anything as a result of that?"

As you continue reading this book you will learn more structures and strategies with the questions that will help you know how and when to start using Clean questions and when and how to stop.

References

Blakeslee, S. and Blakeslee, M. (2008) *The Body Has a Mind of Its Own.* New York: Random House.

Gendlin, E. (1968) The experiential response. In E. F. Hammer (ed.), *Use of Interpretation in Therapy: Technique and Art*. New York: Grune and Stratton, 208–227.

Grove, D. (1998) *Philosophy and Principles of Clean Language*. Available at: www.clean language.co.uk/articles/articles/38/1/Philosophy-and-Principles-of-Clean-Language/Page1.html [Accessed 24/6/2015].

Lawley, J. (2006) When Where Matters – How Psychoactive Space is Created and Utilised, *The Model*, British Board of NLP. Available at: www.cleanlanguage.co.uk/articles/articles/29/1/When-Where-Matters-How-psychoactive-space-is-created-and-utilised/Page1.html [Accessed 2/4/2015].

Lawley, J. and Tompkins, P. (1994) *And What kind of Man is David Grove?: An Interview by Penny Tompkins and James Lawley*. Available at: www.cleanlanguage.co.uk/articles/articles/37/1/And-what-kind-of-a-man-is-David-Grove/Page1.html [Accessed 28/6/2015].

Clean Coaching strategies

Chapter nine

Metaphors that mould us

What is a metaphor?

A picture may paint a thousand words, but a metaphor can impart a whole *landscape* – of images, sounds, sensations and any relationships that exist between them. For example, the statement "When I'm near him I just bloom" carries a wealth of meaning, implied by the metaphoric expression 'I just bloom'. When we hear or read a metaphor like this, inevitably we form our own interpretation about what kind of 'bloom' this may be. Cropping up in our language constantly, in obvious and more subtle ways, metaphors evoke more than the words alone convey. Many common expressions and clichés have metaphorical roots although we no longer notice them. And often, a metaphor is unique and deeply personal to whomever has uttered it, helping the person make sense of what's going on.

People tend to think of metaphors as being obvious, overt and colourful, used deliberately to help convey a depth of meaning. We use them as literary embellishments, describing one thing as though it were something else, such as "She was as good as gold" or "That question was as clear as mud." Each metaphor contains two essential ingredients, the real 'thing' being spoken about (often referred to as the 'source' or 'ground') and the metaphoric thing it is being compared to (referred to as the 'target' or 'figure'). In our two examples, the figure is 'gold' and the ground is 'she'. 'Mud' is the target, the 'question' is the source.

As a communication aid, metaphors work well when we can map across some characteristics from the source to the target metaphor. People will draw out those comparisons for themselves and make assumptions based on them. Gold is precious and pure, presumably like her goodness. And in the second example, we might immediately glean that the question is not clear at all, likened to mud which is thick and opaque.

A simile is similar to a metaphor, which is where the comparison is spelt out more openly and the word 'like' is used to show the connection, e.g. "My head's like a hammer" or "I felt just like a little girl." Apart from the linguistic difference, both metaphors and similes do the same thing: they make comparisons, using one thing to represent another. For Clean Language, the distinction is irrelevant and I will refer to both comparison varieties from now on as metaphors.

Cognitive psychologists have long since recognised that metaphors play a far more important role than a mere communication aid, and at a much deeper level. In the late 1970s George Lakoff and Mark Johnson (1980) first proposed that metaphors are not merely describing our thoughts, but are the very nuts and bolts from which all conceptual thought is based. Prior to this seminal work, metaphors were considered an optional extra within language. Nowadays, most psychologists accept that metaphors play an important role in how people construct their thoughts, although the exact nature of that role is still up for debate.

Doorways to inner experience

Lawley and Tompkins (2000:23) highlight that "Metaphor is a fundamental means of making sense of life." We comprehend one aspect of our experience by likening it to something else. Metaphors allow people to experience the world in many different ways. There is not one single metaphor which corresponds to each facet of the real world, but many metaphors that could each reveal different aspects of the same kind of experience. Each of us is capable of experiencing different meanings from multiple metaphors.

If you listen for metaphors, you will notice that they tend to flow seamlessly and spontaneously throughout speech, rather than as a conscious attempt to embellish language. In everyday conversation, the actual metaphor itself is often only implied rather than fully exposed. Both the figure and the ground within the metaphor can remain unspoken and both the sender and receiver of the message still 'get' the meaning. For example the sentence given previously "When I'm with him I just bloom" infers a metaphor. By implying that a person is capable of blooming, the message sender draws a comparison between herself and things that typically bloom, e.g. flowers. And there is a second metaphor indirectly hinted at: that whoever 'he' is, is providing the conditions for that flower to flourish. Perhaps, like a sun or less likely I suppose, some manure! The point is, we do not need to hear all the explicit metaphoric comparisons spelt out; people understand expressions like this because not only do we talk in metaphor, but we also *think* in metaphor and therefore can make sense of such statements, most often instantly. Think about the expression "I fell in love" – it is also implicitly metaphoric. It implies that love is like a hole or a trap that you accidentally become ensnared or engulfed by, rather than something you consciously decide to happen.

Grove described metaphors as containers that carry information: "Metaphors take information from one source and introduce it to another" (as cited in Lawley and Tompkins, 1996). In Eva Kittay's (1987) philosophical examination of metaphor, she describes them as 'displaced signs'. And she suggests that it is this displacement – of simultaneously seeing one thing both as you would normally and through the 'eyes' of the metaphor that creates a juxtaposition of perspectives. This can result in a reconceptualisation – you notice something different about the source concept because of the metaphor. This reframing could be temporary or more permanent – forever altering what you know about some aspect of your world.

Metaphors are both *constructive*: in that they shape our understanding of the world – and also *constrictive*: in that they structure and limit our thinking into narrow parameters. Lawley and Tompkins (2003) describe them as a double-edged sword, being both "descriptive and prescriptive," a "tool for creativity or a self-imposed prison." In summary, they say: "Metaphors embody and define the intangible and abstract, but this limits and constrains perceptions and actions to those which make sense within the logic of the metaphor."

Kittay (1987) argues that metaphoric language is more than a mere conduit of our thoughts, embellishing and adorning as it goes. Instead, all language originated in metaphor, it is a medium through which we express ourselves, as an artist might use paint. She asserts that metaphors are shaped through the imagination, and don't record pre-existing similarities in things. As we bring together our diverse thoughts into a 'unity' we can reform our perceptions of the world, and it is only through expressing metaphor in some representational system can we grasp its structure and therefore gain understanding of its meaning.

Levels of thinking

James Lawley and Penny Tompkins (2000) suggest that people can experience the world and think about it on at least three different levels or 'domains':

> *Sensory:* The most basic, raw experience of our physical sensations and feelings. Our senses are our 'windows' through which we perceive the external world. This level of thinking stems from our bodies. When we imagine or remember experiences we can also recreate associated physical sensations, without any external stimulus.
>
> *Conceptual:* This thinking includes the kind of rational, abstract logical thought that we use to plan, decide and make judgements. You can think of a concept as the label we give a certain kind of thing. Everything has a label, not just solid real things we see in the world around us, but abstract, intangible things too: for example 'employment' and 'motherhood'.
>
> *Metaphoric:* This is where our thoughts and/or experience about one thing is being explored and compared to another kind of thing. In this way, we often take the abstract and intangible and make sense of it by comparing to something that *is* tangible. For example "employment is like a rat race."

All experience is capable of being thought about, to some degree, on all three levels, but we tend only to notice one level at a time. People often describe which thinking level they are engaged in and by listening to the kinds of things people say, moment by moment, you can identify which level of thinking this person is most engaged with. For instance, here's how your coachee may describe the promotion he wants so badly:

> *Sensory:* I can just *see* the *look* on my wife's face if I could *tell* her I got it. I'd *feel* a huge *sense* of pride. I can *picture* the interview now, Joe was smiling at the end. I really got the *impression* I did really well.
> *Conceptual:* This promotion would mean I could finally be taken seriously as a manager. I've worked really hard for the last five years and I deserve it.
> *Metaphoric:* It's like I'm racing for the finish line. The end is in sight and I just need to take a final sprint to get there first.

When people focus conscious attention directly on each kind of experience, their awareness begins to tune in. When the coachee concentrates his attention on seeing his wife's face, for instance, he starts noticing more about that imaginary picture. Thinking of that huge sense of pride as a physical sensation in or around the body brings out the qualities of that feeling. He may notice whereabouts in his body he feels that sense of pride, and become aware of other sensory factors.

By focusing attention on metaphors, the imaginary symbols used for the comparison can take on a realistic shape and form within the coachee's imagination. The race for the finish becomes a 3D experience that can be seen, felt and touched within the mental cinema of the 'mind's eye'. The finish line comes into clearer focus, within a distinct location somewhere around him. Those rats appear before him, visibly occupying a space in his mind's eye, along with the sounds of scuttling rat feet as they run along the race of employment. Lawley and Tompkins (2003) point out that:

> Neuroscientists tell us there are no actual images, sounds or feelings in the brain, but subjectively it seems like there are. In other words, our representations are metaphors that exist in a mindspace – a stage in the theatre of our mind where the play of consciousness is happening.

All three levels provide useful information for the person experiencing them. Some people habitually pay more attention to one level to the detriment of the others. When coachees are too engrossed with conceptual thoughts in their heads, they may disconnect from their bodies and barely notice any physical sensations they may be feeling. Helping them to engage more with the neglected level is likely to be very worthwhile, however it may take some perseverance and patience. By focusing the coachees' attention on their own sensory experiences, exactly as they describe them, it facilitates a meditative state of awareness. This awareness brings people back to their bodies, by focusing on inner experience and deeper thought structures rather than the external world and surface-level reactions and responses.

The sensory and metaphoric levels often work hand in hand, as coachees turn their attention inwards, they become more aware of their physical sensations and along with that can imagine and explore metaphoric representations more easily. Those people stuck in their conceptual heads can be helped to re-connect with their bodily experience. First, by helping them to find a metaphor that defines and explains an experience they usually conceptualise in a more abstract, logical fashion.

Using Clean Language to help explore metaphors

Using carefully selected Clean questions, you can focus your coachees' attention on different aspects of their experience and help them connect more deeply with their meanings. By uncovering and examining metaphoric patterns of thought, Clean Coaching provides a mechanism for loosening their grip. This allows people to explore beyond the edges of their usual thought patterns, enabling other metaphors to emerge. The key aim for exploring metaphors is *not* so that we, the facilitator, can analyse and understand their deeper meaning. It is so the *coachees* can work out the meaning for themselves, often simply through the process of experiencing the metaphor and discovering what happens when they do so.

Initially the coachees' conversation may not include many metaphors, and those they do use may be implicit and inferred. Clean questions provide a structure for directing the coachees' attention towards any metaphoric words and gestures they *do* use. Through continued exploration, the coachees can notice more about their inner experience, and like a developing photograph, the metaphoric picture is likely to become clearer. Lawley and Tompkins suggest "Metaphors allow people to express and give a form to complex feelings, behaviours, situations and abstract concepts" (2000:5). Having given form to them, they can be explored in more explicit ways. For example, let's return to the 'rollercoaster' metaphor, and say that your coachee describes the last month of her working life has been just like one. That metaphor reveals many different facets about how this coachee is thinking about her working life. For example, it could be: fast paced, running along a single track, with highs and lows, out of personal control, etc. And by exploring the qualities of the rollercoaster, the coachee gains a greater understanding of **how** she experiences her working life, often helping the person see new possibilities or creative solutions. With Clean Language, you help your coachees to *think about* **how** *they are thinking.*

Working with metaphors and symbols

For a metaphor to transform, it needs to have a form (Grove and Panzer, 1989). The tangible forms that emerge within a metaphor are the things that can be seen, heard or touched, at least within our mind's eye. Those tangible parts of the metaphor can be thought of as symbols, capable of having a form and a location. Tompkins and Lawley describe a symbol as 'something' that exists 'somewhere' and 'somewhen' (2000:31). In our mind's eye, symbols are the objects that make up the metaphoric landscape, each with a unique identity.

A symbol can be defined as: A sign or object that signifies something with a deeper meaning not necessarily recognisable from the sign itself. Like metaphors, a symbol is something that stands for – or represents – something else. It's another kind of container that has hidden depths. Apart from a visual image, a symbol could be represented by a sound, or a gesture, or a sense of any kind. But the more obscure kinds of symbols are harder to identify in a coaching context so we will focus our attention on the symbols that appear in the mind's eye as visual images of objects. David Grove differentiated symbols as single, internal parts of the coachee's experience, whereas metaphors were externalised and potentially contained multiple elements, each of which could be represented as separate symbols (Grove and Panzer, 1989).

When you hear a metaphor, the symbols are the elements that you could picture in your own mind's eye. For instance, in the metaphor "like a needle in a haystack" there are two symbols, the *needle* and the *haystack*. Once this metaphor is explored, it is likely further symbols will emerge, presenting contrasting and useful meanings for the coachee to become aware of.

Carl Jung took symbols very seriously. He suggested that we unconsciously form symbols based on our experience throughout our lives. He said that perception was inevitably limited by conscious awareness, but that the unconscious mind recorded everything, storing this vast repository of extra knowledge about the world not in easily identified words or accurate memories, but in symbolic form (Jung and Franz, 1964). Those symbols often contained pearls of wisdom: messages from the unconscious mind that knew considerably more than the conscious could ever grasp. Jung, like Freud, believed that dreams were the 'royal road' to identifying symbols. But, symbols reveal themselves far more frequently during waking moments than Jung suspected, through the everyday use of metaphor. Every metaphor articulated could reveal many symbolic representations.

Often, any symbols are initially hidden within metaphors and need some coaxing to bring to conscious awareness. For example, the following transcript highlights how asking a series of Clean questions helps prompt the coachee to gradually explore her inner experience, unblocking a stuck way of thinking. As the metaphor is explored, the tangible symbols within that metaphor begin to emerge, which can then be questioned further until the coachee gains an insight. In this case what seems like a confusing, unhelpful beginning develops into a useful resource.

Transcript: exploring symbols within a metaphor

This short transcript demonstrates how metaphors can be explored with Clean Language and how that process can lead to new ways of thinking.

Coach: "What would you like to have happen?"
Coachee: "Well, I would like to take more risks. But whenever there is any level of risk, it seems something stops me. Actually, deep down I know that it's actually me. I stop myself."

Coach: "And when you know deep down you stop yourself, what would you like to have happen?"
Coachee: "Mmmm. I'm not sure. That's going to take some more digging, I think, to bring whatever it is out into the open."

'Digging' is a verb and like many verbs contains a metaphor, implied rather than explicit the comparisons are not actually disclosed. It seems that the mental process of uncovering an answer is like the physical process of digging. At the moment, there are no clear representations to help us picture in our mind's eye what this experience is like for this particular coachee. There are vague hints as to elements that could have a shape, form and location, such as the 'whatever **it** is' that seems currently hidden. We make sense of such statements by placing our own objects into the metaphor, for instance the coach could be imagining that there is a noisy 'digger' machine in a vast, empty landscape tumbling through soil to unearth big black roots, which represent the desired outcomes not yet expressed. But, that would be the coach's own meaning. The coach has used the symbols of the digger, the soil and the roots to create a 'landscape' of interconnecting elements that together make up the metaphor.

As we fill in the gaps around the coachee's metaphors, we create the symbolic representations required to give that metaphor some meaning. Our personal meanings are good enough approximations for normal, everyday conversation to catch the gist of what is meant. People often say "I know exactly what you mean" when it's very unlikely that they do. Our mental images of the other person's metaphoric experience are likely to be different from theirs.

Let's re-examine the coachee's 'digging' metaphor, and this time, instead of guessing what the symbols are, let's find out by asking Clean questions:

Coach: "And when it's going to take some digging, what kind of digging is that?"
Coachee: "Hmmm. Hard work. But rewarding work. It happens gradually, I think. Just one scoop at a time."
Coach: "And is there anything else about just one scoop at a time?"
Coachee: "It's like one spade-full of soil."

We now have two actual things to populate the picture of the coachee's metaphoric experience, the *spade* and the *soil*, and already, this is a very different landscape to the one imagined by the coach before. Now we can begin to see what it's like for the coachee:

Coach: "One spade-full of soil. And what kind of spade is that spade?"
Coachee: "It's a little garden trowel. I am digging in the garden on my knees in the soil."
Coach: "A little garden trowel. On your knees in the soil. And what kind of soil is that soil?"

Coachee: "It's rich. It looks dirty, but in fact it is full of nutrients."
Coach: "And when that soil that looks dirty is full of nutrients, and it's going to take some digging to bring it out into the open, *what happens next?*"
Coachee: "I find a seed."
Coach: "You find a seed. And what kind of seed is that seed?"
Coachee: "It's a tiny seed. It looks like nothing. But in that soil it will grow. It can't help but grow, that's what seeds do. It's a risk, but all growth is, what else is there? I've been stopping myself by mucking around too much. I keep churning up the soil instead of just letting it be. I don't need to take risks, I just need to allow things to grow without getting in their way."
Coach: "A tiny seed, looks like nothing. It can't help but grow. And what needs to happen for you to allow things to grow without getting in their way?"
              (Session continues)

The original metaphor developed into a whole landscape – like a 3D picture containing a variety of symbols, each relating in some way to each other. You'll recognise some of the questions from Chapter eight. Others, such as "What happens next?" will be explained further in Chapter twelve.

The spade became a particular kind of spade: a *garden trowel*. The background has emerged as a *garden*, most likely containing more symbols should it be explored further. The *soil* is now placed in a context and two further important symbols have emerged. This coachee has now placed herself in this experience by saying "*I* am digging in the garden." It's all still metaphoric, as the coachee is not really currently digging in a garden, so this is an imagined scenario. She also mentions she is "On my *knees.*" The coachee is imagining a version of herself in her mind's eye and this can also be thought of as a separate symbol for exploration. The final symbol mentioned was the *seed*, and in this example, the coachee seems to draw comparisons between the characteristics of the seed and that of her original outcome about taking risks. The symbols which emerged from the original metaphor of digging offer new ways to interpret and understand the situation, one that feels congruent as it has grown organically from her own exploration, not forced upon her by another's mental model. If the coach had shared her original mental image of a mechanical digger, it is unlikely that the insight about leaving seeds to grow would have emerged so easily!

Spotting metaphors

In Chapter five, I covered the importance of listening skills for Clean Coaching, and specifically listening for metaphors is a crucial part of this. The most effective Clean Coaches are able to notice the embedded and inherent metaphors that people use within their natural spoken language when describing their experience. On average, people use six metaphors in every minute of speech (Tosey et al., 2013). In my experience though, the vast majority of people will fall either side of the norm. Some people use a stream of metaphors in their conversation. Rather than add depth to their meaning, it can be distracting to listen to a jumble of metaphoric terms, with your attention leaping from one bright colourful term to the next, like chasing butterflies. At the other extreme, some people are far more literal with their language, rarely using overt metaphors. Instead their use of metaphors is far more subtle, unconscious and embedded deeper within their language and choice of words.

Let's look more closely at the two extremes. For the mega-metaphoric coachees, you are listening for consistency in their metaphoric descriptions. As they flit from one to another, notice what remains the same, and question that. For example, one coachee described the calmness of approach that she wanted as being like swimming, ice skating and gliding all in the same sentence. All these metaphors depict a similar kind of smooth movement, and by exploring any one of them, the coachee is likely to learn more about what 'calmness' means to her.

It's important to be consistent with your questioning. Once you have focused on one element or metaphor, continue to explore it for a while. This could be for a short series of questions before moving on to another metaphor, or another aspect of the same metaphor. Sometimes a coachee's constant diving around from pillar to post is representative of part of the problem he or she has. You can help the person by holding the focus for long enough in one direction that a clearer picture comes into view.

For the person for whom metaphors are sparse or even non-existent, pick up and play back any subtler metaphoric hints, but don't expect this person to start noticing symbols any time soon. Be patient with these coachees, skirt around the edges of their reality and help them gradually notice their words that have more than one meaning. Help them define their abstract labels and allow them to get a greater sense of any physical sensations and feelings in their body. For these kinds of people, even a small breakthrough in connecting to their metaphoric level of thinking can result in a transformative shift. Let's go back to the earlier example. If the conceptual thinker is lost in his head around that promotion, continuing to question his notions such as being "taken seriously" and "deserving" may gradually help him connect with a deeper, personal meaning. He may begin to notice physical sensations and start describing things in metaphor. For example, "deserving" may conjure up a sense of being small and reaching up. You can then ask, "And that deserving, when it's small and reaching up . . . is like what?" The conceptual thinker might then come up with a metaphor, such as "like Oliver Twist." It doesn't matter that the symbol is borrowed in this way, most are. As the coachee explores the image of Oliver Twist, it becomes unique and personal to him. The key is to accept and value any kind of answer the coachee gives you, whether or not it's metaphoric.

Concepts and categories

Our inner world of objects is constructed not just of imaginary people, rats and races, but also non-tangible concepts, for instance, notions such as 'personality' and 'speed'. The most fundamental concepts are those in connection with time and space, the raw ingredients of our world. There are literally thousands of everyday concepts that enable us to have complex mental reasoning. We share socially constructed meanings about such terms and these meanings can change over time. Underneath the shared meaning will be further layers of personal meaning. Our concepts are shaped by the way we *categorise* them: our mental filing system for classifying the different aspects of the world into different groups of things.

Categorisation is a core human activity and the building block to many human thought processes such as reasoning, judgement and problem solving. People cannot help but compare and contrast everything they experience in their lives. Most of the things we come across in the world are not singular and unique, but part of a set or group of objects. We are instinctive and natural filers – every time we see something new and distinctive, we consider what kind of thing this is: what is it like that we have already experienced? We notice patterns of similarity and difference, and classify it accordingly. Until recently, it was commonly thought that everyone categorised things in pretty much the same way, with our inner mental categories directly corresponding to the external independent reality: that's the 'objectivist' perspective referred to in Chapter five. However, Lakoff (1987) overturned this idea, providing compelling evidence that people make up their own personal and unique categories based on imaginative experience. These remain fluid, diverse and capable of contradiction.

All human mental activity takes place within brains that cannot be disconnected from our human form. We think in certain ways precisely because our experience is always from an embodied perspective (Lakoff, 1987). We use mostly the same neuronal pathways to form sensory perceptions of the external world as we do to form inner, imaginary conceptions about it. We use internal sensory 'representations' within our imagination to represent our concepts and give them substance and structure accordingly. We manipulate these symbolic representations to create complex thought structures. We shuffle them around into different patterns as we imagine a future or remember our past.

Without metaphor, raw experience is just a set of bodily sensations that are felt, seen or otherwise perceived through senses. To *do* something with that perception, for example to reason or rationalise, to weigh up pros and cons, to do any kind of mental thinking activity, we need stuff to think about. That stuff of thought consists of internal representations of both real-life objects and also non-tangible concepts and ideas.

Symptoms with a message

People may reveal their metaphors in ways other than their spoken or written language. For instance, some will use a recurring gesture, speech mannerism or a movement to represent some kind of inner experience. Even more than with spoken, literal metaphors, these subtle stand-ins are likely to be beyond the person's awareness. By drawing the coachees' attention to these metaphors, from exploring the 'figure', they can gain insight into the 'ground'.

Some people have explored the relationship between health, illness and metaphors. For example, symptoms could be understood as the body's attempt to generate a metaphor of a deeper internal experience. Lawley and Tompkins (2002) suggest metaphors are the most natural way to describe illness and health and stress the importance that the medical professionals recognise and use the patient's metaphors to encourage and activate the healing process. On a deeper level, the symptom itself may be a metaphoric translation of an inner experience, which has become manifest. For instance, I remember developing a severe back problem around the time I was most anxious about whether or not I could carry on supporting myself. At the time I felt emotionally weighed down and under strain, and eventually my body seemed to manifest that fear by taking these metaphors and turning them into a living representation. I became someone literally 'unable to stand on my own two feet'.

There has been little research to date into the impact of metaphors on health issues, despite the huge potential that exists. No doubt many unhelpful metaphors about health, illness and recovery are perpetuated by the medical profession. One study explored how doctors referred to patient's illness and symptoms with very different metaphors to those typically used by patients themselves (Skelton et al., 2002). Doctors typically use metaphors that treat the problem as a puzzle and describe the body as a machine. Patients are likely to have their own unique, vivid portrayal of their symptoms and their experience of their illness. One exception is the almost universally used metaphor for cancer treatment, which describes cancer as the 'enemy' and the treatment as an act of war. People 'fight' cancer and tumours, sometimes to the death. From a more post-modernist perspective, a tumour could be considered as a co-existing part of the person, not as a separately bounded entity with a life of its own. All 'parts' could be reinterpreted as having positive intention, and more integrative metaphors around healing could provide a more helpful frame of reference.

Psychotherapist Karen Hurley (2014:312) describes her personal experience of her own journey with breast cancer. She stresses the powerful moment when she was able to reconceptualise her illness by forming an entirely new metaphor:

> The solution came suddenly, in a powerful, unbidden image. I saw my cancer not as an invader, not an enemy to be fought, but as refugee children who had lost their way. The little refugee cells were hungry, dirty, tired, sullen, and needed care: to be fed, cleaned up and comforted before being resettled into a new and better life, elsewhere, where both they and I would be safe. What had caused my cancer was not clear, but the cells had come from my body, and they were mine.

Hurley discovered that the most important question was not about how to 'fight' the cancer, but whether you are empowered by your metaphor to heal, in whatever way that may mean for you. She acknowledged the cancer as parts of herself, and took responsibility to care for them. *"I learned that what I had really taken on was the care of unloved, unwanted parts of myself."*

References

Grove, D. J. and Panzer, B. I. (1989) *Resolving Traumatic Memories: Metaphors and Symbols in Psychotherapy*. New York: Irvington.

Hurley, K. (2014) To fight, or not to fight: A cancer psychotherapist with cancer confronts the battle metaphor. *Women & Therapy*, 37(3–4), 311–318. doi: 10.1080/02703149.2014.897556.

Jung, C. G. and Franz, M.-L. (1964) *Man and His Symbols*. New York: Dell Pub. Co.

Kittay, E. F. (1987) *Metaphor: Its Cognitive Force and Linguistic Structure*. Oxford: Oxford University Press.

Lakoff, G. (1987) *Women, Fire and Dangerous Things: What Categories Reveal About the Mind*. Chicago: University of Chicago Press.

Lakoff, G. and Johnson, M. (1980) *Metaphors We Live by*. Chicago: University of Chicago Press.

Lawley, J. and Tompkins, P. (1996, August) *And, What Kind of a Man is David Grove? An Interview by Penny Tompkins and James Lawley.* First published in *Rapport*, The Journal of the Association of NLP (UK), Issue 33. Available at: www.cleanlanguage.co.uk/articles/articles/37/1/And-what-kind-of-a-man-is-David-Grove/Page1.html [Accessed 3/8/2015].

Lawley, J. and Tompkins, P. (2000) *Metaphors in Mind*. London: The Developing Company Press.

Lawley, J. and Tompkins, P. (2002) *The Mind Metaphor and Health, first published in Positive Health*, Issue 78. July 2002. Available at: www.cleanlanguage.co.uk/articles/articles/23/1/Mind-Metaphor-and-Health/Page1.html [Accessed 6/8/2015].

Lawley, J. and Tompkins, P. (2003) *Clean Space – Modelling Human Perception Through Emergence.* Available at: www.cleanlanguage.co.uk/articles/articles/24/1/Clean-Space-Modeling-Human-Perception-through-Emergence/Page1.html [Accessed 3/8/2015].

Skelton, J. R., Wearn, A. M. and Hobbs, F. R. (2002) A concordance-based study of metaphoric expressions used by general practitioners and patients in consultation. *The British Journal of General Practice*, 52(475), 114–118.

Tosey, P. C., Sullivan, W. and Meyer, M. (2013) *Clean Sources: Six Metaphors a Minute?* Guildford: University of Surrey (ISBN: 978–1–84469–029–9).

Chapter ten

Modelling and systems thinking

Modelling

One of the greatest contributions that neurolinguistic psychotherapists James Lawley and Penny Tompkins have brought into the field of Clean Language is the concept of 'modelling'. They worked closely with Grove from the late 1990s and over a five-year period they scrutinised his client work, which at the time was his traditional Clean Language approach. Lawley and Tompkins developed Grove's often spontaneous and fast-evolving 'artfulness' into a more replicable craft that others could learn and apply more easily. They used the NLP process of modelling to do this, distilling his overall style, technique and specific questions into a blue-printed 'model' that others could follow. They noticed that David's use of Clean Language was in itself a form of modelling, through his questions he attempted to build his own working model of his clients' patterns of thought and behaviour, as revealed through their use of metaphor. This developed into their own process: 'Symbolic Modelling' (Lawley and Tompkins, 2000).

'Modelling' is a term used to describe the replication of something 'real' into a simpler, often smaller-scaled form – usually referred to as a 'model'. There are many everyday examples: think of model aircrafts, model railways or perhaps catwalk models representing a certain designer's style. As a process, modelling works like modelling clay, for instance. You mould something into the shape of something else.

Modelling is very useful when the original article is large and complex and a simpler version could serve the desired purpose. For instance, the 'A to Z' map of London is not London, it's just a model. And as covered in Chapter four, the map is not the territory. But for what models and maps lack in complexity, they make up for in depicting certain information very clearly. A map doesn't tell you everything about the reality of a location, but it provides very specific, albeit limited information such as street names, and where they are in relation to other streets and places. For instance, if you were lost in Holburn needing to get to Finchley, actually being there in person might not help much. Having a map – an artificial small-scaled version of reality – allows you to step back from the detail. You can then see the wider perspective, noticing the connections and relationships between one part of the terrain and another. Models help us make inferences and predictions about what's going on in the real world.

People carry out the process of modelling in many different ways, sometimes with conscious intent and sometimes it just happens. Every time we listen to another person, we automatically build our own internal representation of what we think the person means, creating a model. In a more concrete, conscious way, people apply modelling within many different industries and applications, producing simulations of traffic flow, weather patterns and consumer behaviour for example, sometimes using complex computer modelling programmes. Even the children's entertainer who does balloon modelling is using the same process. In that instance the entertainer is taking the medium of a balloon or two and shaping it into a simple representation of something larger and more complex, such as a giraffe or a gibbon.

Within the field of NLP, modelling is a process for learning to deeply understand how another person is able to achieve a certain result, in order to adopt those strategies and get the same results for ourselves. Often referred to as 'modelling excellence', the process starts from a position of curiosity. The NLP 'modeller' asks the question: "How is it that this person can do that?" Then the modeller pays exquisite attention to what that person (called the 'exemplar') actually does, moment by moment, to achieve the results the exemplar gets. The NLP modeller needs a heightened degree of observation known as 'sensory acuity' to pick up very subtle shifts in the person's behaviour, mannerisms and body posture. By asking specific questions of the exemplar the modeller also attempts to understand exemplars' internal processes. This includes what they are thinking about; their underlying beliefs and values as well as what they see, hear and feel in their mind's eye, step by step, as they do whatever it is they do. When modelling, everything that can be represented as an internal or external experience is written down in sequence for the modellers to then attempt to replicate them all for themselves. They try the model on for size and adopt, as best they can, exactly the same internal and external representations and experiences. This enables them to fast track to the same or similar successful results as the exemplars (Gordon and Dawes, 2005).

Grove studied NLP although he never used the term 'modelling' to describe what he did. But many others as well as Penny and James recognised this aspect of his work, for instance UK NLP trainer Sue Knight (2002). After working with Grove, she said he was one of the most skilled modellers she had ever known.

The principles of modelling are useful within Clean Coaching, as we are attempting to build a model of the coachee's insider perspective, rather than simply use our own personal 'map' of what seems to be happening from the outside. As the coachees describe their inner world, we mentally place their internal representations inside and around *them* – relative to *their* body, rather than (as is normal) stepping into their shoes and imagining it as though we were directly experiencing it ourselves, through our *own* bodies. The coachees you are working with have their own unique map of the world guiding their beliefs and behaviours and belongs with them, in their space and not ours. Through modelling, your aim is to build a model of your coachee's map – which is, of course, in itself only a model of reality! You can perhaps see here why a more interpretivist, subjective view of people can be helpful to adopt (as covered in Chapter five), otherwise you may end up fruitlessly searching for the 'real' truth amongst all of this abstraction!

Models, as you may have already deduced, are also a bit like metaphors and symbols, they are another kind of representation, where something 'real' is replaced by something else. The beauty of metaphors and symbols for modelling is that they provide something rather tangible and definable to focus on, if not actually physically real. And in doing so, it helps the coach to let go of his or her own map and concentrate on something more readily accepted as being owned by another. Using the displacement of a metaphor, the coach is less likely to try and interpret the meaning of any symbols or sensations.

Self-modelling

Grove (2003) said of Clean Language that "When questions are kept clean the client's own model of the world is able to come out and the solutions come from within them." In fact, the value of Clean Coaching could be summed up in this way: it is helping the coachees know more about their own maps of the world. James Lawley (2012) calls this 'self-modelling'. Unlike NLP modelling, Symbolic Modelling aims are not usually for the benefit of the modeller to gain a strategy for success. Instead, Clean Coaches use modelling by asking questions to build up their own model of the coachees' metaphoric landscape. As this happens, the coachees simultaneously becomes more aware of their own map as you direct their attention towards the symbols and their relationship with each other.

Coachees are encouraged to build their own conscious model of part of their unconscious map. This model is another level of abstraction, but has four advantages over the coachee's original 'map' already in place:

1   The coachee has a conscious awareness of his or her model. Whereas maps are largely hidden from any kind of direct examination.
2   Maps all connect together into one almighty and unwieldy mega-map of absolutely everything making it hard to know where to look, but models can be more focused around a specific topic, outcome or issue.
3   It is based around metaphors, providing a simplified version of reality which brings previously hidden aspects about a goal or an issue to the surface.
4   It is more likely to be visual. The coachee can be encouraged to physically draw out the model as part of the coaching process. Tangible visual representations are useful for noticing further aspects of the model and to deliberately redraw and reframe it in useful ways.

Normally, we don't really know much about our own mental maps as they remain largely outside of our conscious awareness. Clean techniques bring those maps to the surface of our understanding. Models formed through metaphor and symbols are available for self-examination. You might think that this would simply reinforce existing unconscious maps, not in the best interest of the coachee, but it doesn't. Lawley and Tompkins (2000:26) suggest that continued self-modelling results in an amazing phenomenon: ". . . the client begins to generate new experience. Describing this in metaphor triggers further experience and awareness, and so on, in a recursive, developmental spiral."

The metaphoric model evolves and change becomes the by-product of the process. The coachees are no longer merely describing their experience, they have reproduced it for themselves right here and now. They can test their own developing model as they sense and experience it, embodied as feelings, images and sounds. In this way, they can "gain a deep insight into why they act and respond the way they do" and "start to notice choice points – places where their process could go in a different direction and result in a different outcome" (Lawley, 2012).

Systems thinking

Systems thinking is a frame through which to think about large systems, such as organisations, societies and groups of people. It is used in many contexts by a wide range of professionals, such as consultants, engineers, social scientists, as well as providing a very useful frame for Clean Coaches. The same core principles of systems thinking can apply to thinking about an individual person, with a mind that behaves as a complex system of interconnecting parts. It is a way of thinking that goes hand in hand with the process of modelling, providing a suitable focus. In many ways, individual minds form patterns and relationships that act just like large group structures, as Lawley and Tompkins suggest, "People can be regarded as self-organising systems" (2000:29).

For a system to be self-organising, it needs to continuously self-preserve and self-adapt (Lawley and Tompkins, 2000:30). In nature, these two core patterns of survival are seen over and over again, replicated in all forms of systems. Examples of natural systems are the weather, the seasons of the year, and patterns of growth and decline amongst the animal and plant kingdom. All these systems can be better understood not by examining individual phenomenon happening in one place at one time, but stepping back and seeing clusters of such phenomena, which together make up a pattern of interactions. These patterns emerge from the relationship between the individual parts, a system of connection that makes up a different kind of thing. With systems thinking, every individual 'something' – whether an idea, belief or a behaviour – is viewed as a single component of a different, bigger 'something else'.

Peter Senge's book *The Fifth Discipline* (1990) provides really useful ways of understanding what systems thinking is about. Like many of the core ideas covered in this book so far, it's as much about unlearning the supposed 'natural' and taken-for-granted ways of relating to the world and learning to see things – especially people – in a new light. Senge (1990) makes the point that most people (in the Western world anyway) are taught from an early age to fragment the world they perceive into separate, smaller parts with clear, definable boundaries. Even time is reduced to a series of bite-sized, disparate events, seen as straight lines which have a beginning, middle and end. But many situations and problems we encounter do not have a clear cause and effect, and are simply not as straightforward or simplistic to conceptualise. Senge (1990) recommends that people think in circles (or cycles), instead of straight lines.

One important kind of cycle to notice in any kind of system is how each individual part influences other parts, usually in some kind of reciprocal flow, rather than a straightforward cause and effect. These patterns of reciprocal influence represent feedback loops that show how actions (or thoughts) either *reinforce* each other and create a snowball effect, or otherwise counteract each other, creating a *balancing*, dampening down effect. These two kinds of feedback loops can work together as multiple reciprocal cycles that co-exist and form a complex pattern. At first glance they may appear to produce random results, but on closer examination, there is a structure of influence that holds the whole system together. Take 'tipping points' for instance. Or to use a more explicit and detailed metaphor: the 'straw that breaks the camel's back'. With systems like these, it appears as though nothing happens for a long time until a sudden, dramatic change is reached. But behind the scenes, reinforcing feedback loops would have eventually outgrown the balancing loop which has been keeping everything in check. Feedback loops may not be visible or explicit within a system. The elements of the feedback loop are not the individual pieces of the system, but the influence that each has on the other.

These kinds of feedback loops can be very difficult to notice when exploring a person's pattern of thinking and behaving. They are like the 'glue' that holds the system together, invisible but connecting and constraining. By using Clean Language to explore the metaphors that people use to describe their experience, it helps strip away irrelevant detail and complex distractions. Instead a clearer form representing the entire pattern of connections can be attended to.

The whole system is likely to be of a different kind of substance or quality than that of the individual parts. And it may take some time, exploring the various parts of the system involved, before a metaphor for the entire system to emerge. You can encourage the coachee to notice the whole pattern after exploring the parts by asking:

"And *all* of that, is like what?"

Building 'rich pictures'

Checkland (1990) recommends drawing 'rich pictures' as a way of simplifying complex systems into a clear and simple summary, captured all on a single A4 piece of paper. And you can adopt this idea for Clean Coaching, mapping out rough diagrams: flow charts, arrows and/or doodles to represent the coachee's emerging metaphors. In many ways this can be much more useful than trying to capture all the words, verbatim and in sequence, distracting you from the essence of what's happening. Rich pictures provide a useful aide memoire and help you pay attention to the 'whole thing'. You are more likely to notice the relationship between the parts rather than get sucked into detailed content.

Be creative but accurate with your picture and find ways to represent the coachee's descriptions in simple but clear ways. You cannot capture everything, aim for an overview which helps you see how each piece of the metaphoric puzzle is related to other pieces being discussed. Use all the space on the page rather than write in a linear fashion, and where possible place things in the same position/scale as the coachee has represented them. Replace complex descriptions with drawings, and keep written language to one or two short word phrases. Senge (1990) suggests simple systemic diagrams should highlight the nature of the relationship between core components with arrows pointing to the direction of influence.

I advise that you capture on paper the first words the coachee says to describe what he or she wants, however vague, as often those initial comments neatly sum up what's going on. It may be awhile before your coachee articulates a clear outcome. When the coachee does, write that down too, word for word as stated. Invariably the outcome has a number of different elements to it and this will help you return to each piece or part in turn during the session, accurately reflecting back the coachee's own words each time.

You can also encourage your coachees to draw their own picture of their emerging model. By representing their thoughts on paper, through words, pictures, shapes, patterns, often coachees are able to mentally step outside of any stuckness, and disassociate from the experience, as the model is now on their paper and in some ways out of their head. In his later years, Grove developed a whole Clean Coaching process around using the coachee's drawing and writing on paper called 'Clean Hieroglyphics' which we will cover in Chapter fifteen.

Top-down and bottom-up modelling

'Top-down' and 'bottom-up' are two approaches to modelling that can be applied to Clean Coaching strategies (Lawley and Tompkins, 2004). Typically, most coaching sessions follow a top-down approach, which generally begins with the end result in mind. The well-known GROW model (Whitmore, 1992; Alexander, 2006) is a top-down approach. Top-down approaches tend to follow a standard pattern or process, taking the big picture and gradually breaking it down into its component pieces. It's a step-by-step, building block approach to reaching outcomes. It's like when as a child, I used plastic modelling bricks to build a model that matched the picture on the front of the box. That was a top-down approach.

The top-down approach suits the coaching philosophy of being coachee-led and outcome-focused, and follows a clear pattern. Top-down approaches, however, are not always effective. They only work if the coachee is capable of imagining and articulating an outcome and believing it is possible to achieve it. In some circumstances, especially when a coachee has been stuck in a problem state for some time, he or she cannot conceive of the outcome without also anticipating further problems. Any solution ideas have become entangled with the problem. In

Clean Language terms, Tompkins and Lawley refer to this as a 'bind' (following Gregory Bateson's (1972) use of the term 'double bind'), where we become stuck within the very circles of thought we have previously used to escape the problem. In these instances, taking a bottom-up approach and starting afresh from within the problem state, can help new solutions emerge.

The bottom-up approach to plastic modelling brick construction is the kind of play that does *not* copy the desired end result and instead experiments with connections and constructions to see what happens. With bottom-up modelling the focus is on what's happening now, in this very moment, and building from that. With bottom-up approaches, we don't know where we will end up, there isn't a neat flowchart to plot our steps. It's an emergent process, no overall aim or direction is established, instead the focus is on developing a depth of understanding about what the current situation is like. As Clean Coaches, by modelling the coachee's current thinking system, we help the coachee become more consciously aware of it. Self-awareness at this level enables the system to self-correct, as change emerges from the exploration, often in unexpected, surprising ways.

With a bottom-up approach, you can help draw the coachee's attention to the here and now through your questions. Notice when the coachee inevitably starts playing out his or her patterns with you in the session. For instance, the person who wants to be more confident shows the pattern of not knowing what to do next, by being unable to answer your question. Whenever this happens you can use the incident to help model exactly what happens for this person in his or her particular system of 'not knowing'. In this way, as the person learns more about how he or she 'does' this pattern of not knowing, some alternative way of being may present itself. If you had used a top-down approach and continued to explore what confidence is like for this person, you may have found the conversation continually loops back to the problem state.

Clean Coaching: structures and strategies

Clean Coaching is above all an approach for working with coachees. You can adopt a Clean approach in any kind of coaching conversation, 'cleaning up' any coaching model or framework by giving greater emphasis to the coachee's own perception and using Clean questions to elicit information and direct attention. Additionally, there are a number of Clean questioning strategies and sequences that are ideally suited for coaching.

Clean Coaching and the GROW model

The well-known GROW model follows a top-down approach to coaching, providing a flexible framework with four core stages to cover with a coaching session:

G: Goal: Help the coachee to establish and clarify where he or she would like to be.
R: Reality Now: Ask questions to clarify the coachee's perception of where he or she is now.

O: Options: Examine the gap between the Goal and Reality, and explore the alternative paths the coachee could take to get from here to there.

W: Will: Help the coachee to choose the steps that he or she definitely will take, and establish the coachee has the motivation and commitment to see it through.

Many other coaching and counselling frameworks are similar in structure, highlighting the same core steps to the coachee's journey, for instance Egan's (1974) Skilled Helper Model names them as:

1 Current scenario;
2 Preferred scenario; and
3 Strategies to get there.

The GROW model is an extension of this framework, which includes the final step of clarifying the 'Will' or determination to succeed.

In a top-down approach, each of these stages happens in succession, e.g. the goal is established before options explored. However each stage may be revisited at any time in the process, as Grant (2011) highlights the actual model probably looks more like GRGROGROOGROWOGORW as each stage is continually revisited as information and understanding emerges. The core difference between top-down and bottom-up approaches is the order in which the stages are explored, in particular whether the goal is explored before or after reality now (Grant, 2011). For Clean Coaching, I suggest taking a top-down approach to begin with. If that proves unsuccessful and the coachee does not make clear progress within one or two sessions, then switch to a bottom-up approach.

The difference with Clean Coaching

As conventional coaching covers a vast array of different styles, techniques and approaches, clearly the difference between Clean and conventional coaching will depend on what kind of conventional approach is being compared. Some non-directive forms of conventional coaching may be very similar. Grove and Wilson (2005) suggest that a key difference is that conventional coaching, with models such as GROW, require a good deal of effort on behalf of the coachee to make change happen. Clean Coaching, because it capitalises on underlying thought structures and unconscious patterns, is able to integrate rather than side-step inner obstacles, such as fear, anger or limiting behaviour patterns, into energies which will participate with instead of working against the client. The coachee's inner world is treated as a system, instead of simply addressing a specific goal in a blinkered, narrow way. The coachee's wider metaphoric landscape integrates disparate elements and consolidates deep, intuitive wisdom, often leading to a greater congruence about the right path to take.

The value of this kind of integration can be immense, as explained by Grove and Wilson (2005) in this way: "The internal changes achieved automatically re-align what the client is able to know, think, feel or achieve in the external world. No effort is required: it is like a train running on different tracks." As a result, following Clean Coaching sometimes goals that the coachee has been obsessively driven towards achieving seem irrelevant, or laughingly easy to reach. They add: "The physiology of effort does not come into play. Clean coaches do not motivate, encourage or challenge their clients; they move their clients forward by facilitating a re-arrangement of their psychescape through emergent knowledge solutions."

References

Alexander, G. (2006) Behavioural coaching – the GROW model. In J. Passmore (ed.), *Excellence in Coaching: The Industry Guide*. London; Philadelphia: Kogan Page, 83–93.

Bateson, G. (1972) Double bind, 1969. In *Steps to an Ecology of the Mind: A Revolutionary Approach to Man's Understanding of Himself*. Chicago: University of Chicago Press, 271–278.

Checkland, P. (1990) *Soft Systems Methodology in Action*. New York: Wiley & Sons.

Egan, G. (1974) *The Skilled Helper*. Pacific Grove: Brooks/Cole Publishing Company.

Gordon, D. and Dawes, G. (2005) *Expanding Your World: Modeling the Structure of Experience*. Tucson, AZ: David Gordon.

Grant, A. M. (2011, December) Is it time to REGROW the GROW model? Issues related to teaching coaching session structures. *The Coaching Psychologist*, 7(2), 1748–1104.

Grove, D. (2003) *Summary of David Grove's Ideas – As of 2003*. Available at: www.clean language.co.uk/articles/articles/278/1/David-Grove-summary-of-ideas-as-of-2003/ Page1.html [Accessed 25/6/2015].

Grove, D. and Wilson, C. (2005) *Emergent Knowledge ΣK™ and Clean Coaching: New Theories of David Grove*. Available at: www.cleanlanguage.co.uk/articles/articles/47/1/ Emergent-Knowledge-and-Clean-Coaching/Page1.html [Accessed 9/8/2015].

Knight, S. (2002, Summer) Modelling: A tribute to Simon and David first published in *Rapport. Journal of the Association for NLP* (UK), Issue 56. Available at: www.clean language.co.uk/articles/articles/77/1/Modelling-A-tribute-to-Simon-and-David/Page1. html [Accessed 15/7/2015].

Lawley, J. (2012) *What Is Self-Modelling?* Available at: wwwcleanlanguage.co.uk/articles/ blogs/71/ [Accessed 8/8/2015].

Lawley, J. and Tompkins, P. (2000) *Metaphors in Mind*. London: The Developing Company Press.

Lawley, J. and Tompkins, P. (2004) *Modelling – Top Down and Bottom Up*. Available at: www.cleanlanguage.co.uk/articles/articles/240/1/Modelling-Top-down-and-Bottom-up-/Page1.html [Accessed 4/9/2015].

Senge, P. M. (1990) *The Fifth Discipline*. New York: Currency Doubleday.

Whitmore, J. (1992) *Coaching for Performance*. London: Nicholas Brealey.

Chapter eleven

The structure of a Clean Coaching session

Clean Coaching: the "A to B" model

As Grove frequently described, coaching is about helping the coachee get from "A to B." Metaphorically, a coach is like a vehicle for coachees to make that journey from where they are now, to where they would like to be. And when coachees' think of their outcome they tend to imagine it as existing somewhere outside of themselves: a destination to aim for somewhere in their mind's eye. There is also another imagined space that signifies where they are right now. Clean Coaching attempts to model these mental spaces, either by exploring them as metaphors using Clean Language, or by helping coachees map them out in the physical space around them.

Grove described these mental spaces as containers for the different sources of information to be explored. The coachees arrives for coaching carrying with them all their previous experiences, for example their beliefs, history, identity, etc. Everything they know about themselves exists in one kind of imaginary mental space which David labelled as "A." This represents our current reality: from here we only see things from our personal perceptive, which may obscure aspects of our chosen goal.

The other mental space of "B" represents all we know about the goal we want to reach. By its very definition, the goal can't be in the same place as A, else the coachee would already have it. Grove and Wilson (2005) highlighted that when people have achieved their outcome, they tend not to represent it as being 'over there' at all, but right beside them or even within them. Goals yet to be achieved are usually separate from and at a distance from A, in a space we can call B. The following diagram (Figure 11.1) highlights the kind of mental 'construction' we form in our mind's eye in order to imagine a desired outcome of any kind. We might not be consciously aware of this structure, however it reveals itself through the metaphors we use when talking about our outcomes:

- I'm reaching for it.
- Just beyond my grasp.
- The only way is up.
- Moving forwards.
- Taking steps.

Figure 11.1 The mental spaces of A and B.

Once the two spaces of A and B are positioned, a third kind of space emerges, in the space between A and B, the gap or the path between is represented by "C." On the face of it, this might appear to be the most obvious route for the coachee to take, straight through the space of C. Most coaching processes look to find the most direct path between A and B, moving towards the goal in as shorter distance/fewer steps as possible. However in the client's mental map, the space between A and B contains not only potential steps forward, but also the obstacles, barriers and traps that the coachee perceives have hindered progress so far, whether real or imagined. It is the separation or distance between A and B which has driven the person to find a coach. If coachees were able to travel that distance themselves, without help, it is likely they would have done so already. For many people, especially if their goal is one that has been unsuccessful in reaching so far, C doesn't just represent the path between A and B. Grove's concept was that between A and B would be everything else we know about where we are now and where we want to be, including what's stopping us. Which means C is not necessarily the best route to take, albeit it seems the shortest and most direct. It is the route where all the problems lie and is likely to be a difficult and effortful journey to take.

Together then, these three letters provide a kind of equation. Typical coaching works by helping the coachee get from A to B, through C. Instead, Clean Coaching suggests exploring outside and around the whole mental map which includes A, B and C in between. And into the space Grove called "D," representing the unknown and/or forgotten. Here lies the opportunities and possibilities not yet considered.

So, with Clean Coaching, we take a different strategy from A to B. Instead of a direct path, we take a more circuitous route, appearing to take us 'all around the

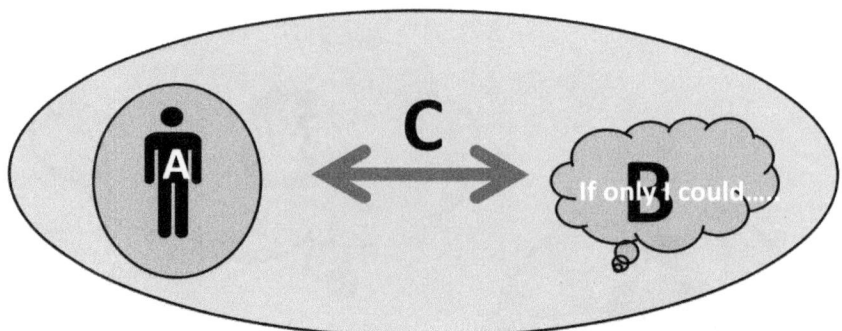

D: *Outside A, B and C*

Figure 11.2 Getting from A to B.

houses'. Clients discover more about themselves and their goal from different mental spaces, some which may seem irrelevant. In this way, less obvious pathways open up revealing an entirely different perspective (see Figure 11.2).

This "A to B" strategy describes the body of work known as Emergent Knowledge, developed by Grove later in his life. This approach incorporated Clean Space, using the physical space around the coachee as an externalised container within which the coachee can explore his or her inner thinking. With most EK processes the coachee maps out imaginary mental spaces in real locations around him or her, taking the internal perspectives and making them tangible so they can be explored physically and moved around within.

As a Clean Coach, you may decide to use Clean Language or Emergent Knowledge, or a combination of the two, to help the coachee understand as much as possible about the three places of A, B and C. As a strategy, Clean Coaching follows three distinct steps to help the coachee make the journey from A to B, focused on how the coachee's attention is being directed:

1   Focus attention.
2   Expand attention.
3   Establish actions.

For the rest of this chapter we will look at how to use this strategy with Clean Language. The next chapter will highlight how to use Emergent Knowledge with the same core three-step strategy.

Clean Language structure

1   *Focus attention:* Establish and continually re-establish the goal and focus attention on it.

2   *Expand attention:* Ask questions that expand attention beyond the goal until a shift in thinking occurs (we cannot *make* this happen but we can notice when it happens).

3   *Establish actions:* Find out what needs to happen to reach the goal. Confirm each action is possible and if the coachee is committed to following through.

As with the GROW model, the coachee's clearly expressed goal is the starting point for any exploration, we anticipate that this may be the first of a series of sub-goals, any of which may replace the initially articulated goal. It's like tracking a course to find a herd of elephants that is constantly on the move! However, being as clear as possible about where that herd is at the outset will enable you to alter direction more quickly and accurately as and when new information emerges. This structure also allows for a *bottom-up* approach (see previous chapter), as the initial 'focus attention' step could attend to the current reality, not the goal, which emerges later in the process, after any shift in thinking has occurred at step two. A further model – the 'PRO' – is highlighted below, which in combination with our broad strategy helps to continually track towards the outcome.

Focus attention: establish the goal

Traditional Clean Language begins with one crucial question to help establish what the coachee wants:

"What would you like to have happen?"

The question can be asked to set outcomes on a number of different levels or contexts, for instance:

"Overall, from the series of coaching sessions we have scheduled for the year ahead, what would you like to have happen?"

"You told me on the phone you are concerned about your job, what would you like to have happen about that?"

"For today's session, what would you like to have happen?"

Listen carefully to the answer. Is it an outcome? Outcomes are statements about the place of B. They describe the effect once it has been arrived at, after things have changed or action has been taken. If the answer fits the bill of an outcome, however unachievable, unrealistic or woolly it might sound to you, write it down, word for word and ask your coachee to do the same.

This is an important part of the coaching process and definitely not to be rushed. Take time to identify where the coachee currently believes he or she would like to be. That outcome may change during the coaching session, however you need an initial focus to provide the momentum for exploration. The goal may be more like a herd of elephants than a single static thing, but knowing where the herd of elephants is right now is a good place to start. Without doing so, you'll be spending a lot of time searching around in the dark, with no idea where to head next.

Some people express their goals as a single word, for instance: "Money." For some, they may prefer to represent their goal as a picture or diagram. It doesn't matter if the goal makes no sense to you, as long as it represents an end result for them.

If your coachees don't know what they want, you can still help focus their attention on whatever vague sense they have and your aim will be to help them articulate an outcome, at some point. For some coachees, it may take a whole coaching session to help them get clear on what they want. You may decide to adopt a more bottom-up approach in these instances, simply exploring whatever comes up for the coachee in the moment, and allowing the outcome to emerge later on in the coaching session.

Focusing attention on the goal

As covered in Chapter five, being attentive is one of the greatest skills for Clean Coaching. In effect your capacity to focus attention enables coachees to focus their attention too. The quality of their attention on their own experiences helps them gain the understanding required to reach shifts in thinking. Our questions help narrow in the focus of attention, as covered in Chapter three, with each question the coach makes a choice on where to direct the coachee's attention. In Chapter eight we covered the crucial Clean Language questions to use in order to focus attention.

Let's say our coachee comes prepared with a clear goal for the session, which is:

"I'd like to develop my levels of concentration so I can get more done and finish on time."

In any outcome statement, there are usually a number of different components, each worth exploring further, and for this reason it's worth writing down the outcome, so you can systematically explore and focus on each area covered. In the above example, you may choose to ask a series of Clean Language questions about:

"Develop"
"Levels"
"Concentration"
"Get more done"
"Finish"
"On time"

As each is explored, more areas for exploration and focus emerge, creating an ever-increasing multitude of possible directions and areas of potential focus.

Where to focus the coachee's attention

There will always be a variety of good choices to make, and it's impossible to know which would be most effective. The following areas of coachee information are generally valuable to focus on and explore further:

- *Resources:* Focus on what coachees say they need to do, be or feel to reach their goal. They are usually things the coachee already has, such as patience or time. In the above example, 'concentration levels' seem like a resource which could be developed further. More resources are likely to emerge as the session continues.
- *Verbs*: As covered in Chapter nine, verbs are the 'doing' part of any statement and often where the action is, as well as being a common source of inferred metaphors. For instance, in the above example: 'develop' and 'finish'.
- *Repetition*: It's encouraging to know that if the coachee says something important and you fail to notice, the chances are if it really matters, the coachee will say it again . . . and again.
- *What's important to the coachees*: They may stress this directly or infer through their voice emphasis, physical reaction, gestures or gaze.
- *Metaphors*: As covered in Chapter nine, metaphors are like doorways to inner symbolic thinking, so always a useful place to focus attention. In the above example, 'levels' are a kind of metaphor, as is 'concentration'. The most effective Clean Coaches are able to notice the embedded and inherent metaphors that people use within their natural spoken language when describing their experience.
- *Symbols:* As any metaphor is explored, more tangible parts may be revealed, for instance, levels may become like the depth levels in a swimming pool, ranging from shallow to medium to deep water. The symbols are the swimming pool and the water, each is capable of taking on a clear form and location, in the coachee's mind's eye. By exploring more about the symbols, the 'levels' metaphor is likely to evolve.

If you are not sure where to focus attention, you could pass the ball back to the coachee by asking: "Is there anything else about that?" to allow the coachee to tell you what matters most.

Expanding attention

You can help expand the coachee's attention beyond what the person currently knows by using more advanced Clean Language questions. These will be covered in detail in Chapter thirteen. Expanding attention questions help the coachee:

- Take things forwards or backwards in time. This enables them to explore the sequence of events that lead up to a particular happening, as well as the consequences afterwards.

- To go back to the origins of a particular piece of the exploration. The source of a resource, for instance, which is often an even more powerful place. This can involve people thinking about their genealogical or historical roots, or a location not previously thought of as related, or the origins of a process long before their previous sequential imaginings.
- To explore the relationships between the parts of the metaphoric system. Relationships reveal the power sources and influence flows, and often further pieces of the system are revealed as relationships are explored.

These specific questions are best used sparingly. One shift in thinking is often all that's required for it to have a chain reaction across the whole system of thinking being explored. As new information comes to light, revert to 'focusing attention' questions to help any new realisations come into clearer form. Sometimes, especially if a bottom-up approach is being adopted, your question may deliberately encourage a complete shift in attention. This can work well if someone appears rigid and stuck within known paths of thinking. The kinds of questions you may ask to expand attention under these circumstances are:

- Rather than focus questions on what appears to be central to the coachee's understanding, it can be very useful to notice, what it is that the coachee is steadfastly ignoring or considering unimportant?
- Words that describe self: Me, myself and I, and combinations: such as I tie myself in knots about this. I am in two minds. Part of me wants to do x and another part, y.
- Words that imply some sense of scale, comparison and/or measurement – e.g. better, closer than, etc. This draws attention to the underlying patterns used to make judgements.
- Grove (1998) suggested often it is the seemingly irrelevant, off-topic 'red herrings' that can lead the coachee to insight, under-the-breath comments or 'asides', non sequiturs and idiosyncratic sounds and expressions.
- Tompkins and Lawley (2009) advise similarly: "Listen to the unusual voice, the suggestion that does not obviously fit, the annoying intrusion. They often contain the gem, the spark, the perturbation the system needs."

The PRO model

Developed by James Lawley and Penny Tompkins (2006), the PRO model provides an extremely useful tool for deciding, moment by moment, where to focus your coachee's attention and in which direction to point for the person. The PRO model offers a choice of direction to follow based on the current situation/coachee's orientation. To figure out that orientation, you need to ask yourself: "Where is the coachee's attention, right now?" and listen for linguistic clues from the coachee.

P is for problem.
R is for remedy.
O is for outcome.

Problem

Problems inevitably turn up frequently during a coaching session. But often coachees are unresourceful and stuck when concentrating on what they don't want. When coachee are focusing on the problem, they tend to:

1   State a difficulty that they are experiencing.
2   Use words that indicate or presuppose that they do not like what is happening.
3   Not mention any desire for things to be different.

Whenever coachees describes a problem, we should respect them by first acknowledging that problem by repeating back their description of it. Then, we re-orient them towards an outcome by asking what would they like to have happen *in light of this problem*: "When (coachee's problem), what would you like to have happen?" This may lead to the discovery of different outcomes at different times during the coaching session. It is an iterative not a repetitive process, each question has a cumulative, generative effect, asking for an outcome that pre-supposes the problem just mentioned.

For example, here is a *repetitive* process:

"What would you like to have happen?"
"I keep losing control."
"And what would you like to have happen?"
"I just said: 'I keep losing control.' Why are you asking me the same thing again?"

This is an *iterative* process:

"What would you like to have happen?"
"I keep losing control."
"And *when* you keep losing control, what would you like to have happen?"
"I'd like to stop losing control, of course!"

With this example, the coachee is no longer focusing on the problem, and has now stated a desire for change, although has not yet articulated this as an outcome. This is a *proposed remedy*.

Remedy

Sometimes, coachees talk about the remedies to their problems, rather than the ultimate outcome they are aiming for. The remedy is a route the coachees are suggesting they take to get rid of, or solve their problem, although it's easy to mistake for an actual outcome. The remedy contains three components:

1   Desire words such as "I'd like to . . ."
2   Words that indicate avoiding/reducing/stopping the problem.
3   A mention of the problem itself.

Remedies are often expressed as wanting less of, or the complete absence of, the stated problem. For instance, "I want to give up smoking" is a remedy. So is "I'd like to reduce my anxiety." People can get locked into remedies, focusing on next steps and ending up going in circles, because the actual end destination has not been thought through. Remedies often contain some of the same language as the problem (e.g. 'smoking', 'anxiety,' etc.) which means the mind tends to run along the same or similar tracks as it usually does when this problem is thought about.

With Clean Language, you can help a coachee work out the bigger picture by asking a question about the stated remedy that takes things forward in time to *after* the problem remedy has been successfully applied:

"And when you stop losing control, what happens next?"

Or

"And when you reduce your anxiety, then what happens?"

This is a great way to test out the remedy. Does it actually lead somewhere the coachee would like to be? Sometimes it does. This end result is the actual outcome the coachee wants. Sometimes the answer will loop back around to the same or another problem, in which case you can keep applying the PRO model until the coachee states an actual desired outcome that he or she *does* want.

Outcome

The coachee may answer:

"Then I will remain in the driving seat of my life, taking charge even in difficult situations."

One can assume this is the real desired outcome, which can be achieved once the remedy of stopping losing control has been successfully carried out. Linguistically, outcomes often contain:

1   A desire, need or preference for something new in the coachee's situation.
2   No mention of the problem.
3   A future event. This has not yet happened.

By focusing attention first and foremost on the actual outcome, the coachee's motivation to remain in the driving seat and take charge is likely to increase. As the coachee's attention is first focused on and then expanded around that driving seat, a completely different path or remedy may become possible for the coachee. Instead of needing to stop losing control, which previously felt like an impossibly difficult struggle, the coachee may discover he or she can drive smoothly through the slippery patches. The resulting action may seem the same from the outsider perspective, but for the coachee, it can feel very different following a shift in focus. Sometimes, remedies remain useful and you may decide to ask questions about the remedy later in the coaching session, when you reach the third stage of the process and are checking actions. Here you may further explore what needs to happen, for instance, to reduce anxiety. The coachee may be able to reframe the remedy in light of the metaphoric exploration so far.

Finally, if the coachee states an outcome, you can focus attention on any part or all of it. The coachee may express different outcomes at different stages of the coaching session, and outcomes may change during the session. It's also possible that the coachee initially seems clear on what he or she wants but at some point changes his or her mind. Using a combination of the Focus-Expand-Actions model and the PRO strategies, you can switch your approach depending on where the coachee's attention is, moment by moment.

Above all, remember this is all explored from the 'insider' perspective. It is not about what you, the coach, see to be a problem, remedy or outcome. It is the coachee's interpretation of the situation as revealed through his or her own words and actual language.

If in doubt

- Go with the simplest, 'stupidest' question.
- Use the two basic questions: "Is there anything else about that?" And "What kind of" up to 80 per cent of the time.
- Ask for an outcome in light of whatever the coachee has just said, this can provide a firmer foothold on which way to go next.
- Focus on one part and drill down: find a symbol and explore it.

References

Grove, D. (1998) *Philosophy and Principles of Clean Language.* Available at: www.clean language.co.uk/articles/articles/38/1/Philosophy-and-Principles-of-Clean-Language/ Page1.html [Accessed 24/6/2015].

Grove, D. and Wilson, C. (2005) *Emergent Knowledge ΣK™ and Clean Coaching: New Theories of David Grove.* Available at: www.cleanlanguage.co.uk/articles/articles/47/1/ Emergent-Knowledge-and-Clean-Coaching/Page1.html [Accessed 9/8/2015].

Lawley, J. and Tompkins, P. (2006) *Coaching for PROs.* First published in the Fenman Ltd publication *Coach the Coach*, February 2006. Available at: www.cleanlanguage.co.uk/ articles/articles/31/1/Coaching-for-PROs/Page1.html [Accessed 10/8/2015].

Tompkins, P. and Lawley, J. (2009) Modelling: Top Down and Bottom Up. Available at: www.cleanlanguage.co.uk/articles/articles/240/1/Modelling-Top-down-and-Bottom-up-/Page1.html [Accessed 1/7/2015].

Chapter twelve

Clean beginnings and endings

Before the first session

Right from the first connection, you and your coachee are forming expectations and predictions about one another, mostly unconscious. Those early perceptions may be useful instant frames of reference, however they also predispose you towards certain assumption and actions. Your understanding of the coachee's requirements and possible ways forward is whittled down with every answer the person gives. The narrower this perspective becomes, the more certain you may feel about the 'right' course to take, however the scope of coaching needs constant review. Continually check out your perspectives and assumptions and ensure your coachee is able to do the same. The contracting stage of the coaching arrangement provides the ideal opportunity to do this.

Whether or not you follow any kind of formal contracting process, your pre-coaching discussions create a contract between you, setting out the scope of your relationship and what you can expect from each other.

Clean contracting

Before embarking on any coaching assignment, it is important to contract openly and clearly, establishing what both parties expect from the relationship. For organisational coaching/mentoring this needs to be a three-way agreement between coach, coachee and the client organisation. Contracts must be continually reviewed as expectations can quickly change once the coaching relationship is established. A contract should "state your intentions as a coach and remove any ambiguity, misunderstanding or misconception" (Hill, 2004:159). At a minimum, the contract should cover:

- The purpose of the coaching.
- How success will be measured.
- What each party expects from the working relationship, e.g. degrees of confidentiality, timekeeping, cancellation terms, broad approach, how difficulties will be managed.
- The scope of this arrangement, what's included and what's outside of it.

This is also the time to introduce Clean Coaching, explaining that it is a method to support a non-directive approach to coaching. You can seek agreement to use this form of coaching and set expectations about the coach's role in advice-giving.

You can also use a Clean approach in the way you go about contracting. This ensures you make no assumptions about what's being agreed, encouraging further questioning. Unlike a Clean Coaching session however, in the contracting stage it is important that you can also own and voice your expectations and limits openly and transparently so the coachee's expectations are set at the right level.

Explaining Clean

There are many ways to introduce and explain the concept of Clean. This book provides lots of examples. Explaining less rather than more tends to work best, as it can be hard to grasp without a direct experience. For example, you could say something along these lines:

> Clean Coaching is an approach that allows you to explore your own thoughts and feelings more deeply than you may usually have opportunity for. The reason it's called Clean is because the questions are wiped clear of the coach's own opinions and assumptions. We'll explore different ways of thinking about your situation and outcome, using imaginative metaphors and everyday items to help you think 'outside of the box'.
>
> The questions are designed to repeat back your exact words and help you reflect further on whatever you last said, bringing your conscious attention on automatic and unconscious ways of talking and thinking. They are structured in an unusual way to help you find unusual answers.
>
> We may use written words and drawings as props to move around during the session, helping you gain fresh perspectives. Some people find they get very immersed and engaged in their own thoughts, almost as if in a dream-like state of awareness. Most people find it to be a very pleasant experience. Would you be happy to try this approach during our coaching?

Pre-coaching questionnaire

Before a Clean Coaching session, I send out a short questionnaire to encourage the coachee to prepare for it. I make it clear that the questionnaire is optional, although stress its usefulness. If the coachee replies to me before the session, it can help me prepare and we may save time during the session as some background information has already been covered. The questionnaire could also be completed face-to-face at the start of the session. The key questions covered are:

- What is your goal?
- What needs to happen next?
- How long have you had that goal, and what was your goal before that goal?

- In this coaching session, what would you like to have happen?
- And how will you know that has happened?
- Is there anything else?

Is the coachee in the right space?

When meeting coachees face to face, it's easily apparent when the environment is unsuitable for coaching, for instance in an open-plan office with many distractions. But over the Internet or telephone, it may be harder to discern. If your coachee is able to connect with you from their own home, this personal space could be ideal for Clean Coaching. Sometimes the space the coachee chooses to be coached in somehow represents or even recreates the problem the person is having. The person who feels trapped and suffocated chooses a tiny office to work in, for instance. This can be useful as it helps recreate the conditions within which the coachee must find his or her way. But it can also be a distraction if it means there are interruptions or barriers to the coaching itself.

A pre-coaching discussion could include agreeing on a suitable place to hold sessions. For instance, it could mean gaining the coachee's commitment to meet somewhere away from his or her usual routine. I also advise coachees to come to their coaching session armed with paper and pens, as well as sticky tack or tape. If they come to my premises, I have various props available for such use.

Right at the start of each session, you can help get the environmental factors just right by asking:

- And are you in the right space?
- Where would you like to be?
- Where would you like me to be? (if face-to-face)

It can make a huge difference to coachees where in the room they are standing or sitting. These questions invite them to notice what kind of effect it might be having.

Clean set-up

Caitlin Walker of Training Attention (2014:30) developed a simple model for contracting that can be used at the outset of any new coaching assignment, also at the start of every single individual session.

- For this (coaching) to go exactly as you would like it to, it would be like what?
- For that to happen, you need to be like what?
- For this to be like (their words) and you to be like (their words) what support do you need?

After each of these key questions you can ask further non-directive, Clean questions to clarify further.

There are other Clean questions that are particularly useful right at the start and can form part of your contracting for each session. Two very useful, and more conversational, ice-breaking Cleanish questions I like to ask are:

- Where would you like to start?
- How would you like me to be?

Setting outcomes

For any kind of coaching conversation, a good place to start is to help the coachee develop a clear and comprehensive sense of what he or she wants. As we covered in Chapter eleven, Grove's 'gold standard' question for eliciting an outcome was:

"And what would you like to have happen?"

Like all Clean questions, the impact of this question is amplified by delivering it with a slow, steady cadence. The question is multi-layered, like many Clean questions. When delivered slowly with longer-than-expected pauses between the words, the listener gets three questions in one:

1   What would you like?

The first four words are a question in themselves, providing a very simple, open request for a preference.

2   To have . . . ?

Now the focus is ownership, 'have' is about things obtained; in your possession – either metaphorical or in reality.

3   Happen?

The final element changes the emphasis to focus on an event or occurrence *in time*. This time reference has an ambiguous feel to it, with past, present and future all possible options, creating a sense that the outcome may have already taken place.

Moreover, recursive questions like these with embedded questions within them act like 'garden path sentences' (see Chapter seven). The 'response inviting gaps' have the effect of creating multiple meanings in the mind of the coachee, opening up a multitude of possible answers. This encourages coachees to continue exploring their thoughts, involving further mental networks of ideas, concepts and memories, going beyond obvious replies and getting to new ways of thinking.

Try this question with your coachee at the start of a session, or whenever any kind of problem or block is mentioned. It is part of the PRO model (explained in Chapter eleven), providing a useful way to focus the coachee: at the start of the session and whenever the coachee appears to lack direction. Referring to any obstacle or block that the coachee mentions, you can ask what he or she would like to have happen instead of that obstacle or block. This helps the coachee decide on the immediate direction to take in light of any problem he or she has.

Stages of Clean Coaching

As covered in the previous chapter, all Clean Coaching follows the same three step 'Focusing-Expanding-Action' sequence. The Emergent Knowledge approach does so in this way:

1   *Clean Start:* Focusing attention is achieved through a spatial set up, establishing the goal (B), current reality (A) and the relationship between them (C).
2   *Clean Intervention:* A sequence of Clean Questions designed to help the coachee think outside the box, expand his or her attention and encourage insight.
3   *Clean Action Space:* To establish what needs to happen, how that can happen and when.

Step one: Clean Start

For the Clean Start, you can ask for the coachee's outcome using the question above, or in different ways, depending on the coachee and his or her circumstances. In his later years, Grove would often start by asking, "What is your mission in life?" expecting people to bring the big stuff to him! You may ask, "What's your biggest business aim for this year?" for instance if this is corporate executive coaching. The exact terminology of this question can be varied according to what feels appropriate.

Once you have asked for an outcome, follow up on the coachee's response with:

> "And can you write or draw your goal on a piece of paper, or choose an object to represent it?"

This excellent question helps the coachee focus attention and consider what the 'nub' of this goal is all about. You can even leave out the first step outcome questions and simply invite the coachee to represent the goal in this way. For instance, in order to preserve total confidentiality. It is possible, with this process, to complete the entire Clean Start without the coachee ever having to disclose exactly what the goal is, giving the coachee complete privacy and uncensored freedom of thought.

It is valuable for the coachee to make an external representation of the goal like this. By putting the goal on paper, the paper becomes a kind of receptacle to hold everything that the coachee knows about the goal. It can be viewed from different physical perspectives and the context around the goal can be explored. It can be explored dispassionately and objectively, disassociating from any difficult emotions attached to the goal, such as fear, doubt or embarrassment. On a practical level, it also becomes a very useful reference point for future sessions.

Often, people will summarise their aim with a single word or a phrase, or a simple drawing or symbol. Inviting people to choose an object can have the most interesting results. It is quite extraordinary how objects and materials that just happen to be around the coachee at the time end up taking on extra significance and meaning in this exercise. It can be especially useful if the coachee is within his or her own environment, with personal items all around. But, it can also be useful in other places as long as there are some bits and bobs around to select from. People are generally great at finding patterns of connection between their inner imagination and the outer world of reality around them.

For example, many years ago when I was first learning and practicing Clean Coaching, I was coached on losing weight. When my colleague asked what my goal was, I could just imagine a picture of me, all slim and svelte-like. When he asked me to write or draw my goal, I had no paper or pens to hand. We were working together in a quiet cafe and there was little around us, but there was a sugar bowl with a silver spoon within. As I heard the question I immediately saw the spoon as representing the slimmer me, there in the middle of all this sugary temptation. It was exactly the right representation and seemed an almost uncanny coincidence. David Grove referred to these kinds of synchronous objects as 'co-inspiring items' (see Chapter thirteen), recognising that people naturally use things from their external environment as symbols to represent and hold meaning from their inner world.

The process continues with a couple of unusual but effective questions:

- "Can you place the goal (or object) somewhere in the space around you, in a space that just seems (or feels) right?"
- "And can you place yourself in a space that seems (feels) right in relation to that goal?"

For people unfamiliar with Clean, these questions may sound strange. Some coachees may initially doubt that it matters where they put their paper. When this happens, I agree with them that it might not make any difference, however I encourage them to experiment and try out some different spaces to see what happens. Usually the coachee quickly gets a sense of the 'wrong' kind of space, discovering some places seem better than others.

Once the coachee has found a space for the goal, you can repeat the second question:

- "And can you place yourself in a space that seems (feels) right in relation to that goal?"

If the coachee found a place for the goal, this question should be easy to respond to. It may be the coachee has already positioned himself or herself in the right space as the coachee experimented moving the goal, but it is still worth checking this out.

Some coachees worry they might misunderstand you and ask for clarification, such as "Do you mean to represent where I am now or where I would like to be?" We want their current representation but however *they* would define it, so best to respond in a vague, encouraging fashion: "Whichever seems right and appropriate for you."

Once they have placed themselves and their goal, they have effectively created a life-sized, physical representation of their inner mental map of 'A to B' (as covered in the last chapter). This is the equivalent of the 'Focusing Attention' stage of Clean Language, and we want to encourage the coachees to reflect deeply about both A and B. We help them experience and embody these spaces by asking the following questions:

- "And is the distance right between you and [goal]?"
- "And are you in the right space?"
- "And is [goal] in the right space?"
- "And are you at the right height?"
- "Is [goal] at the right height?"
- "And are you facing the right direction?"
- "And is [goal] facing the right direction?"
- "And are you at the right angle?"
- "And is [goal] at the right angle?"
- "And are you in the right position?"
- "And is [goal] in the right position?"
- "Are you the right amount of distance from [goal]?"

You may ask all of the questions or just a selection, in any order or sequence. Grove recommended asking around six questions, continuing until the coachee seems certain of the positions and is answering with an unequivocal "yes." I have found that some people need more time to position the places, whereas others do so quickly. Everyone seems to make progress more quickly once they become familiar with the Clean Start process.

When the client seems sure he or she and the goal are in the right spaces, ask:

- "And what do you know now?"

Once the person has answered this question, if the coachee still sounds/appears to be reflective, wait a moment then ask a follow-up question:

- "And is there anything else that you know now?"

I have witnessed this remarkably simple process help coachees unravel a web of complexity into a much clearer form, summing up where they are now, where they want to be and what's in between. For some coachees, it is enough to reframe their perspective so that change inevitably follows. I've seen some people realise their expectations are too high, for instance. I've seen others realise, having initially hidden their goal from view, that in some way they are not facing up to it. How the coachee positions their goal in relation to themselves usually reveals something about that relationship. It is a metaphor created from the space around them. If the goal is a lofty one, it is placed high up. If it feels a long way off, people will place their goals as far away as they can, to reflect how it feels for them. For instance, one coachee placed his goal right at the bottom of his garden, before walking all the way back to the house to stand in the right space for him. Even then, the goal felt "too close." Others put their paper behind them, so they themselves point in an entirely different direction. Sometimes these positional metaphors offer hints of obvious next steps, but these may only become clear to the coachees as they progress through the rest of the Clean Coaching session.

Clean Start: variations and contingencies

Although the Clean Start is a simple process, following a predictable set of questions each time, people react to the questions in widely different ways. Normally people respond positively especially if they understand what to expect. You don't need to go into detail about why this approach works, just take a light, playful attitude and gain the coachee's permission to try something different that involves movement and space.

Deal with any unexpected responses as though they were acceptable and 'normal' and just keep going with the process. For instance, the coachee may choose a 'fixed' object to represent the goal, such as a fireplace. Or the coachee may be unwilling or unable to move much or at all. Trust that any such responses will be just right for this particular coachee and eventually lead to the appropriate positioning. Whatever happens, keep asking the questions. "No" is just as valid a response as "yes" or silent movement. The coachee may simply answer in the negative, or make small adjustments, or even decide to choose a different object.

Starting conditions

Why does this unusual process often result in such a profound shift in the coachees' understanding of themselves and their goal? David Grove was well read on systems thinking and sometimes made reference to terms used within this field. For instance, he referred to the 'starting conditions' of an exploration. This is a concept from 'Chaos Theory', from the study of dynamic systems. It refers to the high sensitivity an evolving dynamic system has to the initial prevailing factors involved at the start of its occurrence. Lorenz (1972) used the metaphor of the 'butterfly effect' to emphasise how the flutter of a butterfly's wings in one part of the world could set about a chain reaction that leads to a hurricane in another part of the world. In reality, this couldn't happen, however a more realistic example would be to think of repeatedly rolling a ball down the side of a mountain. Assuming you could fetch that same ball over and over again and repeat the exercise, it would be impossible to predict the route along which the ball would fall each time. Very slight variations in terms of how the ball was positioned would affect its trajectory, quickly leading to unpredictable knock-on effects. And so it is with our goals and problem solving, we set up the starting conditions as we create our mental spaces about them. We bias our future strategies from what we initially, and mostly unconsciously, select as the relevant information needed. Cognitive psychologist Stellan Ohlsson is a specialist in insight. He argues: "in a turbulent and unknown world, there is no guarantee that the biases laid down in the course of experience are predictive of which knowledge elements are most useful for solving a problem" (Ohlsson, 2011:104).

Clean Start focuses on the framework that the coachee originally created when he or she first discovered or decided on this particular goal. This is Grove's 'A to B' model which is like a 'small world' in networking terms, with a mass of connecting thoughts, memories and beliefs bundled together in a kind of system. Ohlsson (2011) describes the problem space as being like a soap bubble with certain rules of logic about the problem acting like a kind of membrane that holds everything together and keeps everything else you know outside of it. We bring a small selection of relevant data into our conscious working memory rather like a mental whiteboard to manipulate the pieces of the puzzle until we calculate the answer. This is great for linear problem solving, such as mathematical questions. However for non-linear problems with no standard answer, we need to enlist the help of our non-conscious mind, which is vast in comparison to our conscious limit.

The Clean Start's iterative questions challenge the coachee's 'small world' network of knowledge and push the mind to re-evaluate, stretching further to collect what else you also know, but did not initially believe was relevant. Much of this is tacit knowledge, not just factual data but senses and experiences, known through our bodies and by movement and positioning.

Step two: Clean Intervention

The middle of the Clean Coaching session offers wide scope on what to do and how to work with coachees. You can use Clean Language to explore their outcome and any metaphors used. Or you can use one of the many Emergent Knowledge processes developed by Grove for this purpose, for instance:

- Clean Space: Explore the spaces around the coachee:
    - "What kind of space is the space around that goal?"
    - "Is there another space that you can go to from that space there?"
    - "What do you know, from there?"

- Clean Hieroglyphics: Explore the words, letters and pictures on the paper:

    - "What do you notice about the words, letters or pictures on that paper?"
    - "What do you know about that word, *xxx*?"
    - "Is there anything else you know about that?"

In the following chapter, we'll look at specific processes and approaches for expanding attention, using Clean Language and Emergent Knowledge techniques.

Step three: conditions for change

Conditions for change and specific action steps often emerge naturally and easily during the coaching session. But in today's world, many people are overworked, under-resourced and overcommitted, with unrealistic expectations of their time and ability. In the face of overwhelm, learning to let go may be even more important than committing to completing three more tasks this week. With Clean Coaching, a different attitude is taken towards setting actions. They are considered completely optional and not always relevant.

Using traditional Clean Language, instead of actions that are owned by the coachee, at the end of a session we explore 'conditions for change' which does not presume that change comes from the coachee's actions. Conditions for change can include a wider scope of happenings that don't require the coachee to do anything. The questions always build on the coachee's stated possibilities.

There are two important Clean Language questions to use to explore conditions for change. They are:

"And *what needs to happen* for (possible change as described by client)?"
"*And can* (condition described by client) happen?"

With the first question, notice that it doesn't assign responsibility. The question focuses on *what* needs to change, not *who* needs to make the change happen. This depersonalisation helps avoid any blame frame kicking in for the coachee when responsibility is mentioned. This prevents people getting 'cold feet' if the finger is pointing at them.

Some people may start with a change that's really a series of events rather than one specific, tangible thing. The question can then be repeated in an iterative fashion to break the 'happening' down into smaller, clearer things. For instance:

"And what needs to happen for (your) confidence to grow, like that little green shoot?"
"It needs to be nurtured."
"And what needs to happen for it to be nurtured?"

The answer may reveal a series of steps or conditions:

"Well, it needs to keep warm, get watered, have lots of sunshine . . . and above all, believe in itself . . ."

This is an example of the typical kind of actions that emerge during a Clean Language session. Some of these relate to the metaphoric world, and may or may not have a direct translation into the real world, others seem more clearly to belong to the real world, such as 'believe in itself'. But the action is taken on by the metaphoric symbol, not the person being coached.

Rather than worry about interpretation or ownership, we can now break the answer down into clearer steps and for each, check whether it's possible. For this we use the second kind of question to explore conditions for change, this one focusing on possibility:

"And it needs to keep warm. *And can it keep warm?*"

You may notice that this 'possibility' question is a closed question. You are likely to get either a yes or a no to this. A definite 'yes' may require no further questioning. Part of what needs to happen for nurturing is already in place.

A 'no' or even a vaguer 'maybe' requires a follow up, using the 'conditions for change' question again:

"And *what needs to happen* for it to keep warm?"

The iterative cycle continues asking the same questions of each of the conditions mentioned, and any further conditions and/or possibilities that emerge. Rather like a series of Russian dolls, each broad condition for change may contain a number of sub-elements, with further sub-elements within.

What tends to happen with this approach is:

- Some things just happen, there and then in the session, within the person's mind's eye which creates some kind of perspective switch. The action required was a mental shift, the change has now happened.
- Some things turn into requirements needed – a checklist for success rather than an action plan. This may include what's needed from others, and less quantifiable requirements, such as time and patience, for example.
- Some things will become specific and clear actions. Often the same core actions will emerge from a number of different 'Russian dolls' increasing clarity, certainly and motivation to actually *do* something different and take *ownership* required for that.

So, in answer to "What needs to happen to keep warm?" you may hear:

"I just need to be visible, be out there."
"And can you be visible, be out there?"
"Perhaps."
"And what needs to happen to be visible out there?"
"I need to stop hiding."
"And can you stop hiding?"

"I think so."

"What needs to happen for you to stop hiding?"

"When I feel nervous, rather than retreat I need to take one step forward."

"And what kind of step could that step be?"

"Oh, any small action, to volunteer, to ask a question, to hold eye contact. All kinds of things."

"And when all kinds of things, and you need to take one step forward, *how will you know* which step to take?"

"I need to make a list of all the things I could do to stop hiding."

"And can you make that list?"

"*Yes!*"

At the end of this process we have a clear commitment from the coachee. Notice a further Clean Language question was added above: "How will you know?" This is a useful question for helping a person notice what sensations or internal signals he or she uses to track a certain change.

Sometimes, concepts or resources come up in the conditions for change stage that need further exploring. For instance, 'nurturing' is a big concept and could encompass many different actions from different sources. One approach here would be to define this further with the coachee by reverting to some more 'focusing attention' questions: "And what kind of nurturing is that nurturing?"

Clean Action Space

David Grove worked with Carol Wilson when developing his Emergent Knowledge techniques to develop a contrasting model for helping coachees to action plan. It can be used instead of the above approach or in conjunction with it. Like the Clean Start, it makes use of the physical space around the coachee.

This process works well especially if you have already been using space and movement within the coaching session. However, it can also work well if the coachee has been in the same place/position for the whole session. Inviting the coachee to find a fresh place helps him or her shift gear from exploring to committing. My regular coachees will often use this stage of the session as a prompt to get into an appropriate 'action planning' position, by a flip chart, computer or note pad for instance. In support of this, you may want to check whether they have a way of recording their actions, or you may be able to provide them with a recording or brief notes.

The questions are simple and again iterative:

"Is there a space that you could go to that knows about what actions you want to take?"

How can a space know something? With Grove's Clean Space processes, the external space around the coachee is treated as though it's a mirror of an internal space within the coachee. By inviting the possibility that space can contain different information, the coachee often discovers a more useful place in which to decide on actions. Once the coachee has found a space (or decided his or her current space is fine), you then ask:

"And what's the first action that you know you can do, from that space there?"

Once the action has been verbalised, you can fine tune it:

"And how will you do that?"

This excellent Clean question can also be used outside the specific Clean Action Space process to help take complex processes and break them down into specific actions. It works well repeated over and over as the coachee can get more and more specific. Notice with the Clean Action Space, responsibility for taking action is firmly placed with the coachee. This suits some coachees more than others, not everyone responds well to creating an action plan. This process is still gentle on commitment as it can be to used break large, vague strategic actions into specific and very doable chunks of activity. What that means is that any actions the coachee does agree to are very measurable, they have had to walk through the tangible details of action and in doing so, they are much more likely to follow through.

For example, they may answer the question with: "I'm going to take better care of myself" for instance, to which you can repeat the questions again:

"And how will you do *that*?" And so on.

The next question to clarify each doable action step is:

"And *when* will you do that?"

You can then repeat for all the doable action steps highlighted, before returning to the main question sequence:

"And what is the second action that you know you can do?"

And so on through the same sequence as above.

You can continue asking for further actions until the coachee runs out of replies. Generally I find three strategies (with all the subsequent action steps and dates) are sufficient. After a while actions steps begin to duplicate themselves as they crop up as part of more than one strategy.

In summary, this chapter has highlighted in detail the most effective ways to begin a Clean Coaching assignment as well as each individual session. It's also covered detailed steps for ending a session with a clear process for understanding the conditions for change and/or action steps required. Below are two simple summaries of the Clean processes for starting and ending a session. You can practice these in any kind of coaching session, or indeed any meeting or conversation where goals need to be set at the start, and change conditions/actions at the end.

The next chapter explores in depth the middle part of the session, how to expand the coachee's attention and help him or her reframe circumstances to discover insights and new possibilities.

Practical exercise 1

Making a Clean Start (Summary)

- Write or draw your goal on a piece of paper, or choose an object to represent your goal.
- Place it in a space that feels right.
- Now place yourself in a space that feels right in relation to your goal.
- And are you in the right space? Height? Distance? Direction? Angle? Position?
- And is the goal in the right space? Height? Distance? Direction? Angle? Position?
- And what do you know now?

Practical exercise 2

Clean Action Space

Is there a space that you could go to that knows what actions you know you can take?

1   And what's the first action that you know you can do, from that space there?

- And how will you do that?
  - And how will you do *that?*
    - And how will you do *that?*

-
- And when will you do (all) that?

2   And what's the second action that you know you can do?

- •

  - •   And how will you do that?

    - –   And how will you do *that?*

      - ◦   And how will you do *that?*

      - ◦

  - •   And when will you do that?

3   And is there a third action that you know you can do?

References

Hill, P. (2004) *Concepts of Coaching: A Guide for Managers.* London: Institute of Leadership and Management.

Lorenz, E. N. (1972) *Predictability: Does the Flap of a Butterflies Wings in Brazil Set Off a Tornado in Texas?*, AAAS 139th meeting. Available at: http://eaps4.mit.edu/research/Lorenz/Butterfly_1972.pdf [Accessed 31/8/2015].

Ohlsson, S. (2011) *Deep Learning: How the Mind Overrides Experience.* New York: Cambridge University Press.

Walker, C. (2014) *From Contempt to Curiosity – Creating the Conditions for Groups to Collaborate.* Fareham: Clean Publishing.

Advanced applications and transcripts

Chapter thirteen

Expanding attention Cleanly

Clean Language, Clean Space and Emergent Knowledge

This chapter reveals ways to help expand your coachee's attention beyond what he or she already knows and into new ways of thinking and experiencing the world. This covers expanding attention with Clean Language questions, following on from the 'focusing attention' questions covered earlier. We also cover the concept of 'Clean Space' and how this became the springboard for Grove's development of a brand-new set of Clean Questions known as 'Emergent Knowledge'.

Clean Language questions

Building on the basic 'focusing attention' questions covered in Chapter eight, there now follows more advanced Clean Language questions to help your coachee expand exploration of his or her metaphors and symbols. As summarised in Chapter eleven, specifically these questions serve to take the coachee's experience of things either forwards or backwards in time, to explore the origins of a symbol and/or explore the relationships between different parts of the coachee's metaphoric system.

The questions are:

- *To go forwards or backwards in time:*
    - "And when (coachee's words), then what happens? "(or "What happen next?")
    - "And what happens just before (coachee's words)?"

- *To go back to the source:*
    - "And where could (coachee's words) have come from?"

- *To explore relationships:*
    - "And is there a relationship between (coachee's words) and (coachee's words)?"
    - "And when (coachee's words) happens, what happens to (coachee's words)?"

Forwards or backwards in time

Metaphors often tell a story and symbols may evolve over time. Rather than fixed, still pictures, metaphors are more like movies. To help the coachee notice what happens next in the time sequence, we use a question that you have already been introduced to, as part of the PRO model covered in Chapter eleven:

"Then what happens?"

The same question can also be phrased:

"What happens next?"

This question helps the coachee work out the next step in any sequence of events, providing the continuation of the story and the consequences of any action or change. New aspects or symbols can come to light as you track forwards in time. The question works best when it flows from the coachee's own exploration, reflecting back any specific and distinct action, event or happening that the coachee has mentioned, linking with 'And . . .'

Let's return to an earlier example of a coachee's metaphor of the 'rollercoaster' representing her work life. Assuming the coachee has just been musing on what it would be like if the rollercoaster was to grow wings, for example, you could ask:

"And when that rollercoaster grows wings, *then what happens*?"

The phrasing of time sequence questions continually keeps the imagined landscape as 'current time' in the coachee's experience, rather than in the past or future. The questions are all phrased in the present tense, such as "Then what *happens*?" not "Then what *happened*?" or "What could *happen* next?"

The coachee may discover a positive outcome or consequence. Or another aspect of her metaphoric landscape could change as a result:

"Then I can fly into the blue sky. I have complete freedom to do as I want. Now I can see the rollercoaster has a steering wheel so I can change direction."

You could now explore 'blue sky', 'freedom' and/or 'steering wheel', going back to focusing attention questions. You could also continue to move things forward:

"And when you can change direction, *then what happens*?"

You can quickly help the coachee to reach a very different experience by continually moving forwards in time. However, usually the coachee needs to focus attention on each time sequence for a while until it becomes vivid enough for the coachee to take another step forwards in his or her imaginative inner world.

Going forwards in time may reveal binding patterns of thought and behaviour, where the coachee is held stuck in a habitual, circular system that keeps repeating itself. In these cases, asking "Then what happens" could result in the coachee returning to a previously mentioned obstacle or back to where he or she started.

Going backwards in time can also be a very useful exploration. For instance, you might decide to ask:

"And what happens *just before* that rollercoaster grows wings?"

These questions invite people to think of the flow of time in an unusual way. Keeping the question phrased in the present tense brings whatever the coachee is experiencing or thinking about into the here and now, despite going 'before' it. For example, the wings growing are part of an imagined future, therefore any exploration of what happens before they grow could still be future time. This Clean Language question invites a kind of mental time-travel which often leads to the realisation of a previously missing or unnoticed requirement for change. The coachee may discover the next steps required, despite seemingly looking into the past. This useful facet of Clean Language questions is similar to the 'miracle question' used so successfully by therapist Milton Erickson (de Shazer, 1985). He would suggest clients imagines themselves in a future when they have achieved their outcome, then to imagine thinking back in time to remember what it was they did to get there.

Sometimes once an outcome has been fully explored as a metaphor and insights gained from this experience, you can help coachees to work out how they get to the outcome by asking them:

"And what happens *just before* (some useful thing within the metaphor occurs)?"

The time sequence questions help the coachee to see a chain of events as a sequence, leading to an understanding of key actions required. Like pressing the fast forward button and then rewinding, each time you pause the picture it can reveal a moment in time not seen before. It can help the coachee get a shift in perspective, noticing some small piece of the jigsaw not noticed before. With Clean Language the coachee gets to slow down his or her experience and notice what might usually happen in the blink of an eye, capturing fleeting ideas and thoughts not usually available for conscious examination. Going back and forth in time can also help a coachee see things from a wider perspective over a longer time period and beyond any immediate cause and effect.

Getting to the source

This question encourages the coachee's attention to go right back to the beginning, to the first step or origin of a particular event or situation. The question is phrased:

"And where could (coachee's own words) have come from?"

This question is especially valuable when a potential resource has already been explored in depth using the 'focusing attention' questions to develop a clear symbol. The following question sequence provides an example:

> "And when confidence is warm and red, and deep in your heart, that's a warm . . . red . . . confidence like . . . what?"
> "It's like a burning ember."
> "And is there anything else about that burning ember, that's deep in your heart?"
> "As it glows, I feel the confidence radiating about my body."
> "And feel the confidence radiating as that burning ember glows . . . and when that confidence is radiating like a burning ember, *where could that burning ember have come from?*"

The question, asked of a powerful resource, tends to take people to an even more vivid, powerful origin. For instance, the burning ember could come from a raging fire or spring from a powerful erupting volcano. Once this new symbol has been identified, you can begin focusing attention on that (using all the questions covered in Chapter eight) and the coachee is likely to find himself or herself connected to an even greater sense of power and positivity.

Notice that preceding this question, it's useful to carefully reflect back a selection of the coachee's exact words that have led up to this powerful symbol. See the three-part syntax described in Chapter seven, for more information on how to do this.

The source question can take people into unexpected directions, they could reply:

- "From the love of my children" – referring to an abstract concept or quality.
- "From Africa" – referring to a location, real or imagined.
- "From a magic fireplace" – referring to another symbol within their metaphoric landscape, often on a different 'page' or mental space to what was previously explored.
- "From my Grandmother" – taking the origin thread back to its genealogical roots.

It is a potent question and works best when used sparingly and never rushed into. Take your time to first focus attention on an appropriate resource, waiting until the coachee is engaged with the inner symbolic experience. The source question can prompt a profound effect in the coachee; a stirring of a deeper sense of awe or inspiration. Some may cry, laugh or have some huge shift in physical energy. If this happens, just stay Clean. In the unlikely event that the coachee experiences something unpleasant or unhelpful, and says he or she doesn't like or doesn't want something about this experience, use the PRO model and ask, "And when you don't want (coachee's words) what would you like to have happen?"

But don't assume tears are negative or unwelcome. If the coachee is quietly contemplative, just give the person space. Tears can be positive and catalytic, providing a release in tension. Be patient, and when the coachee is ready, continue with the session. There is no need to ask for further explanation or offer extra reassurance or comfort.

You can use the source question to go back to the root of the coachee's stated problem, however it is not generally advisable. For coaching work, it is more appropriate and effective to focus your coachee's attention towards the outcome and/or the emerging solution he or she needs for that outcome to happen. Focusing on the problem could trigger unhelpful memories, which may not help the coachee feel resourceful, instead accentuating unpleasant feelings. Although Grove developed Clean Language to help people let go of past trauma, coaches must work within the scope of their experience and expertise, honouring their contract. If you use this question only to explore metaphoric symbols rather than real-world happenings or abstract concepts, the coachee remains safe to explore his or her imagination without needing to confront painful memories.

Relationship questions

As a person describes the attributes of his or her metaphor, it often develops a clearer form within a wider perspective. The metaphor will likely contain a number of symbols, each having some kind of connection or relationship with each other. Clean Language relationship questions help the coachee notice and explore what's going on between the symbols the coachee has been focusing on. These questions help the coachee see the systems that hold the patterns of thought together.

The first relationship question is:

"Is there a relationship between (coachee symbol A) and (coachee symbol B)?"

It's a closed question, allowing for the coachee to say "no," if they cannot discern any relationship. This is a good failsafe as it is a challenge to be completely Clean when asking this question. Your likely reason for choosing to ask about two particular symbols in this way is because you think there *is* some kind of relationship or connection. As well as allowing for a negative response, you can also take care to ask a number of relationship questions during a Clean Coaching session, paying equal attention to a range of symbols and their possible relationships with each other.

Note that the question is always directed at just *two* symbols. Sometimes, new Clean Coaches enthusiastically try to lump more pieces together in one go asking something like:

"And *is there a relationship* between that burning ember, the blue sky, and the rollercoaster wings?"

If your question includes too many elements, it's harder for the coachee to find an answer. The same is true if the question is too long-winded and complex:

> "And is there a relationship between that confidence like a burning ember that's glowing and deep in your heart and the rollercoaster's wings that it has grown and flown in the blue sky?"

The brain cannot easily compute all the elements of this question. It's difficult to know what comparisons are being asked for. Relationship questions work best when they are short and clear:

> "And is there a relationship between that burning ember and those rollercoaster wings?"

You can also use this relationship question to explore real-world conceptual experience too:

> "Is there a relationship between your confidence and the current workplace?"

This kind of question may simply clarify the obvious 'yes there is a relationship' response, which can be followed up with a focusing attention question:

> "And what kind of relationship is that relationship?"

But, when your attention is not focusing on metaphors or symbols, it's more likely that your own personal biases will steer this question. Remember to ask about a range of different potential relationships, not just those obvious to you.

Another useful relationship question is:

> "When (coachee's words) happens, what happens to (coachee's words)?"

This is very useful in the later stages of a Clean Coaching session, as the coachee begins to explore and notice potential changes and actions. You can use this question to help coachees discover how a change in one part of the metaphoric landscape impacts on other parts.

You can also use this question to relate changes back to the initial, conceptually stated outcome:

> "And when that rollercoaster grow wings and you can fly in the blue sky, *what happens to* being more confident in team meetings?"

Being selective

Use expanding attention questions sparingly. Because expanding attention tend to point beyond what the coachee has already noticed, these questions tend to be less Clean than the basic, focusing attention questions.

Each time you ask an expanding attention question, follow up with more focusing attention questions. As new pieces of the metaphoric landscape come into focus, you can help them become more clearly established by asking more "What kind of" and "Is there anything else about" questions, as well as locating any feelings, images, symbols or senses by asking "Whereabouts is that (coachee word)?". The "shape or size" and "That's like what" questions may be useful too, if any symbol is not clearly defined or a new metaphor is emerging.

Concepts of 'Clean Space'

Grove coined 'Clean Space' for Clean techniques that involve inviting the coachee to physically move from one space to another, so the coachee can explore his or her experience from different places and perspectives. It makes use of the space around the coachee as a universal metaphor, used to physically map out internal thoughts. In the last chapter we highlighted how to begin a Clean Coaching session using the 'Clean Start' process, and how to end with 'Clean Action Space'. In the middle section of a coaching session, as well as using Clean Language, you can help expand the coachee's attention by facilitating the coachee to explore the space around him or her. There are a range of specific Emergent Knowledge interventions to choose from, some of which are covered in this book. More can be experienced and learnt through specialist training.[1]

Space is literally all around us. It's everywhere, although people don't view it as one single feature of the world. Different areas of space have different qualities, from the big black outer space of the universe to the space between your toes. Space is what lies between the material stuff of the world, shaped by what's placed around it. Space has physical qualities, but we have perceptual space too: our subjective experience of a certain space around us. Empty space is an easy target for our imagination to project what's happening within us into what's around us and people do this naturally all the time. Perceptual space includes a blending of both the *physical* space a person directly perceives, immediately around the person, plus *metaphoric* space which includes imaginings beyond any direct experience. This is the true location of our 'mind's eye': a mental 3D cinema screen that exists in all 360 degrees around us, not locked within our physical brains.

Space is the perfect medium for Clean Coaching as people use it in many imaginative ways. It is the universal metaphor that crops up in nearly all conversations about goals and outcomes. We place things in imaginary spaces in our mind's eye, but that space is easily superimposed onto the physical space around us. Our non-physical thoughts are not contained within the physical boundaries of our brains, or even our bodies. All our experience – both internal imaginings and external reality – takes place in our own personal theatre of the world. We use the objects and spaces around us as containers for our thoughts: anchors that trigger certain ideas, memories and emotions. Space is so ubiquitous in language that some psychologists (Pinker, 2007) suggest it's the very medium through which conscious reflective thought can happen. Where we are in space has a fundamental effect on our minds. For example, *Context-dependent memory* (Godden and Baddeley, 1975) is a widely researched effect that demonstrates how people remember more about past events when they are in the same/similar environment to where the events were originally experienced.

The relationship between our imaginative thoughts and our physical environment may seem tenuous, however they are closely connected. Humanity has evolved to have senses that uniquely correspond to our environment. We use mostly the same neuronal configurations for conceiving inner imaginings as we do for perceiving external reality. The brain evolved to enable voluntary movement through space. It is embedded within a body, which is embedded within a wider environment that supports the conditions for life. This embodiment has inevitably shaped the brain's capabilities, with the external environment providing the raw ingredients for thought, as well as the purpose for it. We are constantly interacting with our physical environment: when we use a tool like a pen or a spoon, it's hard to separate where we end and the external world begins.

Clean Language enables clients to access inner wisdom through metaphor. Clean Space does the same through literally moving people around the room. People shape their perceptual space in ways that mirror the way they organise their internal experience. Lawley (2006) suggests that "Our hopes, fears, desires and decisions depend on the architecture of our mind-body space" and goes on explain:

> Just as the invention of the arch, steel girders and concrete changed the kind of buildings we could build, so changes to the way we construct our perceptual space can have profound implications for the way we live our life . . ."

Using space in coaching

Grove (2003) explained how people store their knowledge in various pockets of spaces around them. People can access and 'download' these pockets of knowledge much like your computer can download information by connecting to a certain web address. Even by taking one step forwards, or back, or turning around on the spot, our perspective can be sufficiently refreshed to illuminate new information. He said that when coachees move from one space to another they "leave behind part of themselves in the previous space." Their current mental space stays anchored to this spot, and moving on helps remove them from any emotional connection to information that surfaced there. From any new position, the previous space can be explored dispassionately and things seen differently, with access to a new set of information.

He argued: "It can be very difficult to move someone to another space emotionally, but actually making the person move to a different position in the room can achieve the same objective, sometimes quicker or easier" (Grove, 2003). For this reason, he recommended that even if you are not overtly using space in your coaching work, you should encourage the coachee to sit somewhere different for each session. Otherwise "their problems will always be configured in the same way."

Grove developed Clean Space after noticing how his clients would use their eyes in a session, literally gazing around the room searching for their answers (Grove, 2004). He tried asking questions directly addressed to the space where the answer was coming from instead of to the person. A single sheet of A4 paper was seldom big enough to contain the client's complete metaphoric landscape. So, he would have the client place more and more paper around the original sheet, until he decided to use the room itself as the map. Then he could ask the person to go and stand in the space where a particular answer seemed to be coming from. Problems seemed to unravel as a person moved from one position to the next, like untying a knot.

During a coaching session, particular spaces can take on special significance over and above any other. Some spaces become imbued with energy and have a symbolic resonance that's beyond our usual, everyday experience. Grove (1998) referred to these kinds of spaces as being *psychoactive* and when people physically step into them it's like plugging into an energy source and getting a surge of data. But we seldom notice our perceptual space, distracted by others who occupy our space and engage us in their world, through their physical gestures and movements as much as their spoken language.

Our role as a Clean Coach is to metaphorically and physically stay out of our coachee's way. Lawley (2006) described Clean facilitation as creating the conditions to maintain the coachee's psychoactive space and allow it to emerge. Rather than standing in the shoes of the coachee, the coach's default position is somewhere outside the coachee's perceptual space. This changes moment by moment as the extent of the client's imaginary space is also dynamic and evolving. The coach should occupy a physical position not directly in front of the coachee's line of sight, if possible, and avoid making any distracting gestures or movements.

The opening up of new knowledge can happen with a shift in body posture as well moving to a new physical location. It could come simply from facing a different direction. Coachees can be encouraged to experiment and 'feel their way' (Grove, 2004) into the right space. The body knows what the conscious mind may not acknowledge, like a kind of blindsight: the hand can point to the source of light the mind cannot see.

Co-inspiring items

Grove advocated the use of "Co-inspiring items" that tend to crop up during a Clean session. These were the things that 'just happened to be' in the space around the coachee at the time of the session, like the broken pen not yet thrown away, or last year's diary brought along by mistake. Sometimes a coachee notices these items during a session and becomes aware of their deeper significance to the current situation and goal. The object becomes psychoactive and reflects further information for the coachee. The coachee's inner world is mapped onto his or her external space so it's not surprising that sometimes extraordinary coincidences and synchronous happenings seem to occur. It is as if objects within the space were becoming part of the coaching process. For example, I worked with a coachee once who chose to represent her goal during our session as a pine cone she had found in the garden. The structured shape and pattern on the pine cone made it an appropriate metaphor for the orderly result she was after. She placed the pine cone on the floor to explore it more thoroughly. Very randomly, a cat suddenly jumped in through an open window, ran up to the pine cone and picked it up in its mouth before charging off just as suddenly, taking the pine cone with it!

As the facilitator, I was taken aback and unsure how best to respond to such an odd happening. I took a deep breath and carried on with the Clean Coaching process, asking the coachee what it was she knew now, about her goal. She also seemed surprised by what had happened, but said:

> "Actually it's very typical of what happens to me, at work and in my life in general. I take ages planning a very structured goal, so I know exactly what to do to achieve it. And then someone – or something – comes along out of nowhere and changes the goal posts! It's like they 'steal' my outcome, just like that cat. My goal no longer belongs to me, in fact it feels so distant it just disappears off my radar . . ."

What followed was an 'ah ha' moment, the coachee began to see a pattern in how things had been happening and how she needed to address the wider environment and tackle things differently if she wanted to achieve a personal outcome.

Thanks to the cat, my coachee gained insight that she may otherwise had not. This cat was a great example of a 'co-inspiring item' – although usually they are not quite so animated! But things do have a tendency to come alive during Clean Space, often with the coachee imagining certain objects as capable of intention and emotion. This projected personification can be very helpful in a session by providing another source of knowledge.

Clean Networks

In Chapter eleven we looked at the 'A to B' model of change, suggesting that with Clean Coaching, we take a very different, often circuitous route to the coachee's solution, rather than a straight line between A and B. Clean Networks is a process that enables coachees to map out their imaginary mental spaces into real locations in the physical space around them. The coachees' internal perspective is brought out into the open, so they can experience it viscerally and move around within it.

Following the Clean Start process (Chapter twelve), this process continues the exploration of spaces around the coachee by asking:

1   "And is there another space that you could go to, from that space there?"

Earlier versions of Clean Space questions were more directive, asking the coachee to go to a space that knows something about (coachee's words). But as Clean Space evolved into Emergent Knowledge, Grove replaced the command with a gentler, ambiguous invitation.

Once the coachee has found a new space, you can ask:

2   "And what do you know, from that space, there?"

Depending on how the coachee responds, you could choose to follow up with a further:

3   "And is there anything else you know, from that space there?"

Once the coachee has finished responding, you can repeat the cycle:

4   "And is there another space that you could go to, from that space there?"

This question cycle can be repeated multiple times, with the coachee trying out new locations and taking on different perspectives with each question cycle. The process often becomes iterative, in that the knowledge gleaned from one space informs the coachee where to go next. Invite the coachee to find around six further spaces beyond where he or she ended up with the Clean Start. You can judge the exact number of moves according to the coachee's ease of finding new spaces and whether the person has reached a new understanding.

Over time, Grove noticed that there was a predictable pattern to how information seemed to emerge for the coachee, with each cycle of questions producing a different layer of information that built towards a totally new understanding. He discovered that on average, people required six levels or steps of exploration between their current position and reaching insight. He called this the *"Six Steps to Freedom"* which was a major premise to his 'Emergent Knowledge' work. His concept was based around networking theory and the 'small world' phenomenon, whereby any two points on a network, however complex, can be connected by no more than six intervening 'nodes' in between. Shortcuts can be found by making links between nodes that extend beyond typical local clusters within the network, and Grove tested this notion by treating the mind like a complex network, with the spaces of A and B as points within it.

Once the coachee has finished exploring the spaces, you can bring the exercise to a close by asking:

"And can you now return to the space where you started?"

The coachee might return to the exact same spot where the exercise began, or somewhere slightly different, not quite remembering the original spot. Wherever the person goes is fine. You can bring the process to a conclusion with:

"And what do you know now?"
You can follow up if necessary with:
"And is there anything else that you know now?"

You can add two further follow-up questions to help clarify any change that has occurred:

"And is there a difference between what you know now, and what you knew at the start?"
And/or:
"And what difference does knowing that make?"

When the coachee doesn't move

You can set up the coachee's expectations by explaining at the outset that this technique involves the coachee physically moving around the room. You can encourage the coachee to plan accordingly prior to the session by inviting him or her to choose a space in which he or she can move around freely.

If the person still fails to move or answers your invitation with "no," ask questions 2 and 3 anyway. Sometimes the barest twitch can bring about a change in perspective, or even knowing that the space has not changed somehow produces another layer of understanding. You can also encourage a more intuitive move by asking:

"Is there a space that would like you to go to it?"

Clean Networks moving B

At times you may decide to direct your questions to the goal rather than the person. Although this may seem strange at first, you are inviting the person to gather information from a place outside of himself or herself. This can be very powerful, especially with overly logical and cerebral coachees, as this will encourage them to access thoughts from a more intuitive source.

David's theory was that if your goal was placed somewhere 'over there', you have probably disassociated part of yourself over there too. By asking the question of the goal, the clients will be re-connecting with that separated part of themselves and in doing so, they have access to previously obscured information and understanding.

This exercise normally works best once you have already followed the basic Clean Networks process (as above) with your coachee. This provides time for the space to become psychoactive and the items within it to begin taking on an imagined life of their own. You'll notice when this happens because the coachee begins saying things like "My goal doesn't like being in the dark over there" or "The goal is laughing at me now." This kind of mental 'ventriloquism' indicates that the coachee has imbued the paper or object with some kind of will, indicating that this Clean Networks variation could be useful.

The questions are the same as Clean Networks, except that you replace the word 'you' with the coachee's goal (using the words the coachee used to describe it).

For example:

1   "And is there another space that (goal) could go to from that space there?"
2   "And what does (goal) know from that space there?"
3   "And is there anything else that (goal) knows from that space there?"

After six moves, have the coachee return the goal to the first position and ask:

"And what do *you* know now?"

These two Clean Interventions can be used repeatedly. As the goal evolves you may need to do a new Clean Start, which is likely to take less time as the coachee becomes familiar with the steps.

Grove (Wilson and Dunbar, 2008) explained that to emerge knowledge, you need to be an 'equal opportunity' questioner as there is often more interesting information contained in the space of B than in A. He referred to Einstein's dictums:

1   A problem cannot be solved at the same level in which it is defined. The order or level at which the problem was defined lies in the space of an A B C small world. When using Clean Networks, the physical movement in space corresponds with moving information outside of the problem domain.
2   A quantum physics problem called 'entanglement'. If you have 2 photons of light together and you separate them at a distance, what happens to one also happens to the other. Einstein labelled this 'spooky action at a distance'. This is what happens when the client is at A and moves B, as the goal is moved around and changes its space it is affecting the client powerfully, both psychologically and physiologically at the same time.

In Chapter fourteen, you can read a transcript on coaching for confidence which uses the Clean Networks moving B process.

Clean Spinning

Grove capitalised on the instinctive, natural ways that people use to move their bodies in space to gain different perspectives, and this included turning around in the same spot. He would invite them to revolve slowly in a 360-degree circle, and share what they know from various directions that they stop in. Lawley (2006) saw this have a profound effect on some clients, as I myself have witnessed on many occasions. By changing the body's external orientation to the physical environment, so the internal landscape shifted. Lawley (2006) believes "This works because they are not just moving through physical space but turning through a previously self-generated psychoactive landscape."

The purpose of this exercise is to emerge knowledge which may be uncovered when the client faces different directions. It begins with a Clean Start and (optionally) the Clean Networks processes.

1   Ease into the Clean Spinning process by exploring the space the coachee is currently in:

"And what do you know from that space there?"

2   Then ask one or two Clean Language focusing attention questions:

"What kind of (coachee's words) is that (coachee's words)?"
"Is there anything else about that (coachee's words)?"

3   Invite the coachee to spin slowly around in the space he or she is standing in:

"And turn around now, in whichever direction feels right, and keep turning until it feels right to stop."

4   When the coachee stops, ask:

"And what do you know from that direction?"

5   Repeat the invitation and follow-up question around six times, as with Clean Networks.

As the process continues you may shorten the invitation and question if it feels appropriate:

"And keep turning, again. Until you stop. And what do you know from that . . . direction . . . there?"

This process could combine both Emergent Knowledge and Clean Language questions. As the person explores his or her external surroundings, tangible objects often become metaphors for his or her inner reality. As metaphors emerge, you can explore them with two or three focusing attention questions.

"And is there anything else about that green forest?"
"And what kind of safe is that safe, in that green forest?"

Then move on by turning the client again. Grove suggested asking just two to three Clean Language questions each time, maintaining a 'light touch' to prevent the coachee from becoming adhered to one particular direction or another. Once the coachee has made around six turns, ask the coachee to return to the first direction he or she was in and ask:

"And what do you know about that . . . [goal] . . . now?"
"And is there anything else you know about that [goal]?"

Conclusion

This chapter has provided a wealth of possibilities in terms of expanding attention with Grove's original Clean Language questions as well as the innovative approaches he created later on. Each can be used in a flexible way, creating an endless range of questions and approaches for encouraging people to find creative ways to learn, grow and change for the better. They are simple questions that can bring instant, fascinating results. However, it takes considerable practice to become skilful using the questions. To develop competency and confidence in these approaches, I advise that you work with another like-minded coach and practice together.

Note

1 See www.cleancoaching.com for more details of training content.

References

De Shazer, S. (1985) *Keys to Solutions in Brief Therapy*. New York: Norton.

Godden, D. and Baddeley, A. (1975) Context-dependent memory in two natural environments: On land and under water. *British Journal of Psychology*, 66, 325–331.

Grove, D. (1998) *Problem Domains and Non-Traumatic Resolution Through Metaphor Therapy* (edited by Rob McGavock). Available at: www.cleanlanguage.co.uk/articles/articles/4/1/Problem-Domains-And-Non-Traumatic-Resolution-Through-Metaphor-Therapy/Page1.html [Accessed 30/9/2015].

Grove, D. (2003) *David Grove: Summary of Ideas – As of 2003*. Available at: www.cleanlanguage.co.uk/articles/articles/278/1/David-Grove-summary-of-ideas-as-of-2003/Page1.html [Accessed 30/9/2015].

Grove, D. (2004) *History of David Grove's Work: 1980–2004* (compiled by Jenny Mote). Available at: www.cleanlanguage.co.uk/articles/articles/279/1/David-Grove-history-of-work-1980–2004/Page1.html [Accessed 2/8/2015].

Lawley, J. (2006) *When Where Matters – How Psychoactive Space is Created and Utilised, the Model, British Board of NLP*. Available at: www.cleanlanguage.co.uk/articles/articles/29/1/When-Where-Matters-How-psychoactive-space-is-created-and-utilised/Page1.html [Accessed 2/4/2015].

Pinker, S. (2007) *The Stuff of Thought: Language as a Window into Human Nature*. New York: Viking.

Wilson, C. and Dunbar, A. (2008) *Clean Coaching with Emergent Knowledge* (training course notes).

Chapter fourteen

Changing habits and building confidence

The nature of change

We are all changing constantly. We grow older and hopefully, wiser. Physically, the cells in our body are on average replaced every seven to ten years, although the blueprint remains the same. And brain cells last us our whole lives, explaining why thought and behavioural patterns are remarkably resilient to change. People tend to resist change because we are creatures of habit. Once thoughts and behavioural patterns are formed they become the automatic path of least resistance for the future. The well-known phrase 'Neurons that fire together get wired together' (Ghosh and Shatz, 1992) emphasises how once new pathways of thought become well-beaten, it's hard for them to re-route.

Then why and how do people ever change at all? Ohlsson (2011) suggests the real mystery is how it is that people can sometimes break through learnt patterns, but not always. What is the difference that creates the difference? It is not the past that keeps people from changing, but the way their perceptions are presently organised (Lawley and Tompkins, 2000:36). Prochaska et al.'s (1994) well-researched 'Transtheoretical' model of change highlights the steps of intentional human change. It confirms the importance of reflective contemplation in bringing about a new awareness prior to any action, and also how preparation can increase motivation for doing something different. Once again, change is seen as stemming from inside an individual's imagination, and Clean Coaching provides a practical and worthy process for facilitating such change, aligned with this model.

From a systems thinking perspective, Lawley and Tompkins say "Living systems always change – even if just to stay the same" (2000:36). Our bodies exist in a state of dynamic stability known as 'homeostasis', with local mini-changes maintaining the overall status quo. Our minds do the same kind of thing: we have mental structures in place that help us to stick with the same beliefs and values. Any self-organising system will maintain patterns that have so far preserved survival.

Lawley and Tompkins use the term 'bind' to describe a pattern of self-preservation, which the coachee describes as inappropriate or unhelpful and he or she have been unable to change (2000:36). This pattern could look like an inner conflict, a dilemma, an impasse or even a paradox. For the coachee, simply recognising the binding nature of the pattern in itself can create conditions for change. Change can also happen when a tipping point or threshold is reached within a person's awareness. Grove's 'Six Steps to Freedom' notion (see Chapter thirteen) highlights how people tend to go through six key stages of change which you can track during the Clean Coaching process:

Step 1: *"Proclaim."* The coachee is aware of the situation and talks about what he or she already knows.

Step 2: *"Explain."* The coachee can step back and take a wider perspective, giving examples and considering consequences.

Step 3: *"Reinforce."* The coachee continues to justify what he or she already knows, going into further detail. The coachee begins to get overloaded with information and may get irritated, confused or frustrated.

Step 4: *"The Wobble."* The coachee's system reaches a threshold. The sum of all the coachee knows is still not enough to find a solution. The coachee begins to relax his or her perspective and loses certainty about how things appear to be. The coachee often goes silent for a while and then a different kind of understanding begins to emerge.

Step 5: *"Crash and Burn."* Here the client is likely to experience the 'old way' of looking at the situation dissolving or disintegrating. He or she may feel strong emotions and energy at this point as any stuck patterns are released.

Step 6: *"Out of the Ashes."* This is where something completely new emerges. This is often simpler in form but provides a different, wiser level of understanding. It still contains all the previous awareness steps, together forming a 'network' of information, where new learning and insight seems to flow into the coachee. Like many emergent properties, the whole is greater than the sum of the parts and requires sufficient components to reach a tipping point so as to transcend to another level.

When working with coachees you can often recognise where the coachee currently is along the six steps to freedom. It is important to see that the 'wobble' is a necessary stage and to persevere beyond that stuckness. Often the coachee will get more confused and uncertain before a new way of thinking and experiencing begins to emerge.

Setting up conditions for change

For any coaching work, at the contracting stage you have the opportunity to explore and establish how this person normally makes change happen and how he or she expects to change during this coaching. I like to explain to people a few simple points about the nature of change to set their expectations at an appropriate level. For instance I explain that change happens in different ways for different people. Sometimes it's a slow gradual improvement. Sometimes the pattern is more haphazard. And sometimes, people experience a single, sudden moment of insight which brings about an instantaneous shift in thinking. I invite the coachee to describe how he or she thinks change will happen for him or her.

Transcript: exploring a habit with Clean Language

Building from Chapter ten and the concepts of encouraging self-modelling, what follows is a complete transcript of a Clean Coaching session demonstrating how habits can be explored and changed with Clean Language. It follows a 'bottom-up' strategy: rather than starting with a clear outcome, I let the solution emerge from the exploration. As well as highlighting my questions and the coachee's answers, my own internal musings and emerging model is shown in *italics*. These musings demonstrate how potentially 'unclean' thoughts and personal preferences will invariably influence your approach from time to time, but the use of Clean Language prevents any bias from taking hold.

Angela: Thank you Dave for agreeing to this session. Is there anything else you'd like to say or do before we start?
Dave: My pleasure. You can go ahead.
Angela: What habit would you like to explore and possibly change?
Dave: My smoking habit.
Angela: Is there anything else about your smoking habit?
Dave: I've been smoking for a very long time and I've tried many things, and the more I was thinking about stopping I found I was tending to smoke more cigarettes, so I stopped thinking about it. I know it's not good for me. I've always encouraged my friends to stop and when they do it I ask how did you do that? They all seem to have a different answer.

This sounds like it might be a binding pattern as he has tried many things and still smoking. Rather than explore the conceptual detail and get tied up in the story, I stick with the overall frame of 'habit'.

Angela: And when your smoking habit is like that, what kind of smoking habit is that smoking habit?
Dave: It's a bad habit. I know it's not doing anything good for me.

But he's still smoking, even though he knows it's bad. Something else must be going on in this system, or else presumably he would have already stopped.

Angela: And when you know it's not doing anything good for you and it's a bad habit, is there anything else about that habit?
Dave: There are times when there is a kind of craving. It's those moments when things seem to be on automatic and it's alright. I just light up a cigarette.

'Craving' sounds like it could be a physical feeling and have some kind of sensory location, so I try to explore that.

Angela: And when there is a craving and it's automatic, whereabouts is that craving?
Dave: The craving starts in my head and then it's in my mouth.
Angela: And then what happens?
Dave: Then I head towards where the cigarette packet is. If I don't have one I go out and get one.

It sounds like a straightforward cause and effect process – craving comes before smoking a cigarette. It's all quite conceptual at the moment. I continue to explore craving to see if a symbol or metaphor will emerge.

Angela: And when that craving starts in your head, whereabouts in your head?
Dave: I wouldn't *know* an exact location, but some kind of feeling at the start it's from there.

*He's already mentioned knowing. Perhaps this is a resource for him. I am starting to form a very rough model in my mind of what I imagine his mental 'system' for smoking might be like. I am seeing 'craving' on one side and 'knowing it's bad' on the other. I am imagining the habit as a kind of system with these two parts of it that are currently keeping things the same. **NOTE:** These are only my musings. I know this is not likely to be how the coachee sees it or feels it or hears it, but it is my imperfect model of what is happening for the coachee and I expect it will change as the session continues.*

Angela: And you know it's bad for you and the craving is automatic and it starts in your head. And when you know it's bad for you, what kind of knowing is that knowing?

I am trying to help the coachee develop a clearer sense of the 'knowing' now.

Dave: That's a conscious knowing.
Angela: And whereabouts is that conscious knowing when you know it's bad for you?
Dave: That's also in my head.

Both 'craving' and 'knowing' seem to be in the same place. I want to get a clearer sense of what each element is like to help me form a clearer and more accurate model in my mind. In doing this, I'll be helping the coachee develop his own model too.

Angela: And when that conscious knowing is in your head, does that conscious knowing have a shape or size?
Dave: No.

Oops. I'm finding it difficult to draw anything. I am wondering how Dave is modelling this for himself. Maybe I can ask a question to find out.

Angela: And when that conscious knowing is in your head, how do you know it's in your head?
Dave: It's more like a voice.

It's a sound and not a picture! That explains why there are so few visual impressions. My musings have been very visually oriented which is my preference. Clean Language helped ensure I didn't push my coachee into visual descriptions. However, we do have something more tangible to work with now. 'Voice' is a metaphor that we can now explore further.

Angela: And what kind of voice?
Dave: It is my voice.
Angela: Is there anything else about that voice?
Dave: It's always there.
Angela: And that voice that's always there, that's a voice like what?
Dave: That's a voice like – gives me a direction. As to 'do it this way'.

I thought we might have got a more distinct symbolic representation for this metaphor, but this didn't happen. 'Direction' might have been an interesting word/ metaphor to explore further, however I stuck with the craving/knowing 'system' I had started modelling.

Angela: And in your head is craving. It starts in your head, and craving is automatic. And when craving is in your head does that craving have a shape or a size?

I'm still trying to get a symbolic form, this time for the 'craving' part.

Dave: No.
Angela: And when craving is in your head, how do you know it starts in your head?
Dave: It's the voice.

I tried the same question as before as it seemed to work last time, and got another sound.

Angela: What kind of voice is that voice?
Dave: It's my voice.

It feels a bit like I am going in circles. 'My voice' sounds like a single thing, however it comes from two different mental representations. How is Dave experiencing this?

Angela: And that voice of craving . . . is that the same or different to conscious knowing voice?

This is a specialist Clean Language question to identify whether two similar things mentioned are in fact one and the same or separate distinct elements.

Dave: Voice seems to be the trigger, it starts from there.
Angela: And when the voice is the trigger, is that the same or different to your voice that gives you direction?
Dave: The voice that's inside my head is my voice, that's where the direction comes from. The voice that you hear me saying, it's also me: the voice in my head is my inner voice, really.
Angela: And inner voice gives you direction, and is that inner voice the same or different to the trigger, the craving that starts in your head?
Dave: It's the same voice, direction and trigger.

It's one voice but with different intentions . . . what does that look like? Or for Dave, how does that sound? I still don't really 'see' how it works yet! My model needs to include sounds and physical sensations, not just visual images.

Angela: And when there's the same voice with the direction and trigger, is there anything else about a voice with direction and trigger?
Dave: Seems to do most of my thinking, the inner voice.

The voice definitely sounds like one and the same thing now. But 'inner direction' and 'trigger' sound like two opposing outcomes. How do they both maintain their existence? How does one impact on the other?

Angela: And when that inner voice does most of your thinking, gives you direction and knows it's bad for you . . . what happens to trigger when inner voice knows it's bad for you?

Starting to explore the relationship/connect-ness between what I am imagining to be two parts of the same system.

Dave: It's in safety mode.

'Safety mode' sounds like the default position of 'knowing it's bad', when presumably craving can be controlled. But as he has not been able to stop smoking yet, this 'safety mode' is unlikely to be a permanent solution.

Angela: And what kind of 'safety mode' is that safety mode when inner voice is in safety mode?
Dave: It's like everything is fine, nothing to worry about.
Angela: And when inner voice is in safety mode, whereabouts is safety mode?

Dave: It's inside my head.
Angela: And inside your head, the inner voice in safety mode, that's like what?
Dave: It's like a pistol with the safety latch on.

Now we have a clear, overt metaphor containing the symbol of a pistol. Maybe this represents the whole system, both the craving and the knowing? So far we have no outcome: we are still just exploring the current habit. I am taking my time.

Angela: Is there anything else about that pistol with the safety latch on?
Dave: I have an image of the pistol my dad has: a small, tiny little thing.

We have a picture! This felt to me like a big step as we have something quite tangible to work with now. Grove suggested that for symbols to transform, they need to have a form. Often this is visual but in fact could be in the form of a sound or feeling. At this point I was thinking that guns, even with safety latches on, to me sound quite scary and dangerous – that's perhaps why they need a safety latch? I wonder if that's how Dave is experiencing this pistol? His experience could be very different from mine and so I explore further.

Angela: Is there anything else about that small, tiny little thing?
Dave: It looks more like a toy.

I don't know how Dave was experiencing the gun, as already the symbol seems to be shifting, changing from his father's pistol to a harmless toy. Toys don't need safety latches! This shift happened very quickly but much groundwork had been done with the exploration of the voices, I suspect. Looking at this from a systems thinking perspective, is the system starting to self-correct as it discovers more about itself?

Angela: And when that pistol looks more like a toy, what happens to craving that starts in your head?
Dave: I'm not aware of that at the moment, I don't know where that is.

I refocused on the craving to see if anything had changed. The fact it cannot be located could be a positive sign. Let's check what's going on now.

Angela: And that small tiny little thing that's more like a toy . . . what's happening now?
Dave: I'm looking inside my head.

This was very interesting, Dave is now 'looking' – so clearly now he is trying to use visual representations, which he wasn't before.

Angela: And when looking inside your head, then what happens?

Dave: I'm unable to see any image inside my head right know, but that voice
is there and it's looking for that toy.

*The 'voice' has taken on a life of its own: it's the voice that's doing the looking.
I don't know what this has to do with smoking, but it does sound like something is
shifting in the moment and Dave is engaging with his internal metaphors and the
symbols are taking on a life of their own. I trust that the story will unfold if I stick
with Clean Language.*

Angela: And what kind of looking is that?
Dave: It's like the voice is in a dark room and trying to look for that toy in that
dark room.

*We have a new, previously unmentioned symbol of a dark room, containing
the toy, and the voice. It seems we are chunking up to a wider context, with
more of the metaphoric landscape coming into focus. Plus it's 'dark' which
indicates maybe more is happening that is hidden and could be revealed if
attended to.*

Angela: Is there anything else about that dark room?
Dave: It's dark. Can't see anything else here.

*Dave is now referring a lot to the visuals. Even 'dark' is a visual representation
in itself. I assumed here that 'can't see anything' was a problem and decided to
ask for an outcome, but rather than risk bringing Dave back to more conceptual
thought, I ask what 'voice' would like to have happen.*

Angela: And when that voice is in that dark room looking for that toy, what
would voice like to have happen?
Dave: Voice would like to have a light on.

*Voice has generated a metaphoric solution. Again I do not know how this relates
to smoking, but I assume that having light and finding the toy gun will somehow
clarify the puzzle.*

Angela: And what kind of light could that light be?
Dave: Any kind of light to bring some light into that dark room.

*This question might have developed greater awareness of this new symbol 'light'
but Dave does not seem able to sense much yet about the light. What question
could I ask next to help him discover more?*

Angela: And where could any kind of light come from?
Dave: Somewhere outside that dark room.

This is great! His attention is going still wider, thinking beyond the current (and evolving) 'system' of 'voice looking for toy in a dark room'. I will continue to focus attention on this wider view.

Angela: And that somewhere outside the dark room, what kind of outside, is outside of that dark room?
Dave: It's like opening a window and looking outside and seeing the trees and outside surroundings.
Angela: Is there anything else about that window? What kind of window is that window?
Dave: I'm sitting right in front of a window so . . . the window in my head that I can see is quite similar to the one in front of me.

Dave's using the 'real' window to draw inspiration for the symbolic window. Often people notice real things around them that can lend a hand to their internal land-scape. I want to be careful to focus attention on the metaphoric window though, not the real one.

Angela: And whereabouts in the dark room is that window in your head?
Dave: Right in front of me I guess.

'I guess' does not sound that sure, so let's check out what Dave would like to have happen now.

Angela: And when that window is right in front of you, what would you like to have happen?

Asking for a metaphoric outcome again.

Dave: To walk up to it and open the window.
Angela: And when you walk up to it and open the window, what happens to smoking habit?

Now I am checking if any of this has anything to do with the habit.

Dave: There's lot more fresh air, like taking a big deep breath.
Angela: And when you take that big deep breath, what happens next?

I'm helping the change to mature, moving things forward again.

Dave: There's light in the room.
Angela: And when light in the room, what happens to automatic craving?

Again I checked back, has this metaphoric change made a difference to the prob-lem, i.e. 'craving'? It could also have been useful here to ask further questions about the light to really ensure the full effect of having light in the room has been realised.

Dave: I don't know.
Angela: And opening the window and light in the room. What needs to happen to open the window?

I wasn't sure whether the metaphoric change has already happened for Dave, or whether he needs to do something to make the window open.

Dave: I have to keep it permanently open.

The answer he gives implies it had already happened as he wants to keep the window open rather than try to open it.

Angela: And can you keep it permanently open?

Moving to action questions (within the metaphor).

Dave: Yes I can.

Dave sounded quite certain about this. But let's check more about how he will do this. I am responding to Dave's metaphors quite literally. Instead of thinking about smoking habits, I am wondering how you can keep a window open.

Angela: And what needs to happen for you to keep it permanently open?
Dave: Just let the windows be as they are now.

Sounds easy enough if the windows are in Dave's control here. I wonder what's happening to the other parts of this system now the window is open. On reflection it may also have been useful to check in on the 'room', as well as the gun.

Angela: And when you let the windows be just as they are now, what happens to the small tiny little toy?
Dave: It doesn't make any sense. It's like a real toy. Kind of one of those plastic-y thingies that kids play with. Just like that.

I could hypothesize here that the transformation from a dangerous gun to a child's toy may have re-framed how Dave was viewing this whole scenario, and therefore changing the thinking patterns around his smoking habit. But it doesn't really matter if it makes no sense to me. Dave has found a metaphoric solution. What purpose does this 'toy gun' have now, if there is no longer any 'craving'?

Angela: And what needs to happen with that plastic-y little toy?
Dave: It needs to be filled with water.

Of course, it's a water pistol! This is an example of how symbols can change and evolve during a session. Water sounds like another part of the system, and possibly a resource.

Angela: And where could that water come from to fill that plastic-y little toy?

Dave: I need to step outside and find the water source. I haven't explored my head that much.

Again sounds like Dave is thinking outside the usual pattern of thinking again. Perhaps I could have developed this a little more and checked that the water was found and then what happens. However there are always time constraints and this seemed a good place to begin drawing things to a close.

Angela: And as we draw this session to a close, what do you know now about all of that?

Dave: I stop myself, and kept the windows closed. And probably I need lots more water.

Angela: And what needs to happen next?

Dave: Go to the fridge and grab a bottle of water!

Water became a resource in the real world too for Dave, and drinking water became an alternative behaviour to smoking. The transformation of the gun seemed to be a key shift, enabling Dave to think beyond the dark room. It does not matter that I do not understand what the gun represented, or even that Dave understands it. I simply trust that if Dave's mind generated this image in response to my questions there is some significance and the change in thinking will ultimately affect the wider system connecting those thoughts to behaviours, i.e. smoking.

Angela: And would this be an okay place to end our session?

Dave: Absolutely. Thank you Angela, that was great.

Angela: Take all the time you need to know everything you need to know about that window, the light and the toy . . .

Coaching for confidence

Gaining more confidence is a common goal within both personal and organisational coaching. Directly or indirectly, it seems a key outcome for many coaching sessions, either as an end in itself or as a resource required in order to achieve something else. Research suggests it's one of the most common issues brought to coaching, and this has been my experience too.

So, how do we tackle confidence issues Cleanly? To begin with, when coachees mention confidence, or lack of it, this can encompass a wide range of different meanings, associations and metaphors. It could be a feeling or physical sensation they feel in their body; it could be a memory; or it could be something they only see in others, rather than connect with themselves.

A very good place to start is to ask, "When you say confidence, what kind of confidence is that?" Listen carefully to the coachee's descriptions and explore each in turn. For instance: "When confidence for you is about having energy and feeling committed, is there anything else about having energy?" and further explore what it's like to have energy like that, for instance.

And then: "And confidence, for you is also feeling committed. What kind of feeling is that when you are feeling committed?"

Once you have explored a number of different avenues about what it's like (for this coachee) to be confident, you might want to explore the consequences or effects of that confidence. Is confidence a means to an end or the end in itself?

"And when there is that confidence, and you have energy and feel committed, then what happens?"

This question might point towards a greater aim. If explored further, it could open other possible paths to progress, not just confidence. That does not necessarily mean you would not focus on confidence in the session, it just means that you can do so in context with the wider picture and be more easily able to switch attention to other possible resources/strategies if they emerge within the session.

Transcript: to feel more confident

This transcript demonstrates Clean Networks (see Chapter thirteen). This variation moves the goal at B rather than the person at A. David Grove described this as being like Einstein's theory of entanglement or 'spooky action at a distance'. Each time the goal is moved, there is some transfer of information between A and B. What's happening for the coachee will inevitably change what's happening at B.

Angela: What's your goal?

Helen: My goal is to feel more confident about today. I'm doing an assessment in London and it's my first time for this company and I'm nervous and quite worried about it. I want to feel better about it and more confident.

Angela: Could you write or draw that goal on a piece of paper or choose an object to represent that goal?

Helen: I've chosen one of my old business cards . . .

Angela: Now place that in a space that feels right to you. And how would you like me to refer to that goal?

Helen: Confidence.

Angela: Could you now place yourself in a space that feels right in relation to confidence? And is the distance right between you and confidence?

(The session continued with a complete 'Clean Start' – see Chapter twelve *for full details)*

Angela: And what do you know now?

Helen: It's in a very smelly place that's cold. It's not very nice: feels abandoned, under the kitchen sink, a place that doesn't get much attention. It's not that far away, but there's a cupboard door between it and me. Feels like it's had a lot of crap around it for a while.

Angela: Is there another space that confidence could go to from that space there?

Helen (moving her business card): Yes, it's somewhere else now.

Angela: What does confidence know from that space there?

Helen: That if she follows a recipe she will be successful. So if she wants to do something well if she focuses and follows the process that will generally ensure a good outcome. Actually she's quite skilled at what she chooses to do.

Angela: And is there another space that confidence could go to from that space there?

Helen: Okay.

Angela: What does confidence know from that space there?

Helen: Quite a lot really. I'm in the study and there's a lot of resources around me: text books, folders filing cabinet, also the computer. And if I need any information I know where to get it from. And that there's also something in here about focusing on what I'm doing at the time, and trusting that I can do this. Because it's a different assessment . . . a lot of it's around how the company I'm doing work for have doubts about me. Last session, the person requesting assessment wanted someone else to do it, which didn't help. It's about my wanting to prove to them I can do a good job. Feel like this new company has "seen through me" as such, and I know why, I had my interview on a day when I wasn't feeling great. I can understand why they have their slight reservations. Maybe I need to imagine I'm doing it for the old company, then that would help.

Angela: And is there another space that confidence could go to from that space there?

Helen: Not moving very far . . .

Angela: What does confidence know from that space there?

Helen: I've actually put it on a picture of a dream board I did about two years ago when I was feeling very positive and confident about things, same time the business card was made as well. Surrounded by images very positive I used. It's only two years ago, what I'm feeling is it can't be that hard to get back to that feeling. It does feel on some days it's a world away . . . not sure what the missing thing is . . .

This is a lot of variety in this place, very strong images. There is something about being a bit more solid and letting things grow, at a more natural healthy rate. Although I associate this dream board with confidence, behind it there was a lot going on that was on a wing and a prayer. What's happened since has taught me a lot about doing ground-work, and put some solid stuff in place, rather than just an image I have of that time.

Angela: And is there another place that confidence could now go to from that space there?

Helen: Take it up to the studio.

Angela: And what does confidence know from that space there?

Helen: (laughs) I've got an awful lot of things I should feel confident about, my painting is one of them. I brought this goal up here because there are lots of examples of success up here, I suppose. Some days I don't feel like that about my painting but today I feel quite good about it. The thing that jumped into my mind was . . . just because this new firm don't know me very well, there's actually a lot of things that I'm good at and I really need to own those things and put them in the 'pot' rather than just see the insecurities around that tiny little thing. If I add all of the things together there is actually a lot of success and there is something about why I don't allow sucking up from other areas of my life . . . they could help out quite nicely.

Maybe if I'm feeling wobbly today about the special report I need to write, maybe I could remember I have a lot of things I can say I'm good at. This assessment today is not rocket science. I've done this kind of thing lots of times before so no need to be worried about it really.

Angela: And is there another space that confidence could go to from that space there?

Helen: Not sure why it's going in the bathroom . . . I'll put it there and see what happens . . .

Angela: What does confidence know from that space there?

Helen: The bathroom is being re-done at the moment. There's something about designing and building confidence, starting it from scratch. We tore the bathroom out entirely and re-built it. I don't know. I'm a bit stuck. That's all that comes to mind . . .

It's only half-built! It's half-way done, which doesn't help in lots of ways. With the confidence side of things it's really only a couple of years ago maybe it's half built now which is why I'm not 100%, but lots been done so far that's good. Things take time, quite a lot of things that take time to do, as we always do with working on many areas at once. The message I'm getting here is that I'm not just working on my confidence, I'm working on lots of other things all at once. It will take longer that way. But that's how it is and that's how I tend to do things. I like the variety of doing lots of things at once. But just to remind me that if I do it that way it will take a bit longer.

Angela: And is there a final space that confidence could go to from that space there?

Helen: Back downstairs. It's in quite an interesting place now.

Angela: And what does confidence know from that space there?

Helen: Couple of things, it's something about celebrating success. I've brought it down to the front door. There's a canvas here waiting to be stretched and framed, I know that I had another painting framed a few weeks ago when I looked at it I was really chuffed, gave me a fantastic boost. In the other way, the work stuff with confidence, there's something about seeing or celebrating a finished product, that will help my confidence. And re-visiting that, maybe actually even look at one of the other reports I have written, remind myself that I can do this and do it well. Something I could take with me actually on the train, read one of the typed-up, finished reports that my last company were really pleased with, that will give me a similar feeling to when I got my painting framed. That's about it from here.

Angela: Could you now return confidence to the first space, where it started?

Helen (moving the card back to its original position):   Okay.

Angela: And what do you know now?

Helen: I have a choice whether to leave it there or not. I don't think it is helpful to leave it there. I'm going to probably take it out of there quite quickly and give it some sunshine I think. To really own all of the successes I've had over the last couple of years, which have been under really very difficult circumstances, I've still managed to do some amazing things and if I can do that under difficult circumstances, then when things are a bit easier then other things will flow better as well. I think celebrating things I've done is really important but also knowing that I've got the resources to tackle things that aren't so easy. I've done a lot of things in my life that weren't so easy, but I've managed them. I shall take it out of there now.

Angela: Is there a space that knows about what actions you want to take?

Helen: Yes.

Angela: And what's the first action you know you could do from that space there?

Helen: Take out the report to read in train (etc.).

Angela: And what's the second action you know you could do?

Helen: Framing the picture, plus emailing this woman about an exhibition (etc.).

Angela: And are there any other actions that you know you could do from that space there?

Helen: Not immediately that spring to mind.

Angela: Would that be an okay place to bring our session to a close? And take all the time you need . . .

References

Ghosh, A. and Shatz, C. (1992) Involvement of subplate neurons in the formation of ocular dominance columns. *Science*, 255(5050), 1441–1443.

Lawley, J. and Tompkins, P. (2000) *Metaphors in Mind.* London: The Developing Company Press.

Ohlsson, S. (2011) *Deep Learning: How the Mind Overrides Experience*. New York: Cambridge University Press.

Prochaska, J., Norcross, J. and DiClemente, C. (1994) *Changing for Good: The Revolutionary Program That Explains the Six Stages of Change and Teaches You How to Free Yourself from Bad Habits*. New York: W. Morrow.

Chapter fifteen

Coaching on paper

Many coaches encourage the coachee to write or draw during coaching sessions, but Grove turned this into a technique in its own right. He encouraged clients to represent their goal or issue on paper. They would select from a wide range of different sizes and shapes of paper as each would frame the problem/solution spaces in different ways. Once on paper, the goal can be stepped away from and examined from a physical distance, helping to create emotional distance.

Eventually, Grove and Wilson developed this into a Clean Coaching process in its own right: Clean Hieroglyphics. Grove encouraged clients to treat their goal as a work in progress, and regularly asked them to add or change what was on their paper, as they expressed their thoughts and gained insights. As the original outcome statement gets added to, words begin to take on deeper significance, generating an energy of their own. As the coachees focus on their written words, they often begin to notice more than what was initially apparent to them. Sometimes even the letters, or the spaces between the letters take on meaning. These aspects of the written words are like ready-made, embedded metaphors through which meaning can be explored. Rather like Egyptian Hieroglyphics, the letters that make up the message could contain meaning in their own right.

Case study: I'm getting fatter

The following case study highlights my own personal work with David Grove on 9 October 2006.

This session took place as part of a demonstration to a group being taught Clean Coaching training, and so David adds some explanation during the process. We were told that this was an exercise in coaching 'B'.

Demonstration

DAVID: Write down on that paper a particular goal, or specific issue that you would like to use as your experience for this. You could either: write down the words; illustrate it or find an object that is in the room around you that seems to represent the problem. This will be called 'B' your goal which we will coach today. Place the paper or object somewhere in the room that's away from you at a certain distance, and find out where you want to be in respect to the problem. How far is your paper away from you?

ANGELA: At the moment, I've placed mine on me. It's on my tummy.

DAVID: The question set will go either to you at A or to the statement at B. So I'll ask these questions, and as you hear them where you feel you need to change something, please go ahead, you don't need to answer.

(David then asked the Clean Start Question Set, to check that both me and my goal [or problem] were in the right space and at the right height, angle, direction and position.)

DAVID: So that is a Clean Start. What was your experience?

ANGELA: I had to change a couple of things. I had scribbled some words on A4 paper and balanced it on my tummy. But it didn't feel right. It had to be attached in a different way so I wrote it on a yellow sticky. Now it is a little flap tucked into my trousers 90 degrees from my body. My issue is I am getting fatter, so if I stick my stomach out I can see that even more clearly!

DAVID: You can see the types of coincidences that occur. The circumstances of where you place the statement are often very indicative of the issue you are addressing. How you can begin with almost any client and any issue is by making this simple Clean Start and allowing 10–20 minutes for the person to set it up. Let's make sure . . . (David went through the Clean Start process again). Did anyone have to make any other adjustments?

ANGELA: I had to put my hand on my tummy.

DAVID: Now we will coach the space of B. All the questions will be directed towards the space of B. Then we will find out how that progresses towards the space of D that has other information in it. First we will add what else needs to go in there.

And what else could also go on that paper?

Are there any other words that also need to be on that paper as well as the ones that you have?

If there are then put those on.

(David also asked me to add any words or phrases that could be there before the words or phrases we had, and also what the next word or sentence might be.)

What changes were made in your statement? Are any of the words and sentences going to the edge of the page? If you have any writings or drawings that are really close to the edge, put a piece of paper there. Place a piece of paper there and keep adding what should be on that paper. Sometimes the paper is not big enough to contain all the information. The problem will be limited by the paper, so new information will occur at the top, the bottom or two sides of the paper, and that gets us into the information supplied by D.

ANGELA: My piece of paper is quite small because it needs to be portable and attached to me. The statement of the problem 'I'm getting fatter' did not need any more words, as that really says it all. What came before was another 'I'm getting fatter' and I think there are probably about 6 but I haven't written them out in full.

DAVID: You will need to write them out in full. Put all those words down in full and follow the angle at which they go up and put the age that is connected with each of those statements. I am expanding the domain of the statement by finding out what are the words before and what are the words after. It helps to set the context of the nature of those words.

Now the next part – we are still on coaching the words on the page. Now we are going to look at the source of those words. Where did those words come from before they were on that paper? Place the answer up on the paper or top, bottom, sides to the one you have got and place your answer. Did those words come from you and if they did, how old were you when you first had those words? And if they came from someone else, what kind of someone else gave you those words? Whatever the answer is, either place or draw yourself, or that person, on the same piece of paper or add another piece of paper that's around that.

(At this point, I drew myself in the words of "I'M GETTING FATTER"; I drew me on the "A" of "FATTER" giving it a head and arms and turning it into a tiny fat person.)

DAVID: As I am coaching where the words come from in the source, I am taking those phrases and asking her to place them on the statement. This then becomes like a very living document. The fact that you repeat something is crucial. What it means is that one of those phrases is not enough.

ANGELA: The words came from me. About a year ago. It was going back in two month intervals. I think they are just getting louder.

DAVID: Where was the original one from?

ANGELA: The original was just over a year ago and that was I am in good shape.

DAVID: We have coached the words on the page by expanding the context – the words before, the words after, and what was the source of the words before they appeared on the page. Often the goal you have now may not be the goal you had before. The origin of where those words are stored gives you a greater context for the meaning of those words. Now we are going to look at the space around those words or around the statement you have made. In the same way you have a frame round a picture it gives the picture a different perspective.

(David then asked further Clean questions directed at the spaces, and the boundaries of those spaces, around my words. This process is called 'Clean Boundaries'.[1])

DAVID: Now I am going to download to you at A. For the first time I am going to ask a question with the pronoun 'you'. So what do **you** know now?

ANGELA: All I know now is that it is all a matter of scale. The problem does not seem very big at all now. It seems quite small and so do I.

DAVID: Place that on the statement. If you need to rewrite it then do so.

(I then changed my little drawing of me to look like a thin person, so scribbled over my "A" until it looked like an "I.")

It wasn't until later that I realised my overall statement had changed from "I'M GETTING FATTER" to "I'M GETTING FITTER." It felt quite extraordinary, like the letters themselves had decided to change the words, and so change my reality. I lost 2.5 stones in weight over the next year and started to swim twice a week. This radical change of behaviour and result seemed effortless. The "I'M GETTING FITTER" seemed to have a life of its own and just happened.

Clean Hieroglyphics: the process

The purpose of the exercise is to find the origin of the words which have been written down. Each of the letters, words and spaces have a history to them.

1   Clean Start (see Chapter twelve).
2   Ask questions to the space of B:

> "And what else could also go on that paper?"
> "Are there any other words (or letters, drawings or symbols) that also need to be on that paper as well as the ones that you have?"
> "If there are, then put those on."
> "Is there anything else that could go on that paper?"

You can continue with this for as long as it seems to be yielding more. Encourage the person to add more paper around the original piece if he or she runs out of space:

> "Are any words or pictures near the edge of your paper? If so, you can add more paper around the piece you started with."

Finish with the download question:

> "And what do you know now?"

The following separate steps can be used individually, in conjunction with other EK exercises or all together following on from each other.

3   A simple exploration of the letters, words and spaces between:

> Focus attention, using a selection of Clean questions:

> "What do you notice about the letters or the words that are on [goal]?"
> "Is there any letter or word that looks different?"
> "What kind of x is that x?"
> "Is there anything else about that x?"
> "What do *you* know about that (curly) letter [C]?"
> "And what does that *letter* [C] know?"
> "And what does the [yellow space] know?"
> "Are there any other interesting letters?"
> "Is there anything else interesting about the letters, words or the spaces between the letters and words?"

Continue exploring for as long as useful, new information appears to be emerging. Have the coachee write down anything that comes up that seems new or important by saying:

> "And put *that* down on your paper."

End by downloading:

"And what do you know now?"

4   Expanding attention.

Before and after questions:

Use these questions on the whole piece of paper or have the coachee select a phrase that he or she is drawn to, or interested in:

"What words are you noticing now?"
"What other words or phrases could there be before the words or phrases you have on that paper?"
"What words or phrases could there be before these words or phrases?"
"If there are other words or phrases then put them on before the sentence you have got there."

Or, you could explore what's next:

"And what other words or phrases can go on the end of the words you already have?"
"What might the next sentence or paragraph be?"

From this selection of questions, if any seem to engage the coachee particularly well, you can continue asking the same question around six times. As this is an iterative process, although the question remains the same, each time it is asked of the next piece of emerging information.

By asking the coachee to add further layers of detail, we are 'overdriving' B. The aim is to reach a level of complexity that's too full for the coachee's 'small world' understanding of it to contain. The coachee can no longer hold all the information and as it bursts at the seams, another higher level of understanding can emerge. By asking the client to add each piece of information on to the piece of paper, we are having the client 'upload' his or her thoughts, ensuring everything is captured and we/the client doesn't have to remember it. Hence after every articulation we say "And put *that* down."

Sometimes the piece of paper will not be big enough to contain all the information. The problem will be limited by the paper and the client will be limited by the physical boundaries of the page. Say:

"If you have any writings or drawings that are really close to the edge, put another piece of paper up to that edge so you can continue onto another sheet."

The piece of paper could be thought of as like a single page of a story book; these questions help the coachee to turn the page and find out the rest of the story.

5   "Download" any new client information.

Once all the information seems to be present, *check for any new understandings*:

"And what do you know now?"

Grove called this the *download* as it is inviting new understanding. Have the client capture this information on the same piece of paper:

"And put that down too."

6   Expand attention to the source.

If this process seems to be working well you can do further overdriving and uploading of the information at B. You can take this a stage further by selecting a specific word, phrase or symbol to explore the source:

"Where did those words come from that are on that paper?"

Possible variations:

"Did those words come from you?"
"And what kind of you first had those words?"
"And if they came from someone else, what kind of someone else gave you those words?"
"And where did they get those words from?"
"So where did those words come from before that?"

As the coachee answers, ask the person to add or alter the piece of paper in whatever way seems right. Coachees could place or draw themselves, or that person, or they may want to cross out and change some of the words. Remind them they can add more paper if needs be.

7   *Download* again with:

"And what do you know now?"

If things have changed radically, you may invite the client to write out a new goal and do another Clean Start.

8   *Finish* by selecting any or all pairs of questions from this list:

"And what do you know about that . . . [goal] . . . now?"
"And is there anything else you know about that [goal]?"
"And what difference does knowing that make?"
"And what would you like to have happen, next?"

9   Use *Clean Action Space* if relevant.

Clean Iterations.

This is a more flexible approach you can use when doing any Clean Coaching process involving paper. It's helpful to use if the coachee says something that seems to warrant further exploration. With this approach, you simply focus attention on whatever the word or phrase is by asking: "And what does (coachee's word) know?" and "Is there anything else that (. . .) knows?" If, after two questions not a lot has come up, you may decide to stop. If fruitful, you can continue to ask the same question six times.

Where might more knowledge be?

When observing Grove, I noticed he would often question:

- *Repeated words:* If it keeps coming up, chances are there's more to say.
- *Plurals:* Start with "And how many (. . .) are there?" Then "And what does the first (. . .) know?" "And what does the second (. . .) know?" And so on. You could ask the same six questions to the same 'x' if it appears to hold more information.
- *Parts of the body:* This fits with David's idea that we have separated off from parts of ourselves over our lifetime, and this process helps to re-integrate those lost parts. It might be a part of you in that wiggling toe, or your itchy ear!
- *A sound or a gesture:* As above, a possible 'part' trying to make itself heard.
- *Ambiguous words:* David loved words that had more than one meaning, an obvious indicator of a hidden source of new knowledge.

Sometimes Grove encouraged the coach to develop metaphors around the words, but in later life he seemed to move away from this approach. If your coachee responds well to metaphor exploration you could incorporate this into your paper exploration:

"What kind of words are the words on that paper?"
"Is there anything else about those jumbled words?"
"What kind of jumbled is that jumbled?"
"And that's jumbled like what?"

Within an Emergent Knowledge framework you want to keep this kind of delving quite light. We do not want a coachee to become immersed within a metaphor, simply to explore around the edges, keeping his or her whole 'network' of available thoughts active.

Case study: Jane's eye contact

Jane worked as a business coach within a coaching consultancy. I coached her using the Clean Hieroglyphics technique. This picture (Figure 15.1) is a representation of Jane's goal, not the real drawing/writing:

I want to overcome my bad habit of avoiding eye contact when people ask me questions I find challenging

See how visual I am

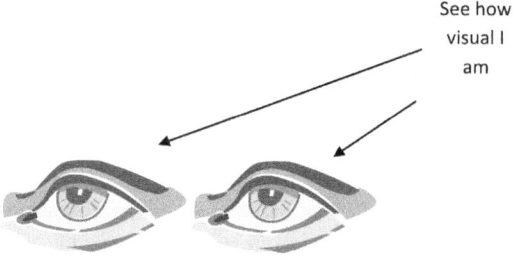

Who <u>do</u> I think I am?

Writing this makes me feel exposed.

This came to me as I was preparing this. As my eyesight deteriorates what am I going to do ~2~...if I use my visual reasoning so much?

Figure 15.1 Jane's drawing.

Jane came across as a confident, assertive and highly competent woman. Her issue was about finding it difficult sometimes to hold direct eye contact with certain people. This was something she admitted she had explored previously with other coaches, and not yet found a solution.

I asked her what letters on the page were drawing her attention, and she commented on the 'I's. So, we explored the various 'I's on the paper, including the 'eyes', which also seemed to hold significance. "Eye" and "I" sound the same, and perhaps the ambiguity pointed to something more to know. I asked the EK question "And what does that 'I' know?" Although it sounds like a strange question, if the question delivered correctly, the coachee will be capable of answering. To do so, the coachee must mentally project herself into the letter then imagine what the world is like from there. The question grants permission for the subconscious mind to 'fill in the gaps' and the reply to come from a deeper, inner wisdom. In Jane's case, she replied, "It knows but it won't tell me." It seemed as though the answer could be just beyond her conscious awareness so I persevered and continued to ask if there was anything else that the 'I' knew. After six attempts, Jane realised that she actually needed to trust herself enough to admit out loud that sometimes she feels small and insignificant. This was quite different to how she appeared, which was strong and confident.

After exploring the 'I's and the eyes, we then looked at what words could come after the words that were on the paper, and Jane began to tell more of a story, as she felt emotional and angry about how she felt, and said, "How dare you make me feel like that!" then afterwards adding, "But it's only me making me feel this."

Everything that Jane said I asked her to put on the piece of paper. Then I asked, "And where could all those words have come from?" She quickly said, "Me" … but then a few seconds later the knowledge finally broke through to the surface and she realized that most of the words were from someone else in her past who had indeed made her feel small and insignificant. Having recognized this, she could now deal with it, and she scribbled out some of the words on the paper.

At the end I asked, "And what do you know now?" and she said, "I feel taller. I am stood next to the wall, and there is a place where I have previous marked my height, and weirdly, I seem to be looking down on that … how strange."

I have kept in touch with Jane and she no longer has a problem with direct eye contact.

Transcript: maintaining Space in my life

The following transcript highlights another example of Clean Hieroglyphics in action. The session began with a Clean Start, which has not been included in this transcript. The outcome was originally written down as "Maintaining Space in my life for a richer life" (see Figures 15.2, 15.3 and 15.4).

ANGELA: Is there anything else that you know now?

CATHERINE: No, it just makes me feel good, looking at it. I like looking over it, that bottom part where the goal is.

ANGELA: What do you notice about those words … and the letters in those words, or even the spaces between the words or letters?

CATHERINE: Well it's very important to have that whole sentence close to me. I wrote it at the top of the page where I normally do, and then ended up having to re-write it at the bottom of the page to have it closer to me. It's also like they are a foundation so everything goes at the top of it. Then those bits at the top, I had to draw a line, they are kind of doubts as opposed to what I want, so . . . there's a little bit of thought up there but I've separated them off. I like the fact I've got a gap between my 'main' and my 'taining'. It's suddenly caught my eye.

ANGELA: Is there anything else about that gap?

CATHERINE: The 't' nearly grabs it. I'm going to take that 't' across to that 'n'. That's nice. Like it's connected itself properly now.

ANGELA: What does that 't' know that's connected across to that 'n'?

CATHERINE: It's caused me to panic about the other spaces now! The space has got larger between 'maintaining' and 'space' now. I don't like that. My spaces are out of control, I don't like all those spaces any more . . . which is a tad bizarre!

ANGELA: And what does that larger space know?

CATHERINE: I think it knows it shouldn't be there, funnily enough. It's almost like if the spaces grew, that whole sentence, I'd lose it, and that's what I'm worried about. I don't want it cramped either. It is about having space, but not a massive amount of space where it just then loses that thread, so there's that kind of richness in the space. The space between 'maintaining space' is a little bit too large. The bit where it's 'for a richer' that's the size the spaces should be. The beginning of the sentence has larger spaces and they get a little bit smaller towards the end where I've put what it's all around . . . That's really interesting.

ANGELA: Which space are you drawn to now?

CATHERINE: I like the space between the 'for' and the 'a', and the 'a' and the 'richer'. It's a good space. Big enough for richness but haven't got so far apart that they are losing that thread, a nice paced space. And it's just started to unravel on me . . . it's like that first space is unravelling too quickly. I need to get it back and control it a little bit more.

ANGELA: That good space between 'for' and 'a'. What does that good space know?

CATHERINE: It knows it's very achievable, it's very solid, and it's kind of drawing me in. It knows it's got that tension. It's very achievable, got a very good feeling about it.

ANGELA: Is there anything else that good space knows?

CATHERINE: Just a good, solid . . . yes that's it, that's what you want. That's where it is.

ANGELA: What do you know now?

CATHERINE: So . . . I know I've got it. I know it's that feeling again. It's always that feeling that gets me back again . . . It's interesting when I view what I'm doing with that feeling I have a very different ability to handle what I'm doing. And, what to say no to and what to agree to, and how to handle my assumptions about how other people might think about what I'm doing or not doing. It's about making sure I'm in that right space with that right feeling around it, and then it becomes easier to maintain that space with the rich line.

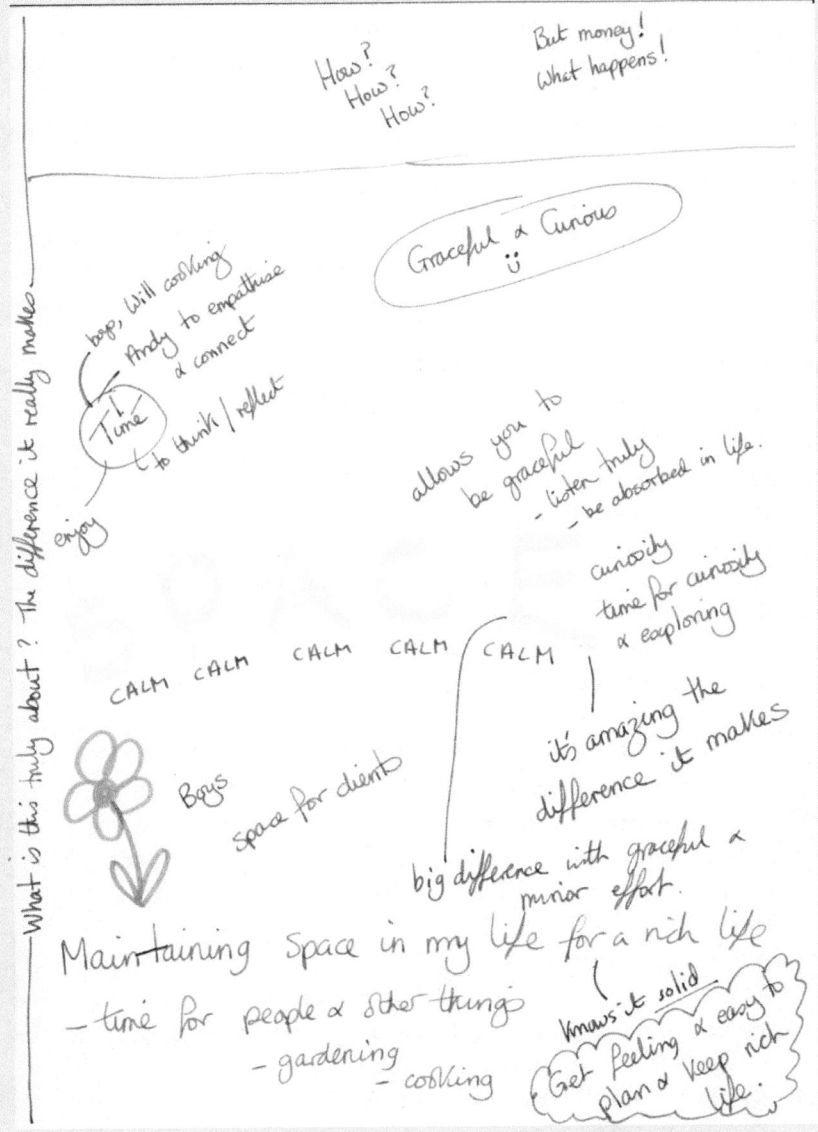

Figure 15.2 Maintaining space in my life.

ANGELA: And put that down on your paper. And if at any point, if you want to add another piece of paper around that paper, just feel free to do that too.

CATHERINE: Okay.

ANGELA: And what words, or letters, or spaces, are you noticing now?

CATHERINE: Interesting that being absorbed. I'm also noticing my 'E' has got a very long leg.

ANGELA: Is there anything else about that long leg?

CATHERINE: It's quite a relaxed look of the 'E', quite arching and graceful in its own way, really. The 'E' is a little detached from the rest. Do you know if you take the 'S' of the SPACE you get PACE, which is very interesting! That's what it's all about, the pacing, isn't it? That E extends it, the SPACE . . . a little bit more linger . . . slower, not a rush. That 'E's had time to be drawn. Just that little extra time, amazing what you get, like you've got extra time without realising you've got extra time, gracefully as well, it brings it all together. So important to keep where I'm at, having just had that opportunity. It's amazing the difference it makes.

ANGELA: And put that down.

CATHERINE: Just put that along the bottom there . . .

ANGELA: And what does that relaxed, lingering 'E' know?

CATHERINE: It's taking its time, and it's very attention seeking, so it's got a lot. Just that little bit extra is quite impactful. It's around . . . take a little time and you actually get further. Being active is not the same as proactive. I'm thinking about the value of the activity and how that all blends together. And what a big, big difference just something small can make. That 'E' has it because it's got that extra piece of work with it.

ANGELA: And put that down too. And if you need an extra piece of paper you can use more paper. What words are you noticing now?

CATHERINE: Calm calm calm calm underneath, that's supporting that space. They kind of work together. The space supports the calm and calm supports the space.

ANGELA: What other words could there be before those words?

CATHERINE: Before those words is a phrase around: "What's the difference you are really making?" That detached "What's this truly about?"

ANGELA: And put that down.

CATHERINE: I've turned my paper. The left hand side has just become the top for a second. That forms a nice 'backstop', that's my protective left arm, holding it on the page there.

ANGELA: What words could there be before those words?

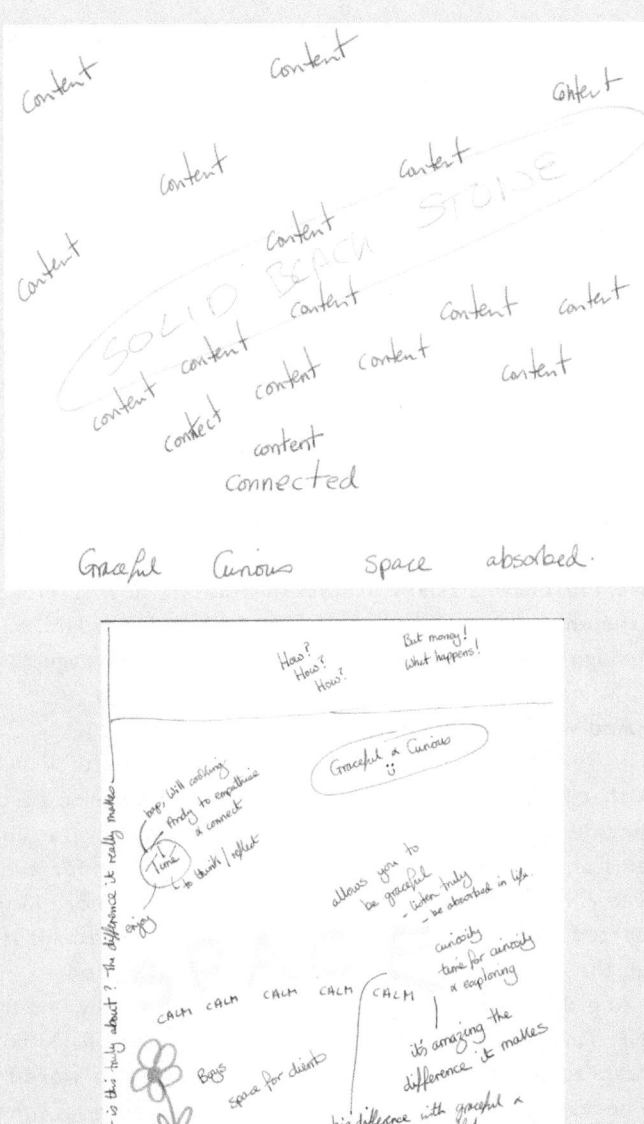

Figure 15.3 Maintaining space in my life – 2.

CATHERINE: It's a feeling really. It's just a real connected. So, connected is the word that comes before it.

ANGELA: Put that down.

CATHERINE: Yes.

ANGELA: What words or phrases could there be before that word 'connected'?

CATHERINE: 'Black's the word, but ... I think it's 'content' actually ... yeah.

ANGELA: Put that down too.

CATHERINE: Yeah ... smaller word, smaller writing.

ANGELA: And what words or phrases could be before that smaller word?

CATHERINE: I like content. If we had more time, I could write 'content' across the whole of that page. The whole new page could have content written all across it ... that's a good word ...

ANGELA: Are there any words or phrases that could go before that word 'content'?

CATHERINE: No. I have a galaxy of stars of 'content' now ... Floating off into the universe now, that's how they feel. And they kind of funnel in through content and connected onto the other page ... that's nice. I've gone onto an A3 sized piece of paper now.

ANGELA: And what do you know now?

CATHERINE: That it's a great place to be, and I hadn't quite worked out what that feeling was ... that is true ... and that makes a big difference. It's amazing the difference that makes in everything I do. When I am that, everything seems to work better for everyone. Bizarre. And the 'content' is me connected, much more intuitively connected to people that keeps me focused on what this is really about, the other stuff happens below that. That's good.

ANGELA: And that word 'content': where did that word come from?

CATHERINE: Deep inside. Comes from deep, deep inside. Took me forty-six years to get there! That's a different word. Not a word I would have necessarily connected to me, but that certainly ... the end of a journey, that one is ...

ANGELA: Is there anything else about that connect, deep inside?

CATHERINE: It's really nice, solid, grounded feeling right down in my sternum. Slightly heavy in that reassuring way. Slightly warmer, and a real nice solidness you get a polished black stone, when you feel it, just weighs the right weight. It has that good feeling.

ANGELA: Can you put that on your piece of paper? Put whatever you need to, to represent that feeling deep inside.

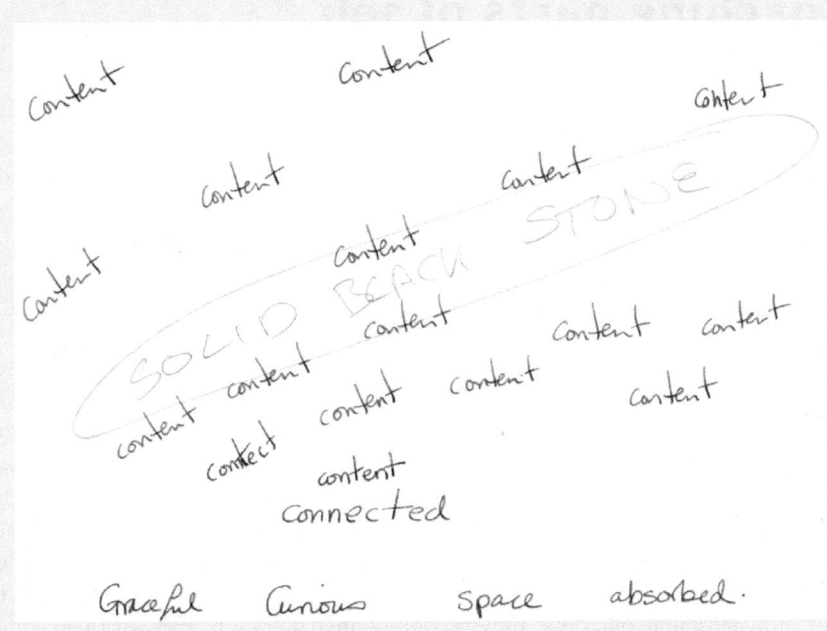

Figure 15.4 Maintaining space in my life – 3.

CATHERINE: Switching to a pencil, I want to draw something. Solid black stone. Hmmmm.

ANGELA: Is there anything else you'd like to add or change to your piece of paper?

CATHERINE: Just separating them. If I take away my first piece of paper, then I'm left with my second piece of paper but there is something missing . . . just adding 'grace' to my 2nd piece of paper . . . curious . . . space (whispering) yes, I quite like that, that's it. Second piece of paper's good.

ANGELA: And what do you know now?

CATHERINE: This is a really, really nice place to be. I've just finally pieced those last bits together that make it easy to stay here. And just maintain it. Much more grounded. A very grounded place.

ANGELA: Would this be an okay place to bring this to a close?

CATHERINE: Yes that's fantastic, thank you.

Note

1 See www.cleancoaching.com for details of distance learning courses to learn Clean Coaching techniques, including 'Clean Boundaries'.

Chapter sixteen

Coaching parts of self

Who are you and how do you know?

People tend to think of themselves in the first person as a single, fixed identity, capable of change but with a core sense of self that's enduring. But many post-modernist perspectives view people as having multiple selves that are flexible, fluid and potentially in conflict. People reveal their different senses of self in the language they use, highlighting metaphors that describe the multiplicity of who they are. For example, coachees may admit that even though they want to achieve a particular outcome, they recognise that there's a 'part' of themselves that doesn't. Or that they are in 'two minds' about what to do next. Or use examples like "On the one hand, I feel trapped. But on the other, I'd actually like to be told what to do." Often people describe and verbalise two sides of themselves, like opposite sides of a coin in conflict.

Many psychological theories have addressed the dualistic aspect of identity. Mead's (1934) influential 'interactional' theory claimed that people have two core identities: the 'I' that interacts with the world, and the 'me', which is the self we see reflected back to us through others' actions, descriptions and responses. In coaching terms, the concept is well represented by Gallwey's (1974) Self 1: the teller and Self 2: the doer. We are both observer and observed, subject and object; each side of the coin presents a very different version of self. Often people describe themselves in a series of I and me (or myself) statements, which could reveal inner conflict, such as "I am holding myself back" or "I wish I was kinder to myself."

Freud claimed we have three not two core selves, the ego (the conscious and rational knowing observer), the 'id' (the primitive, subconscious drive) and the idealistic 'superego'. The 'superego' is the internalised version of the significant others in our lives, usually parental figures that have become our personal in-house rule-enforcers.

Many other theories are based on dual or triage identity formations. For instance, Eric Berne (1964) developed 'Transactional Analysis' based on Freud's tripartite model, with his version of 'ego states' featuring an Adult, and sub-categories of Parent (both nurturing and critical) and Child (natural, compliant and rebellious).

So, from Berne's standpoint we have no less than *five* core selves. Jung highlighted there are an even wider number of universal 'archetypes' – typical prototype characters drawn upon to form the key roles we each adopt in life. All these models are useful for gaining a general understanding of identity, but each of us is unique and so are the selves that we are formed from. Whether people are *really* made up of different parts is not what matters. From a modelling perspective, your coachees may have multiple views of themselves and each 'part' can be explored 'as if' it were a separate piece of the overall whole self.

There is, in fact, some evidence to support a physical separation between parts of self. Functional magnetic resonance imaging (fMRI) shows that certain 'clusters' of neural networks correspond to different states of being. Tsai et al. (1999) studied the brain patterns of a woman with Dissociative Identity Disorder (DID), who switched regularly between her 'normal' personality and an alter ego called 'Guardian'. Each acted like an autonomous person, with separate memories and very different behaviours and beliefs. The fMRI brain scan confirmed that for each personality, different areas of the brain were active. When the woman pretended to switch personalities, there was no change in the area of brain activity. It was only when the alter ego really took control that different brain areas were activated. You do not need to have DID to have multiple selves. In fact, it can be of tremendous value to have different self facets available for a variety of occasions and purposes, enabling us to be more flexible and adapt better to our environment.

People often reveal the existence of different parts through the way they describe their sense of self. You may notice that the personal pronouns they use could be thoughts of as separate symbols, each playing a part. For instance, in a statement like: "If only *I* could let *myself* try something new" or "*I* need to find a way to bring more of *me* into my creativity."

Different senses of self may be formed through the social and occupational roles we take on. We also 'introject' or absorb the role models we look up to and emulate to become inner 'ego ideals'. We avoid, disown or at least ignore the 'shadow' side we don't like or are ashamed of. We are different people at different ages, but perhaps our previous selves never vanish, but instead remain within us, hidden from our awareness.

Grove was a firm believer that people consist of multiple selves. He would search the background of the coachee's metaphoric landscape and perceptual space for signs of any fragment of the person, embedded into the fabric of his or her surroundings (Grove, 2003). He believed, as do many psychotherapists, that whenever a person experienced any kind of trauma the person would disassociate from the experience in the height of fear, detaching from a little piece of who the person is. These 'lost selves' appear in the metaphoric landscape as symbols with a will of their own; in our perceptual space as personified objects, or locked within our physical bodies as a sensation or a symptom. When Clean questions focus attention on those symbols or objects, the part within can emerge and have a voice. As a person moves into different spaces he or she can 'reclaim' these lost selves.

Lawley discovered an old, wise Native American in his metaphoric landscape, watching him from a distance. He explains:

> When I physically moved to sit in the position of the Indian I was shocked. Not only could I see where he (me down there) had come from and was going, but for the first time I also felt a strong sense of detached compassion for myself.

Finally his insight was "I know that I would not have had such a pure experience if I had not physically moved to a place that symbolised the position of the overseer high up on a cliff top" (Lawley, 2006).

Exploring parts with Clean Language

The NLP technique 'parts integration' allows for exploration of selves, but unfortunately is quite prescriptive in assuming that the parts must be somehow squashed together into one. Clean Coaching makes no pre-suppositions about the value of parts or what needs to happen, other than encouraging greater awareness of different selves, so they may be able to better integrate. There is no forced assimilation.

Our model of Clean Coaching pre-supposes the coachee is a collection of parts, using a 'systems thinking' frame to guide us. We do not assume that this person will always have the same identity with the same values, beliefs and behaviours. We watch for changes in a person's demeanour which might indicate that another part has taken centre stage. We need to be an 'equal opportunities' questioner – asking about all aspects of the person's inner world, bringing multiple parts into focus. We watch and listen for symbols that seem to have their own volition and intention, as these may represent a part of that person's sense of self.

Using Clean Language, we can ask the parts for their purpose, through the 'outcome' question, slightly re-phrased and addressed to the part, named exactly as the coachee has named it:

"And what would (coachee's part) like to have happen?"

Another strategy with NLP is to 'chunk up' – by searching for a common value or purpose. Conflicting parts may all be seeking the same end result but believe different strategies will get them there. As these parts have different neural networks, beliefs and memories each may be surprised by the opinions of other parts. The coachee can become more integrated simply by having increased awareness of what each part wants. This can be achieved with Clean Language questions:

"And when (Part A) wants freedom, what would (Part B) like to have happen?"
"And when (Part A) would like to feel more secure, and (Part B) would like more freedom, what needs to happen next?"

Emergent Knowledge techniques hold the pre-supposition that multiple parts of the coachee will likely have a vested interest in any particular goal. By moving into physical spaces the coachee can reconnect with lost parts that he or she has disassociated from and reclaim knowledge from these older and potentially wiser selves. The question "What does (coachee's object, space or symbol) know?" presumes that it is possible for the coachee to see inside these externally placed entities and know what they know. Like a kind of mental ventriloquism, this process usually works well to open channels of thought between the conscious ego 'in charge' and the unconscious sub-personalities vying for attention, influence and/or control. In Chapter thirteen the notion of 'spooky action at a distance' was explained relating to coaching, and it's a helpful model for understanding how parts are both separate from and attached to a person's identity.

'Clean Pronouns' is a specific Clean Coaching process that explores the different facets of who the coachees thinks they are. The coachees use paper and pens to map out their body and then identify the parts of themselves they refer to as their 'I' and 'me', and also their 'myself' and their 'you'. Grove recommends this as a valuable way to coach people at 'A', helping them understand more about where they are now. The more coachees understand where they are, it can influence where they see the destination at B.

Clean Pronouns

The purpose of this exercise is for the coachee to understand that he or she has more than one sense of self, and each may experience the world differently and want different things from it. The same set of Clean questions are asked of the coachee's different senses of self. Some of these may turn out to be parts of the client's psychological system which have become disassociated at some point in their lives.

The process makes use of the usual personal pronouns people use to talk about themselves: I, me, myself and you. If appropriate, you could use other descriptors, such as 'one' or the person's name.

1   Invite the coachee to draw a 'body map'.

   If necessary, explain that this is a picture to represent an outline of the person, and it does not have to be detailed or accurate. A stick-man or simple outline shape is fine, no artistic talent is required. Invite the coachee to use whatever size or shape paper he or she would like, and have available any drawing materials the coachee might like to use, including a range of different colours to draw with during the process.

2   Ask the following questions about 'I':

   "When you say 'I', whereabouts is your 'I'? Is it in your head, your body or outside?"

"Whereabouts is your 'I'? And when you know, can you place that 'I' on your body map, in whatever way you would like to represent it?"

Ask these developing questions:

"And when 'I' is [in your head], does it have a shape or a size?"
"And when it's [egg-shaped], is there anything else about an 'I' that is [egg-shaped]?"

To develop the pronoun still further for a more extensive exploration, you can ask further questions:

"And how old could that 'I' be?"
"And what kind of space is the space around that 'I'?"
"And what could that 'I's goal be?"

(Originally the question "And what would that 'I' be wearing?" was included here. It was removed as it is more appropriate for therapy than coaching, as it potentially encourages childhood memories.)

3   Ask about 'me':

"When you say 'me' whereabouts is your 'me'? Is it in your head, body or outside?"
"And when you know, can you place that 'me' on your body map, in whatever way you would like to represent it?"

Use a selection of developing questions as given above.

4   Ask about 'you':

"When someone says 'you' to you, where does that word 'you' go to? Is it in your head, body or outside?"
"And when you know, can you place that 'you' on your body map, in whatever way you would like to represent it?"

Use a selection of developing questions as given above.

5   Ask about 'myself':

"When you say 'myself', where could your 'myself' be? Is it in your head, body or outside?"
"And when you know, can you place that 'myself' on your body map, in whatever way you would like to represent it?"

Use a selection of developing questions as given above.

6 Download all the knowledge from each part:

"What does your 'myself' know?"
"What does your 'you' know?
"What does your 'me' know?
"What does your 'I' know?"
"And what does that outline/picture/body map know?"
"And what do *you* know now?"

If appropriate, you can go into Clean Action Space after this exercise and tie new knowledge and energy into some actions. Or, you can continue the exploration using another EK exercise such as Clean Networks or Clean Spinning (see Chapter thirteen).

Complete session transcript: to have more options for responding when I am being affirmed

This transcript demonstrates how parts can emerge during a coaching session and how they can be explored Cleanly.

Angela: What's your sense of what you'd like to have happen . . . today?
June: I'd like to start exploring what happens internally for me, when I'm in a situation when either someone is affirming me, or giving me recognition for something that I did.
Angela: So, what's happening internally when you get that recognition . . . and when you do that, when you explore what happens internally for you, then what happens?
June: I guess I would have a better sense of the parts of that process. I think I'm curious about which part of the process is making me cry. I'm not sure what's happening right now, it just happens. It happens instantaneously, like a balloon has been pricked . . . and the tears come! I am not sure where that prick is coming from, or even where that prick is hitting . . . so that the tears come. And I'm curious to know about that part of it . . . so I guess I can have more options about how I would like to respond.
Angela: Okay. So, the outcome is to have more options about how you'd like to respond.

(June first expressed her goal 'to start exploring . . .' which sounded like a remedy rather than an outcome. So I asked, "Then what happens?" to find out the

consequence of taking this remedy. This led to an actual end result: "Have more options about how I would like to respond.")

Angela: And if you did have more options to know how to respond, how would you know? What would be different?

June: I think one of the ways I would know is that crying wouldn't be my default. I guess there would be a kind of pause before deciding "Yes I'm going to tear up because it's appropriate to tear up" (Laughs) . . . or "No, I can choose not to tear up because it's not appropriate to tear up!". And I can choose to accept this gift of affirmation in a space of calm centeredness.

Angela: And there would be a kind of pause. What kind of pause could that be?

June: It's like a space, I guess. I'm trying to locate it . . . I just have a sense of the space. It's like I step into some kind of space where everything else is suspended and I can choose how I'm going to respond. It feels to me as if outside of that space is where the default happens, and it gets a bit volatile and then if I move into this other space it's just kind of quiet and calm and this pause. There's less frenetic energy moving about. I guess I have the option to be able to move into that space where it's quiet and calm.

Angela: There's a kind of space that's quiet and calm that you move into. And is there anything else about that space?

June: I see myself standing in the space. It's not a very large space, I realise. It's a bit like space in a lift. I don't feel claustrophobic, but at the same time it's not a large expansive place. Just a space I step into when it's calm and quiet.

Angela: And it's not a very large space. And you step into that space. And when you say "I see myself step into that space" What kind of myself is that, that you can see in that space?

(June described a representation of her 'self' as 'myself'. As she can see it in her mind's eye, it sounds like a symbol that we can explore further to help raise her awareness of this particular part. June had also mentioned in her preparation documents that she felt there was a 'part of herself' that she didn't understand.)

June: Right now it's just a three dimensional shape of a person, no features, like a computer generated outline of a person. I don't actually see my hair, my face or my clothes I'm wearing, just an image standing in the lift.

Angela: An image, an outline, a 'myself'. Is there anything else about that image that you can see?

June: There's light around it and the image has light inside of it as well. It's not a dark space, it's a light space, quiet and calm. And me standing in that space is also light.

Angela: And that quiet calm space that's light, and you can see 'myself' standing in that space. Whereabouts is that space?

June: I see it in front of me. Yeah, because it's not very big, the figure is not
the same height as me in real life. It feels like it's far away from me.

Angela: Seems like it's far away from you. And the 'me' in real life is seeing
myself in that space. What kind of me in real life is seeing myself?

*(I'm now exploring the other aspect of June's sense of self that's now emerged:
the "me.")*

June: I think it's a 'me' who's decided I want to investigate this! (laughs) It's
a me that's standing and watching and is curious, and rather determined
(laughs).

Angela: And that 'me' in real life who's rather determined, what would that
'me' in real life like to have happen now?

(What is this part's intention? Does it want the same as June does?)

June: That 'me' in real life would like to know, I think, two things for now.
One is: Where is all that frenetic energy coming from, that's outside
that space? To get a deeper understanding of what that's about. And
then, if I can find a way to calm it down, I wouldn't have to step into
another space. Secondly, how can I create this space, this lift, that's
calm and quiet and bright so I can step into that space, whenever I feel
emotionally unstable?

Angela: And two things, Deeper understanding, and if not, how can you create
this space and step into that. And there is the 'myself' that you can see
in that space, and that graphic outline, the image of 'myself'. And that
'myself' that's in the space, what would that 'myself' like to have happen, now?

(Now I'm checking the other part's intention. Is there any conflict?)

June: It would like to stay in that space, indefinitely.

Angela: And is there anything else about that 'myself' that would like to stay in
that space indefinitely?

June: It feels safe in this space. It feels like it's in control of the situation
when it's in that space.

Angela: And 'me' in real life . . . two things, where is all that frenetic energy
coming from, that's outside of the space . . . And would 'myself' be
interested in a deeper understanding of the frenetic energy?

(I wonder whether the two parts can agree on the way forward here?)

June: The 'myself' in the lift? Yes.

Angela: And the frenetic energy that's outside of the space, is there anything else about that frenetic energy?

June: It's really fast, so quick. I can't even stop it even though I don't want it to happen. It's like with lightning speed, I imagine that there is a lot of energy in there, it's just . . . a prick, it pierces me and that's it!

Angela: And it's so quick, like a prick and that's it. And what kind of fast, frenetic energy could that be, that's outside the lift?

June: I'm not quite sure yet . . .

Angela: And when there's that prick, is there anything else about that prick?

June: What's interesting about the prick when I think about it, is that it's happened so many times in my life and yet it doesn't lose its power. Sometimes when you do something repeatedly, you get used to it, it loses its sharpness or the pain gets dulled. Every time it happens it feels like a fresh, new experience, even though I must have gone through it hundreds and thousands of times.

Angela: And is there anything else about going through it hundreds and thousands of times?

June: I guess the 'me' that's standing and watching is getting a little bit tired of it, like that's the only response I know. And I think I want to give myself a break from it.

Angela: Give yourself a break from it. And going through it hundreds and thousands of times and each time it's like fresh and new, that prick. And when there's a prick, then what happens?

June: Then I start to tear up and then I wonder why am I tearing up? (laughs) and then I pull back tears because rationally it doesn't make sense that I'm tearing up. There's this battle and my head is saying stop it.

Angela: And so you tear up and then wonder why I am tearing up. And what happens between tearing up and wonder why I'm tearing up?

June: There's this rush . . . Like a rush of tears. And there's a kind of rush of emotion too, to the front.

Angela: Okay, and there's a rush of emotion to the front. Is there anything else about that rush of emotion to the front?

June: The thought that came to my mind, it's as if it's grabbing me and shaking me I guess and saying 'pay attention to me'.

Angela: And it's grabbing 'me' and saying 'pay attention' and when '*it's*' grabbing '*me*', what kind of 'it' could that be?

(It sounded like another part of June was emerging. It seemed a good idea to explore this further.)

June: Hmmm. Feels like it's a part of me, and it's a small part of me. And it feels like it's a very old part of me.

Angela: And it feels like it's a small, old part of 'me', and it's grabbing. And is there anything else about that small, old part of me that's grabbing and says 'pay attention'?

June: Well, it keeps getting knocked back because I'm stopping the tears and I'm like I don't want to experience this, so it keeps getting knocked back.

Angela: And keeps getting knocked back. And a rush of emotion to the front. Whereabouts is that old, small part of me?

June: For some reason it feels like it's coming from the right side. Like it's leaping up from the right side of my body.

Angela: And what kind of leaping up is that?

June: Kind of like superman when he decides to leap up from the earth and fly into space, that kind of energy.

Angela: Like superman, that kind of energy and leaping up. And what happens just before leaping up?

June: It's just waiting. It feels as if it's waiting for an opportunity.

Angela: And that small old part of me on the right side, waiting for an opportunity. And does that small, old part of 'me' have a shape or a size?

June: It's another figure. And it's about this size, from my pointer finger through to my thumb.

Angela: It's about that . . . and it's another figure. Is there anything else about that figure?

June: It feels like it's a child.

Angela: It feels like it's a child. And when it feels like it's a child, what kind of child could that child be?

June: Like a child who hasn't been heard.

Angela: Like a child who hasn't been heard. And what kind of child is a child who hasn't been heard?

June: Hmmm. So, it's an intelligent child and er . . . it's quite a determined child.

Angela: An intelligent child and quite determined child, who hasn't been heard. And what would that intelligent, determined child like to have happen?

June: It wants attention, it wants to be heard. And I guess it wants to be acknowledged in some way: accepted.

Angela: Okay. Acknowledged in some way . . . wants attention, to be heard. And that child that wants attention, what kind of space is the space around that child?

June: It's a light, airy space.

Angela: It's a light airy space and the child wants attention and waiting for an opportunity. And is there anything else about that child, that wants attention and is waiting for an opportunity?

June: It seems to be saying 'Pay attention to me, because I can help you do this'.

Angela: Hmmm. It seems to be saying 'Pay attention to me because I can help you do this'. And is there anything else about 'Pay attention to me because I can help you do this'?

June: So, the child is a bit perplexed I think that nobody has paid it any attention, and it feels like nobody believes that it can be useful. And because it is a determined, intelligent child, it's just going to keep trying, I guess.

Angela: It's going to keep trying, And that child who's a bit perplexed and is going to keep trying, is there a relationship between keep trying and the prick?

June: It feels to me that the prick is about the child calling attention to it, yeah.

Angela: And the prick is the child calling attention to it, and that attention that the child wants, what kind of attention could that be?

June: It's like, the attention would be a kind of acknowledgement that would sound something like "Oh hello, there you are!". Yes, that kind of attention.

Angela: "Oh hello, there you are!" And is there anything else about that kind of attention: "There you are!"?

June: Yes, there's a kind of a . . . "Well come along then, let's do this together". Let's just go do this together, there's a kind of companion component or teamwork component to that.

Angela: And when that happens: "Oh come along let's do that together", what happens to that intelligent and determined child?

June: Then it doesn't get knocked back. Then all that intelligence and determination, it doesn't get stored up like it's a coil. So that the intelligence and determination is kind of more . . . not coiled up any more, I guess.

Angela: It's not coiled up any more. And when it's not coiled up anymore, what kind of intelligence and determination is that, when it's not coiled up?

June: Well then it's relaxed and it's spread out. And I'm getting this image, you know how when you put on new sheets on your mattress and you throw out those sheets and there's a nice kind ripple and a flow, and it's all nicely spread out like that.

Angela: And like sheets nicely spread out, and the ripple . . . and relaxed. Is there anything else about relaxed?

June: *It feels like that part of me doesn't have to be a superhero of some kind, I guess. It doesn't have to expend super human energy in order to get attention.*

Angela: And that part doesn't have to expend super human energy to get attention. And relaxed, spread out and ripple. And when relaxed, whereabouts is relaxed?

June: It's here right now. On the shoulders, here.

Angela: And it's here. And when relaxed and when that part of you doesn't have to expend super human energy to get attention, what happens to tearing up?

(I'm checking that this new resourceful way of being has actually solved the issue that June brought to coaching.)

June: So when it's relaxed, and the energy isn't coiled up, so then that part of me doesn't leap up and prick me. And I am guessing that if the energy isn't coiled up in that way, and doesn't get expressed in this kind of "whoosh", then I'm guessing I won't feel pricked. And I don't know yet, I'm just guessing that maybe I'll stop tearing up if there is no prick.

Angela: Okay, and you're guessing, there's no tearing up if there's no prick. And that intelligent and determined child that wants attention, what needs to happen for that child to get attention?

(Now we are moving into the third and final part of the coaching session, to identify conditions for change and establish any actions that June can take.)

June: I think 'me' who's kind of watching the space and noticing this other part of me, I think I need to know what this part is about and what is it that it wants to do, I guess.

Angela: And me that's watching the space needs to know what this part is about. And what needs to happen for 'I' to know what this part is about?

June: I think it needs to stop piercing me! Which is kind of like, which one comes first, right? Because it's piercing me, then I get this rush of tears, and I don't want to keep getting this rush of tears and so I knock it back. And when I knock it back, I don't know what it is, I can't figure out what it's offering me. So, if there was no more pricking I could just feel it or see it and there wasn't this rush of tears and emotion. I could be in a calmer, quiet space to say: "Okay, this is what it's all about" and say "Oh hello!" and "Let's go do something together".

Angela: And that child who wants attention, can 'I' feel it or see it when no more pricking?

June: I am getting a sense that just doing this coaching with you, is a way of paying attention to it. Beyond this I'm not sure what else could happen in order for me to acknowledge and pay attention to the child.

Angela: And just generally when you think about acknowledging and paying attention to the child, what could you do differently?

(Coming out of Clean Coaching and being more conversational)

June: I'm not sure I know at this moment, yet.

Angela: Okay. And as we bring our session to a close today, what do you know now, that perhaps you didn't know when we started?

June: I didn't know that the tears, that I was kind of perpetuating the cycle myself by trying to stop it or push it aside or swat it away. It seems to me now that if I kept doing that then the prick is going to keep

Angela: And now you have that awareness, what difference does it make?

June: I think next time I feel pricked, and if it's appropriate, to let that prick take the full course . . . or run of it. And then pause and go inside and see what it's trying to say to me, instead of the automatic reaction of feeling the tears and pulling myself back and stop it, then it stops. Maybe if I didn't do that, if I just . . . Just to see what happens.

Angela: Yes, just to see what happens. And does that feel okay, if it's appropriate to take the full course of that and see what happens?

June: Yes, because I have a clearer purpose, to let that course run itself. Just my curiosity, I'm embarking on this investigation.

Angela: And embarking on this investigation. And see what happens to that child . . . And is that an okay place to bring our session to a close?

June: Yes, thank you! So incredible . . .

Angela: Is there anything else you'd like to say or do before we finish?

June: What happens next?

Angela: Well, we have our next session booked, and you've decided on some actions, so I would add, just pay attention to what happens next, any pricks, any tearing up, any sense of the child, anything that has resonance with what happened in the session. Some of this may continue to evolve or change or just happen over the next couple of weeks. Maybe have a notebook or a journal and make some notes so when we speak again we can explore further.

June: Okay, good.

Angela: Okay, speak to you in two weeks.

This transcript highlights how parts can be explored within a coaching session and provide a source of tremendous insight. For this coachee, by the third coaching session the 'prick' had greatly reduced and the poignancy she had been feeling had evolved into a sense of curiosity about this little girl.

References

Berne, E. (1964) *Games People Play – The Basic Hand Book of Transactional Analysis.* New York: Ballantine Books.

Gallwey, W. Timothy (1974/1997) *The Inner Game of Tennis* (Revised ed.). New York: Random House.

Grove, D. (2003) *Summary of David Grove's Ideas – As of 2003.* Available at: www.clean language.co.uk/articles/articles/278/1/David-Grove-summary-of-ideas-as-of-2003/Page1.html [Accessed 25/6/2015].

Lawley, J. (2006) *When Where Matters – How Psychoactive Space Is Created and Utilised, the Model, British Board of NLP.* Available at: www.cleanlanguage.co.uk/articles/

articles/29/1/When-Where-Matters-How-psychoactive-space-is-created-and-utilised/Page1.html [Accessed 2/4/2015].

Mead, G. (1934) *Mind, Self, and Society*. Chicago: University of Chicago Press.

Tsai, G. E., Condie, D., Wu, M. T. and Chang, I. W. (1999) Functional magnetic resonance imaging of personality switches in a woman with dissociative identity disorder. *Harvard Review of Psychiatry*, 7, 119–122.

Index